That They May All Be One

The Call to Unity

Walter Kasper

BURNS & OATES
A Continuum imprint
LONDON • NEW YORK

BURNS & OATES
A Continuum imprint
The Tower Building,
11 York Road,
London SE1 7NX

15 East 26th Street,
Suite 1703,
New York, NY 10010

www.continuumbooks.com

First published 2004

British Library Cataloguing-in-Publication Data
A catalogue record for this book is available from the British Library.

ISBN 0 8601 2379 0

Typeset by Tradespools, Frome, Somerset
Printed and bound by Cromwell Press Ltd, Trowbridge, Wilts

Contents

Introduction   1

1   The Binding Nature of *Unitatis Redintegratio*   6

2   The Current Situation in Ecumenical Theology   14

3   The Nature and Purpose of Ecumenical Dialogue   33

4   *Communio*: The Guiding Concept of Catholic Ecumenical Theology   50

5   Open Questions in the Ecclesiology of Sister Churches   75

6   The Renewal of Pneumatology in Contemporary Catholic Life and Theology: Towards a Rapprochement between East and West   96

7   The Joint Declaration on the Doctrine of Justification   122

8   A Discussion on the Petrine Ministry   136

9   Spiritual Ecumenism   155

10   The Church and Contemporary Pluralism   173

Abbreviations

Conciliar and Papal Documents

AA	*Apostolicam actuositatem*	Decree on the Apostolate of Lay People
AG	*Ad gentes*	Decree on the Mission Activity of the Church
CA	*Confessio Augustana*	Augsburg Confession, Lutheran Confession of Faith
CD	*Christus dominus*	Decree on the Pastoral Office of Bishops in the Church
DI	*Dominus Iesus*	Declaration on the Unicity and Salvific Universality of Jesus Christ and the Church
DV	*Dei verbum*	Dogmatic Constitution on Divine Revelation
GS	*Gaudium et spes*	Pastoral Constitution on the Church in the Modern World
LG	*Lumen gentium*	Dogmatic Constitution on the Church
NA	*Nostra aetate*	Declaration on the Relationship of the Church to Non-Christian Religions
OE	*Orientalium ecclesiarum*	Decree on Eastern Catholic Churches
PO	*Presbyterorum Ordinis*	Decree on the Ministry and Life of Priests
SC	*Sacrosanctum concilium*	Constitution on the Sacred Liturgy
UR	*Unitatis redintegratio*	Decree on Ecumenism
UUS	*Ut unum sint*	Encyclical Letter on the Commitment to Ecumenism

Other texts

BEM *Baptism, Eucharist and Ministry* (The Lima Declaration)
DH Denziger–Hünermann, *Kompendium der Glaubensbekenntrusse und kirchlichen Lehrentscheidungen*

Introduction

The articles gathered in this book are mainly based on conferences given on different occasions. After extensive revision, the papers are now published in a new, extended version. This volume is founded on the conviction that the very shape of the future Church depends to a significant degree on the ecumenical endeavour aimed at visible unity among divided churches, and that there is no realistic alternative to ecumenism.

This conviction clearly contradicts the spirit of resignation that has often developed over recent years. Those advocating such a critical approach hold that the ecumenical movement, after a short 'spring' and blossoming in the 1960s and 70s, is now experiencing a phase of hibernation. Some even argue that ecumenism was destined to oblivion from the outset. It is often held that today only a limited number of people are interested in the theological differences between the churches; according to these voices, ecumenism is only for a small circle of theologians and church 'insiders', who are, moreover, reined in by the institutions of the Church.

The fact that ecumenism is facing a critical moment cannot be denied. There is a widespread conviction that traditional differences are irrelevant for the majority of people today and could be simply overlooked. The 'wild ecumenism' that has ensued has led, as a counter-reaction, to the emergence of a new confessionalism. The ecumenical movement has been held responsible for the development of relativism and indifference in questions of faith. In reality, a sound ecumenism as defined by the Second Vatican Council is the victim, rather than the origin, of this widespread apathy. Thus a new atmosphere of mistrust, self-defence and withdrawal has often emerged within confessional compartments. This phenomenon can be observed in the ecumenical discussions with the Reformed churches of the West, as well as with the Orthodox and Old Catholic Churches of the East.

However, even 'sound ecumenism', which endeavours to take the unresolved theological questions into serious consideration, seems to be blocked in many respects. In the second half of the twentieth century it certainly accomplished more than it had in previous centuries. Not only were many misunderstandings overcome, but a certain degree of convergence and consensus was attained in questions of faith which had been clearly divisive in the past. After centuries of drifting apart and a lack of mutual understanding, divided Christians today no longer see each other as hostile adversaries but as friendly brothers and sisters. The atmosphere between the churches has profoundly changed. Of course, there are still isolated old-style confessional 'trench fights', but these are perceived as anachronistic and embarrassing by the majority of Christians.

Despite the many encouraging results achieved so far, however, there is one point on which no major progress has yet been accomplished: the question of ecclesiology. This old and complex issue came publicly to the fore when, during the Jubilee Year 2000, the Congregation for the Doctrine of the Faith declared that the churches of the Reformation are not churches in the true sense of the word. Although, on the linguistic level, this could have been expressed in a more sensitive way, from the point of view of the content all participants in the ecumenical dialogue have always been aware of this ecclesiological difference. The Protestants do not wish to be considered as Church in the same way as the Catholic Church sees itself. At the beginning of the ecumenical movement, the well-known 1950 Toronto Declaration of the World Council of Churches already stated that a consensus on the ecclesiological question was not a pre-condition for ecumenical dialogue. Thus the difference between the respective understandings of the Church, and the declaration of the Congregation for the Doctrine of the Faith on this matter, should not be perceived as obstacles, but rather as impulses to ecumenical dialogue.

With regard to relationships with the Orthodox churches, the conflict emerged earlier, within the context of the breakdown of the Eastern bloc. Initial aspirations had led many to envisage a rapprochement between the churches. The so-called 'uniate' churches in full communion with Rome resurfaced after the brutal repression of the communist system, which had forced them into an 'underground' existence, and reclaimed their church property. This led to a painful loss to the Orthodox churches, especially in the Ukraine and Romania, and sometimes to bitter controversy on the question of so-called uniatism. It became clear, however, that the underlying reason for this conflict was the issue of papal primacy and the importance of communion with the pope – a particularly sensitive issue which has stirred emotions over the centuries both in the East and the West. This is indeed one of the most delicate questions on the agenda of the ecumenical dialogue, on which no consensus has yet been achieved despite an undeniable rapprochement.

The different understandings of the Church have necessarily led to different conceptions of the envisaged unity of the churches. This, in turn, has burdened and hampered the ecumenical dialogue. Certainly, all agree that the united Church cannot be a unitary Church but a unity in diversity. We often speak of reconciled diversity.

This formula can be understood in different ways. The Catholic Church, respecting all possible and legitimate traditions, aims at unity in faith, sacraments and church ministries. The churches of the Reformation refer instead to the Augsburg Confession, which states in article 7 that the preaching of the Gospel in its purity and the administration of the sacraments according to the Gospel are sufficient conditions (*satis est*) for the unity of the Church. There is today a widespread interpretation that this means that unity only requires an agreement on the fundamental understanding of the Gospel, and that church communion does not rule out differences in understanding of ministries, in institutional forms and in confessions of faith, which are sometimes even contradictory. According to this position, each church can be in eucharistic and church communion with the others while keeping its own independence and structures.

This approach blurs the fundamental difference between legitimate diversity in the expression of the one faith, on the one hand, and the contradiction between opposite positions on the other. Thus, one should more properly speak of an unreconciled diversity and a union of churches without real unity rather than of a reconciled diversity. Visible unity has been replaced by peaceful co-existence and friendly co-operation, full communion by intercommunion.

The conviction on which this book is based is that aiming at this form of unity is theologically too modest and even contradictory.

The churches should certainly remain churches, but also progressively become one Church (J. Ratzinger). Theological work is a necessary precondition for this. Although ecumenism does not merely and exclusively consist of discussions led by theological experts, it cannot progress without serious theological reflection which, whenever possible, seeks to shape opposite positions into complementary and mutually enriching tensions. In this sense we can speak of catholic evangelicalism and evangelical catholicity.

In line with this understanding and in the spirit of the School of Tübingen – the spirit of scholars like Johann Sebastian Drey and Johann Adam Möhler – the following articles take their starting point from the tension between ecclesiology and eschatology. The Church is seen as a historical reality which, guided by the Holy Spirit, transcends itself to move towards its eschatological future and fulfilment. Within history, this self-transcending activity is to be found in mission and ecumenism. In both these realities the Church is the rich giver and, at the same time, the rich receiver. In mission, the Church makes room in itself for the richness of peoples and cultures in a creative way; likewise, in ecumenism, it is enriched by the gifts of the other churches and enriches them with its own. In this exchange of gifts, the Church becomes concretely and fully what she has always been: the all-encompassing *una sancta catholica et apostolica ecclesia*.

Such ecumenism, which is turned not towards the past but to the future, is a spiritual process. Spiritual ecumenism is the heart of the ecumenical movement. This is why the future ecumenical identity of the Church cannot be concretely defined beforehand. We cannot set exact dates and time schedules for it. We should allow the freedom of the Spirit. But since the Church of the future cannot be a new or different Church, but only the renewed 'one Church' of Jesus Christ of all times, we can be sure that the Church of the future will be in line with tradition – tradition understood not as a fixed reality but as a process of living transmission, the self-transmission of Jesus Christ in the Holy Spirit.

This is not, as some critics say, the same spirit as the spirit of the times, but the Spirit of God. As the Second Vatican Council explicitly stated, it is the Spirit of God that has inspired the ecumenical movement and still leads it forwards. It is the Spirit of God that makes us increasingly aware of Jesus Christ's commandment of unity to his disciples (cf. John 17.21). The Spirit of God is trustworthy, we can rely on it. Amidst difficulty and pain, this trust instils in us the hope that the Spirit will bring to completion the work that it has started (cf. Rom. 8.22ff.). Nor do the 'signs of the times' leave us with an alternative to ecumenism. The following articles want to do justice to this hope (cf. 1 Pet. 3.15). They want to foster this living hope in those who read this book and encourage them to preserve it with patience, which is the little sister of hope (Charles Péguy).

I wish to express my heartfelt gratitude to all those who have constantly strengthened this hope in me, as well as to the colleagues and collaborators who have contributed to this book.

Cardinal Walter Kasper
Rome, Easter 2004

1

The Binding Nature of Unitatis Redintegratio

In the decree *Unitatis redintegratio*, the Second Vatican Council recognized that the ecumenical movement is a sign of the Holy Spirit's action and said that it considered the promotion of this movement to be one of its principal tasks. Today, 40 years later, the ecumenical movement is in a different situation. Alongside the progress, the burden of old and new divisions can be felt: the process of rapprochement has been drawn out far longer than many expected in an earlier, optimistic phase. Then there are impatient voices which, contrary to the Council's declared intention (cf. *Unitatis redintegratio* 11) and hiding behind the mirage of presumed solutions, are creating problems and mis-interpreting the ecumenical movement by mistakenly believing that they will further it by surrendering to dogmatic relativism, indifferentism and pure pragmatism.

At times, the difficulties and the misunderstandings lead people to regard the ecumenical movement with mistrust and often cast doubt on the theologically binding character of the conciliar decree *Unitatis redintegratio*. The argument used alleges that this document is not a dogmatic constitution but merely a decree, that is, it has no binding doctrinal character – or if it does, it is minimal – and its only importance is pastoral and disciplinary.

Ecumenical 'Rapprochement', the Main Purpose of Vatican II

At first sight the argument seems clear. In fact, a closer look shows that this is far from being the case. However, it is impossible to deduce an argument of this kind solely from the use of words. Indeed, the Council of Trent issued nothing but decrees; yet it approved documents with this title that were both dogmatically important and binding. Compared with Trent, the Second Vatican

Council made a distinction between constitutions and decrees; but it did not explain this differentiation, or at least not in a way that justified the above-mentioned argument. Pope Paul VI's declarations on the act of the solemn promulgation of *Unitatis redintegratio* took another direction. At the beginning of the second session of the Council, the Pope had already declared, in a fundamentally important address, that ecumenical rapprochement was one of the purposes – the spiritual requirement, so to speak – for which the Council had been convoked. If due consideration is given to this declaration, all the texts of the Council should be read in an ecumenical perspective. When the Decree on Ecumenism was promulgated at the end of the third session (together with the Dogmatic Constitution on the Church), Pope Paul VI said that the decree explained and completed the Constitution on the Church: 'ea doctrina, explicationibus completa in Schemate "*De Oecumenismo*" comprehensis ...' Thus, with regard to theological importance, he closely linked this decree to the Constitution on the Church. Lastly, in his closing address on 8 December 1965 (in agreement with what Pope John XXIII had said in his opening address) he declared that the Council as a whole – hence including the Dogmatic Constitution – had a pastoral orientation. And he left no room for doubt that the pastoral orientation neither excluded nor relativized doctrinal pronouncements but, on the contrary, was founded on the teaching of the Church.

Effectively, there is no pastoral service worthy of the name that is not anchored in the teaching of the Church; nor is there any teaching of the Church that consists solely of doctrine and is devoid of pastoral aims. The First Vatican Council had already declared that the teaching of the Church must be interpreted in the light of the ultimate destiny of the human being (*DS* 3016). Therefore, just as pastoral work must be guided by the teaching of the Church, the teaching of the Church must be interpreted by observing man and his destiny, that is, in a pastoral sense. The viewpoint of the '*salus animarum quale suprema lex*' is a fundamental principle for the interpretation not only of canon law (*CIC* 1752), but also of the Church's teaching.

This has important implications for the hermeneutics of the conciliar texts. Just as it is not permissible to separate *Unitatis redintegratio* from *Lumen gentium* or to interpret the decree in a spirit of dogmatic relativism or indifferentism, *Unitatis redinte-gratio* likewise indicates the approach to be taken in explaining the assertions of *Lumen gentium* (an attitude of openness on more than one point): that is, a spirit of theologically responsible ecumenical openness. Thus there is no opposition between the doctrinally binding character, on the one hand, and the pastoral or disciplinary character on the other. Rather, any wish to discredit the theological aspect of the Decree on Ecumenism would be contrary to the overall ecumenical intention of the Second Vatican Council.

Judgement of the Document's Binding Character must be Differentiated

Rejection of the overall devaluation of *Unitatis redintegratio* does not mean that a solution has been found to every problem. On the contrary, it is at this very point that the task of correctly interpreting the decree begins. And if this is the case, we must differentiate and classify its binding nature. This can already be deduced from the Theological Commission's response at the end of the discussion on the binding character of the Constitution on the Church: 'Clearly a Council text should always be interpreted in accordance with the general rules, known to all.' This means that we have to accept and maintain the Council's assertions 'in conformity with the intention of the Holy Synod itself, as shown, in accordance with the foundations of the theological interpretation, from the subject addressed or from the form of expression used'.

The Council's extensive discussion of the title of the 'Pastoral Constitution on the Church in the Modern World' (*Gaudium et spes*) led to the same result. In this debate the term 'pastoral' and its theological significance were broadly discussed. As a result, a note on this title expressly establishes that 'It [the Constitution] is called "pastoral" because, based on doctrinal principles, it desires to illustrate the relationship of the Church with the contemporary world. Hence, the pastoral purpose is not absent from the first part nor the doctrinal purpose from the second', even if this part 'not only contains unchangeable elements, but also elements condi-tioned by history'. In brief, it is affirmed: 'The Constitution must therefore be interpreted in accordance with the general rules for theological interpretation.'

Unitatis redintegratio was debated in a similar way, although the discussion may not have been as broad as that on *Gaudium et spes*. The result was objectively the same. The Council, precisely to avoid a false irenicism and a purely pragmatic ecumenism, did not accept the proposal of certain Council Fathers to eliminate everything theological from the text.

The Council wished to retain the principle that pastoral affirmations rest on dogmatic principles and, moreover, that pastoral affirmations relate these dogmatic principles to concrete historical situations. As a rule, historical situations are complex and as such need to be evaluated in the light of deeper investigation. Affirmations on historical events which affect the theological context must therefore be understood in accordance with the theological rules of interpretation, so as not to jeopardize the value of the doctrinal elements that may be present in them.

Unfortunately – and this is not the least important point that has emerged from the discussion of the theologically binding character of *Unitatis redintegratio* – in the post-conciliar period knowledge of the rules for the interpretation of theology and the doctrine of theological qualifications has all too often been forgotten The Second Vatican Council made its contribution in *Lumen gentium*, distinguishing between infallible declarations and the authentic magisterium and explaining that the degree to which they are binding is to be recognized 'by the character of the documents in question, or by the frequency in which a certain document is proposed, or by the manner in which the doctrine is formulated' (*Lumen gentium* 25).

These distinctions must be taken into account when dealing with the theologically binding character of *Unitatis redintegratio*. The question, therefore, is not merely: 'Is this Council text binding or not?' Rather, a distinction must be made within the documents between the different forms and degrees of obligation, and this distinction must be emphasized as appropriate.

If this is done, it will be hard to dispute that the first chapter of *Unitatis redintegratio* (in which the 'Catholic principles on ecumenism' are expounded) contains binding affirmations that either sum up or develop further the corresponding assertions in *Lumen gentium*. Explicit citation of the dogmatic affirmations of earlier Councils (the Fourth Lateran Council, the Second Council of Lyons, the Council of Florence, the First Vatican Council) confirms that we are dealing with theologically binding affirmations, although these may not always constitute ultimately binding infallible definitions. On the contrary, the third chapter in particular (on 'Churches and Ecclesial Communities which were separated from the Apostolic See of Rome') contains historical affirmations which by their nature cannot be theologically binding, even if there are also statements that leave no doubt as to their implicitly binding meaning, such as 'This holy Synod solemnly declares' (*Unitatis redintegratio* 16); 'this sacred Council ... declares' (17); 'after taking all these factors into consideration, this sacred Council confirms' (18). This wording is in no way inferior to corresponding wording in *Lumen gentium*.

Consequently, the hermeneutics of *Unitatis redintegratio* and the judgement on this document's theologically binding character cannot be global; they must be differentiated. To succeed in differentiating every single case demands concentrated work that no one can dispense with by resorting to generalizations.

Examine Individual Documents in the Context of their Reception

Nevertheless, the interpretation of *Unitatis redintegratio* cannot be limited to ascertaining the degree of obligation of every individual affirmation. After ascertaining the formally binding character of an affirmation, the problem of the interpretation of its content arises. For this too there are rules, and they obviously also apply to ecumenical theology. To treat this here would take too long and would require the exposition of an entire theological methodology. We shall briefly mention three of these rules.

A historical interpretation is fundamental
You cannot invoke a vaguely conciliar spirit but must start with how affirmations are expressed. At the same time, this means that we must pay attention each time to what the Council wanted to say. This becomes particularly clear from an examination of the Acts of the Council. Moreover, single affirmations cannot be considered on their own. The positivist citation of single sentences or even phrases taken out of context is not adequate. Instead, individual affirmations should be interpreted in the context of the council documents, in connection with all the mysteries of the faith (*DS* 2016) and according to the 'hierarchy' of truths (cf. *Unitatis*

redintegratio 11). This historical and systematic interpretation confronts many historical and hermeneutical problems: we should not evade them to take refuge either in a purely positivistic way of citing them or in the disputable distinction between the spirit and letter of the Council.

An interpretation in the light of the tradition

No council is independent but every council follows in the wake of the tradition of all the others. Thus, the decree *Unitatis redintegratio* refers to the confession of the faith of the Church and to the earliest councils. It would therefore be erroneous to interpret the Second Vatican Council, and especially the Decree on Ecumenism, as a break with tradition. Actually, one of the most important reasons for this council was a *resourcement*, a return to the sources; the Council dealt with a new actualization of the tradition, and in this sense, with its *aggiornamento* (a concept nowhere to be found in the documents of the Council). We should, of course, ask ourselves what 'tradition' means in the theological sense and, in so doing, it is necessary to distinguish between the one tradition and the many traditions. The ecumenical openness of the Second Vatican Council is not a break with the tradition in the theological sense of the word; but it is certainly an intentional modification of individual traditions, which are for the most part relatively recent. Thus it is indisputable that the Council consciously went beyond the defensive and prohibitive assertions of Pope Pius XI in *Mortalium animos* (1928) and, in this sense, made a qualitative leap. Understood in this way, tradition and innovation are not in opposition.

On the subject of tradition, in the Dogmatic Constitution on Divine Revelation (*Dei Verbum*) the Second Vatican Council made its own the deep understanding of tradition as presented by J. A. Möhler and J. H. Newman, who made it the foundation of their respective theological reflection (cf. *Dei Verbum* 8). The Council understood tradition to be a living reality, full of the Holy Spirit; that is, both as fidelity to '*depositum fidei*' that we received as our inheritance once and for all, and as an ever-renewed 'youthfulness' in eternally new situations. This living interpretation, made under the guidance of the Holy Spirit, has nothing in common with an easy adaptation to the spirit of the times: often, on the contrary, the only way it can express the timeliness of tradition is by a prophetic witness against the spirit of the times. The Second Vatican Council document *Unitatis redintegratio* must therefore be interpreted in continuity with all the councils. This continuity must not be understood as a dead or fossilized reality, but as a living event through which the Holy Spirit introduces us again and again into the fullness of the truth (John 16:13). It is he, says St Irenaeus of Lyons, who keeps the '*depositum fidei*' young and 'dewy', who preserves the one and the same Gospel not as something eternally out of date, but possessing inexhaustible youth.

The importance of the reception of the Council

Understanding the tradition as a living reality implies that not only in *Unitatis redintegratio* but also in many other texts of the Second Vatican Council (together with *Lumen gentium*), old and new are often found side by side.

This looks like a compromise, but this is not necessarily a bad thing. An intelligent compromise can be an intellectual undertaking of high value and an expression of great wisdom; while it clearly excludes error on the one hand, on the other it permits the existence – for the time being and for love of unity in the essentials – of insurmountable intra-ecclesial differences, deferring their solution to future discussion. As every student of the history of dogma knows well, not even the earliest councils could dispense with these expressions of compromise that led subsequently to a laborious process of assimilation. The Councils of Nicea (325) and Chalcedon (451) and subsequent history are eloquent examples of this.

People who criticize *Unitatis redintegratio* for its use of some 'immature' wording should also criticize the dogmatic constitutions of the Second Vatican Council and essential elements of the most ancient history of the councils. The wording of a conciliar pronouncement, despite the absolute certainty that it is exempt from error, is always open-ended; defining it sparks a lively process of reception.

In this sense, *Unitatis redintegratio* cannot be read merely as a historical text, isolated from the history of its reception in the post-conciliar period. Associated with this reception are the many magisterial documents that confirmed and further developed ecumenical openness, in particular the encyclical *Ut unum sint*

(1995), and the acceptance of *Unitatis redintegratio* in the faith and life of the Church, in theology and in ecumenical dialogue. Without a doubt, several points are not yet fully mature; in fact, in the face of certain erroneous developments, the magisterium of the Church has had to take a firm stand, as evidenced by the declaration *Dominus Iesus* (2000). Yet this declaration should not be interpreted out of context either, but in the light of all the other magisterial documents and within the framework of the whole process of their reception.

In the past 40 years, *Unitatis redintegratio* has been assimilated by both the authentic magisterium of the Church and the *sensus fidelium*. During that time the Decree has made a great contribution to developing ecumenical awareness in the consciences of many Christians. Of course, there has been no lack of exaggerated interpretations and inappropriate applications; but although wild growth must be controlled, one cannot uproot the good wheat along with the weeds (cf. Matt. 13.29). Thus to underestimate *Unitatis redintegratio* 40 years after its promulgation would be to set ourselves above an ecumenical council, above the authentic magisterium of the Church, above the life of the Church (which is guided by the Holy Spirit); it would mean resisting the very Spirit who has pushed this process forward through its high and low phases, through its problems but even more through its many hopeful aspects. Therefore, in fidelity to the tradition of the Church and in the light of Catholic doctrinal principles, but also with courage and creativity, we have every reason to ensure that in the changed ecumenical situation *Unitatis redintegratio* will develop its vitality both in theology and in praxis.

2

The Current Situation in Ecumenical Theology

An Ambiguous Situation

In a situation where the term globalization characterizes our condition in all its ambiguity, ecumenism becomes a response to the signs of the times. Through the new means of communication and travel, people are closer to each other; nations and people are much more interrelated and they are, so to speak, in the same boat for better or worse. For the Catholic Church, especially for the present Pope, ecumenism is one of the priorities of her pastoral work.[1]

Much has been achieved over the last decades. Separated Christians no longer regard one another as strangers, competitors or even enemies, but as brothers and sisters. They have largely removed the former lack of understanding, misunderstanding, prejudice and indifference; they pray together, they give witness together to their common faith; in many fields they work trustingly together. They have experienced that 'what unites us is much greater than what divides us'.[2] Such a change was hardly conceivable only half a century ago; to wish to go back to those times would entail being forsaken not only by all good spirits but also by the Holy Spirit. It has been the Holy Spirit that has reminded us that Jesus wanted *one* Church and that, on the eve of his death, he prayed that 'all may be one' (John 17.21)

Nonetheless, after the first rather euphoric phase of the ecumenical movement which followed the Second Vatican Council, the last decade has seen us experiencing signs of tiredness, disillusionment and stagnation. Some even speak of a crisis or a new ecumenical winter.

To some extent such a situation is a sign and a proof of the achievement of the ecumenical movement. The more Christians of different churches and church communities move closer to each other, the more they feel the differences that still exist and the transitory difficulties faced in overcoming them, and the more they suffer because they cannot yet participate in the one table of the Lord. Thus the frustration can also be understood in a positive sense.

But why has the ecumenical movement slowed down? Different answers can be given. Here I will limit myself to one reason, which brings us to the heart of the question: the issue of new identity. Even in a world which is characterized by globalization, many ask: Who are we? Who am I? Nobody wants to be absorbed in an anonymous and faceless whole. The question of identity arises in individuals as well as in entire cultures, ethnic groups and religions; and it arises finally within the Christian churches, where a wrongly understood ecumenism has sometimes led to relativism and indifferentism.

This misunderstanding and an ensuing wild ecumenism has led to understandable hesitations vis-à-vis the ecumenical dialogue and sometimes even to fundamentalist attitudes. But, correctly understood, the question of identity is fundamental and constitutive for the human person, for the Church and for the ecumenical dialogue as well. Only partners with a clear identity can undertake dialogue without fearing the loss of their identity within the dialogue. Thus in the last few years questions about the theological and ecclesial foundations of a healthy dialogue and a healthy ecumenism have once again arisen. Therefore, before outlining an overview of the contemporary ecumenical situation, I would like to mention briefly the current debate on the the theological and ecclesiological foundations of ecumenism.

The Ecclesiological Foundation

The Declaration of the Congregation for the Doctrine of Faith, *Dominus Iesus*,[3] took up this question of identity, recalling some of the fundamental Catholic principles of ecumenism. Correctly interpreted, the content of this text is in its substance in line with the Second Vatican Council. However, the highly abstract and compact style of the document has given rise to doubts about the ecumenical commitment of the Catholic Church. Many people were disappointed, wounded and hurt by its tone and style. In particular, the following sentence from the document caused some difficulties: 'the ecclesial communities which have not preserved the valid Episcopate and the genuine and integral substance of the Eucharistic mystery, are not Churches in the proper sense'. No doubt it would have been possible to formulate it in a more sensitive way. However, informed people are aware that the Protestant communities do not want to be 'Church' in the same way as the Catholic Church understands itself.

Yet the resulting irritations are no reason for resignation. References to still existing and undeniable differences do not mean the end of dialogue; on the contrary, they represent a challenge to further dialogue. Nor does the document contradict the ecumenical spirit, because ecumenism can be undertaken only in the spirit of love and truth. Honesty is one of the first presuppositions of dialogue. Thus the document does not represent any fundamental change in the attitude of the Catholic Church and her irreversible engagement in the ecumenical movement.

The affirmation that the Church of Jesus Christ *fully* subsists *only* in the Catholic Church[4] does not deny that outside the visible structure of the Catholic Church there are not only individual Christians but also ecclesial elements which, as gifts belonging to the Church of Christ, are forces impelling towards Catholic unity.[5] Or, as the encyclical *Ut unum sint* states, 'It is not that beyond the boundaries of the Catholic community there is an ecclesial vacuum.'[6] Both the Second Vatican Council and the encyclical acknowledge explicitly that the Holy Spirit is operating in the other churches and church communities;[7] in particular, the Oriental churches are recognized as particular churches and as sister churches.[8] Consequently, there is no idea of an arrogant claim to a monopoly on salvation.

Besides, the Council is aware of the sinfulness of the members of its own church and the sinful structures existing in the Church itself;[9] it knows about the need for reforming the shape of the Church. The Church is a pilgrim church, an *ecclesia 'semper purificanda'*, which must constantly take the way of penance and renewal.[10] The Catholic Church too is wounded by the divisions of Christianity. Her wounds include the impossibility of concretely realizing fully her own catholicity in a situation of division.[11]

Several aspects of being Church are realized better in the other churches. Therefore ecumenism is no one-way street, but a reciprocal learning process or – as stated in the encyclical *Ut unum sint* – an exchange of gifts.[12] The way to it is therefore not a simple return of the others into the fold of the Catholic Church.

In the ecumenical movement the question is the conversion not only of the others but of all to Jesus Christ. Conversion always begins with ourselves. We Catholics too must be ready for an examination of conscience, self-criticism and repentance. As we move nearer to Jesus Christ, in him we move nearer to one another. Therefore it is not a question of church political debates and compromises, of some kind of union, but of a common journey from a still imperfect communion towards full communion, of spiritual growth in faith and love and of reciprocal spiritual exchange and a mutual enrichment. The *oikoumene* is a spiritual process, in which the question is not about a way back but about a way forward.[13] Such unity is ultimately a gift of God's Spirit and the result of his guidance. Therefore the *oikoumene* is not simply an academic or diplomatic matter; its soul and its heart is spiritual ecumenism.[14]

It is precisely this aspect of spiritual ecumenism that our Pontifical Council for Promoting Christian Unity wants to stress in the future. For without such a soul, ecumenism becomes either soulless activism or merely an academic exercise in which the great majority of the faithful cannot take part; unable to understand what is at stake in the ecumenical dialogue, they become estranged and indifferent or even reject the whole thing, so that a real reception of the results in the body of the Church does not take place. We must, at the same time, deepen and widen the ecumenical dialogue. In other words: we can only widen the ecumenical dialogue when we deepen it. Only spiritually can we overcome the present crisis.

Ecumenism with the Oriental Churches

After these few remarks on the foundations and heart of ecumenical theology, I will proceed to the concrete ecumenical situation. In so doing we cannot limit ourselves to Protestant–Catholic relations. In the *oikoumene* we must overcome a unilateral 'Western-oriented' ecumenical theology and include the Oriental churches.

Besides the Orthodox churches, the Oriental churches also include the Ancient Oriental churches which separated from the then imperial Church as early as the fourth and fifth centuries (Copts, Syrians, Armenians, Ethiopians, Malankara). To us Westerners they make an archaic impression; but they are lively churches, deeply rooted in the life of their respective peoples and cultures. By joining the ecumenical movement they were able to overcome their perennial isolation and resume their place within the whole of Christianity.

The reasons underlying their separation, besides political motives, lay in the dispute about the Christological formula. While the Council of Chalcedon (451) held that Jesus Christ is true God and true man in one person, that is, one person in two natures, these churches adhered to the formula of Cyril of Alexandria whereby the one divine nature was made flesh. After intensive preparatory work involving historical research on dogmas[15] and discussion mediated by the 'Pro Oriente' Foundation in Vienna,[16] this controversy was settled in recent times through the bilateral declarations of the Pope and the respective Patriarchs.[17] It was recognized that when speaking of one person and two natures, the starting point was a different philosophical conception of person and nature, but with the same meaning as far as the content itself is concerned. This understanding has enabled the churches to maintain their common faith in Jesus Christ without imposing on each other their respective formulae. The ultimate outcome has been unity in a diversity of ways of expression.

In the meantime we have also initiated a second phase of dialogue, this time with all the ancient Oriental churches together. Having dealt with the Christological problems, we are now focusing on the issue of the Church as communion. We hope that successive concrete steps can be taken and that perspectives on possible full communion can be developed in the future.

No such official agreement has yet been reached with the Orthodox churches of the Byzantine and Slavic traditions. However, the excommunication of 1054, the symbolic date of the separation between East and West, was cancelled 'from the conscience of the Church'[18] on the last day of the Second Vatican Council (7 December 1965). Of course, the year 1054 is rather a symbolic date. East and West had received the message of the Gospel differently and had developed different traditions,[19] different forms of culture and different mentalities. Yet despite these differences, all were living in the one Church. In the first millennium, East and West had already grown increasingly apart, understanding each other less and less, and this estrangement was the very reason for the separation in the second millennium.[20]

Even today, in every meeting with the Orthodox churches we see that while we are very close to one another in faith and sacramental life, we have difficulties in understanding each other culturally and mentally. In the East, we encounter a highly developed culture, but one that has experienced neither the Western separation between church and state nor the modern Enlightenment, and which has been culturally and mentally marked most of all by 50 or 70 years of Communist oppression. After the changes at the end of the last century, these churches are now free for the first time – free from the Byzantine emperors, free from the Ottomans, free from the Tsars and free from the totalitarian Communist system; but they see themselves facing an entirely transformed world, in which they must first find their way. This will take time and require patience.

The three documents produced by the Joint Catholic–Orthodox Commission for Theological Dialogue between 1980 and 1990 show a deep community in the understanding of faith, church and sacraments.[21] Along this line, important elements of the ancient church communion with both the Orthodox and the ancient Oriental sister churches could be renewed: reciprocal visits and regular correspondence between the pope and the patriarchs, frequent contacts at local church level and – importantly for the strongly monastic Oriental churches – at the level of monasteries.

The only seriously debated theological issue between us and the Orthodox Church, besides the *filioque* clause in the creed (which according to our understanding is more a complementary than a contradictory position),[22] is the question of Roman primacy. As Popes Paul VI and John Paul II have often said, for non-Catholic Christians this issue is the most serious stumbling block.[23] From this perspective, John Paul II in his ecumenical encyclical *Ut unum sint* (1995) extended an invitation to fraternal dialogue on the future exercise of the primacy.[24] A quite revolutionary step for a pope! The resonance was great. The Pontifical Council for Promoting Christian Unity collected the reactions to this initiative and sent a summary to all the churches and ecclesial groupings involved.[25] The outcome of the first phase – as was to be expected – was far from a consensus; but there seems to be a new atmosphere, a new interest and a new openness. Now we hope to initiate a second phase of the dialogue. In May 2003 the Pontifical Council for Promoting Christian Unity convened a theological symposium on the Petrine ministry with theologians of the main Orthodox churches; as expected, we did not find a solution but promising openings were obvious on both sides. Consequently, both sides agreed to continue this kind of dialogue on an academic level.

Unfortunately, after the 1989/90 political changes in Middle and Eastern Europe, relations with the Orthodox churches have become more difficult. In Ukraine and Romania the Oriental churches in union with Rome, which had been violently oppressed and persecuted by the Communist regimes, have come out of the catacombs and returned to public life. Old hostilities on proselytism and so–called uniatism re-emerged and since then have made the dialogue more difficult and sometimes even polemical. At the last plenary meeting of the 'Joint International Commission' in Baltimore in 2001, it was unfortunately impossible to make any progress on the thorny problem of so-called uniatism. Regrettably, since Baltimore it has not been possible to convene the International Commission. Problems and difficulties have arisen particularly with the major Orthodox church, the Russian Orthodox Church, after the erection of four dioceses within the Russian Federation.

In the meantime, however, the dialogue has in no sense come to a standstill. Through personal visits and fraternal contacts, the so-called dialogue of love, we have been able to improve our bilateral relations with the Orthodox churches of Romania, Serbia and Bulgaria. High-ranking delegations have paid mutual visits. In particular, after the historical visit of the Pope to Athens in 2001, our relations with the Church of Greece, until then rather cool, have warmed up and developed into an increasingly intensive co-operation. A further step was the visit of a Delegation of the Holy See to Athens and a visit of a Delegation of the Holy Synod of the Orthodox Church of Greece to Rome, visits which only two years before would have been totally unimaginable. In our relations with Moscow there are signs of détente and improvement, and my impression is that we have managed to turn the page.

The main theological problem we now face is our shared and different understanding of *communio* (*koinonia*). Here we confront the very core of our difference: on the one hand, the Petrine ministry and a universalist conception of the Church, and on the other, the idea of the autocephaly of national churches. In order to overcome this difference, we for our part should work towards a reinterpretation and a re-reception of the First Vatican Council which safeguards the gift of the Petrine ministry for the unity and freedom of the Church, while at the same time maintaining the oriental tradition of churches *sui iuris* with their own theological, spiritual and canonical tradition, but without falling into the trap of national autocephalous churches. Orthodox theologians themselves see this as a weakness in Orthodoxy today. A new solution needs to be found for the longstanding problem of unity and legitimate diversity. Although we will continue to be confronted with difficulties and problems in the future, my own impression is that we stand at the beginning of a promising new phase.

Ecumenism with the Churches of the Reformed Tradition

I am convinced that improvement in our ecumenical relations with the Oriental churches is also essential in order to overcome the divisions within Western Christianity. Since its separation from the East, Latin Christianity has developed unilaterally; it has, so to speak, breathed with only one lung and is impoverished. This impoverishment was one cause, among others, of the serious crisis in the Church in the late Middle Ages which led to the tragic division of the sixteenth century.

The following remarks are limited to the dialogue with the Lutherans which, together with the dialogue with the Anglican Communion, is the most developed. Much has been accomplished with the Lutheran World Federation in the last decades in many dialogues at the international, regional and local level.[26] Based on considerable preparatory work,[27] the 'Joint Declaration on the Doctrine of Justification' was solemnly signed in 1999.[28] This – as the Pope rightly said – was a milestone, that is, an important step but not yet the end of the journey. Of course, there are still a number of unresolved issues on the question on justification. However, the churches do not have to agree point by point on all theological issues. If there is substantial agreement, some differences need not necessarily divide the Church; some can be understood not as contradictory but as complementary. In this sense a differentiated agreement, a reconciled diversity, or whatever we call it, is sufficient.[29]

Some, especially Protestant theologians, have expressed disappointment about the Joint Declaration. They miss concrete ecclesial consequences. My own view is that this critique is unjustified, for the Joint Declaration itself states very clearly that it does not intend to solve the ecclesiological questions. The Joint Declaration brought about a new and deeper dimension and intensity in relations with our Lutheran brothers and sisters, a dimension we do not have with other Protestant denominations. Ultimately, this enables us to give common witness to the world about the essence of the Gospel: Jesus Christ and his salvific meaning. In our largely secularized world this is no small thing.

The actual 'inner core' which remains concerns the linked questions of the Church and its ministry. These are now on the agenda. In the reformatory sense, the Church is '*creatura verbi*';[30] she is understood primarily through the proclamation of the Word and the response of faith; she is the assembly of believers, in which the Gospel is preached in its purity and the sacraments are administered according to the Gospel.[31] Hence, the centre of gravity is no longer in the Church but in the community as the 'central reference point of the basic reformatory insights and mental structures'.[32] For that reason the constitution of the churches of the Reformed tradition is not episcopal but community-synodical and presbyteral; theologically, the episcopate is a pastorate with the function of church leadership,[33] an understanding which is even more strongly marked in the Reformed churches than in the Lutheran churches.[34]

However, in the last two decades there has been some shift. The Lima documents on *Baptism, Eucharist and Ministry* (1982), in which the apostolic succession in the episcopate is considered 'as a sign, though not a guarantee, of the continuity and unity of the Church',[35] are welcome. Meanwhile, in dialogue with the Anglican churches, which ecumenically hold an important intermediary position,[36] the Scandinavian and the USA Lutheran Churches have taken up the issue of the historical episcopate.[37] The continental European Lutheran Churches of the Leuenberg Community have a different stand; for both of them, the episcopal and synodical–

presbyteral order are legitimate within a plurality of church orders and structures.[38]

Thus we are confronted with two different approaches: on the one hand, the universally-oriented, episcopal approach of the Anglicans and some Lutheran churches, inspired by ancient church tradition; and, on the other hand, a more local, community-centred, presbyteral approach. Behind the two approaches lie different interpretations of the precise intention of the Reformation. Did the Reformers intend to renew the then universal Church, maintaining continuity with its fundamental structure, as the Augsburg Confession (1530) suggests?[39] Or was the development of a new type and paradigm of the Church an inevitable and deliberate consequence of their actions? Is there a fundamental consensus or – as many state nowadays – a fundamental difference?[40]

Currently we receive different signals from our partners, and it is not easy for us at the moment to distinguish the direction in which they are moving in ecclesiological terms. There is still a need for clarification on ecclesiological issues, especially on the ordained ministry, both ecumenically and within the Protestant world itself. The Joint International Dialogue Commission with the Lutherans is now working on these issues and the Faith and Order Commission has also initiated a consultation process on The Nature and the Purpose of the Church[41] which – we hope – will build constructively on the Lima documents on *Baptism, Eucharist and Ministry* (1982).

Unfortunately, while we are engaged in overcoming these and other traditional differences, new problems have now arisen in the field of ethics, where there had previously been a general consensus. As well as the issue of women's ordination, which Luther strictly denied, the Anglican and Protestant worlds are also deeply divided today on the ethical problems being debated in our modern Western culture, including abortion, homosexuality and euthanasia. This creates new barriers, which make common witness, which our world needs so much, more difficult and sometimes even impossible.

With regard to the questions of church ministry and ethics, there is one common concern of Reformation theology: Christian freedom. Luther's famous treatise of 1520, one of his main reforming publications, *On Christian Freedom*, once again becomes relevant. Luther was often understood, but also more often misunderstood, as a liberator from the yoke of papacy and from all institutional constraints, and to that extent as a pioneer of freedom in the liberal modern sense.[42] Thus, with regard to the dialogue with the churches of the Reformed tradition, after clarification of the doctrine of justification, the issues still outstanding are pre-eminently those dealing with ecclesiology. But a solution of the ecclesiological questions has to be seen in the much wider context of how to relate to our modern and post-modern culture and how to understand Christian freedom as compared with liberal Western freedom.

Pneumatology as a Fundamental Problem

The objection is often made that the question of church ministry – priesthood, episcopate, Petrine ministry – cannot be the only reason why we have to live in separate churches and not participate together in the Lord's Table. And yet it is! Theologians of the Orthodox churches and the Reformed tradition point out that a deeper difference is becoming clear on the issue of ministry. We shall only progress in the ecumenical dialogue if we succeed in defining that deeper difference more precisely, not in order to cement the diversity but to overcome it in a better way.

For some Orthodox theologians this basic difference involves the argument about the *filioque*, the Latin addition to the common Niceno–Constantinopolitan creed of the ancient Church. At first sight, this seems a somewhat odd thesis. But in the view of some Orthodox theologians, the *filioque* has concrete consequences for the understanding of the Church. For them, it seems to link the activity of the Holy Spirit fully to the person and work of Jesus Christ, leaving no room for the freedom of the Spirit; the *filioque* chains the Holy Spirit, so to speak, entirely to the institutions established by Christ. According to that reading, the *filioque* is the root of the Catholic subordination of charisma to the institution, of individual freedom to the authority of the Church, of the prophetic to the juridical, of mysticism to scholasticism, of the common priesthood to the hierarchical priesthood, and finally of episcopal collegiality to the Roman primacy.[43] This reproach of a unilateral christomonism is not justified with regard to the Catholic tradition as a whole, but there is a significant kernel of truth in it with regard to the post-Reformation ecclesiology, which was indeed often more a hierarchology.[44]

We find similar arguments based on quite different premises on the Protestant side. The Reformation churches are no doubt in the Latin tradition and they generally keep the *filioque*; against the enthusiasts they affirm with energy that the Spirit is Jesus Christ's Spirit and is tied to word and sacrament.[45] But for them, too, it is a question of the sovereignty of God's Word in and over the Church, as against a juridical–institutional view of the Church. So they proclaim Christian freedom as freedom from church mediation through indulgences and the whole priestly–sacramental system. This Christian freedom, an issue so dear to the Reformers, corresponds to the freedom of God and his Spirit.

The development in the Reformation of the revivalist and pietistic movements and the Free churches, with their emphasis on the freedom of the Spirit, was in part a reaction to what very soon became the equally institutionalized and established Protestant churches, and to some extent had its inner historical logic in the fundamental decisions of the Reformers. After the various revival movements and the classical Free churches (Methodists, Baptists, Mennonites, Adventists, Disciples of Christ etc.), we are today witnessing the emergence of new and vigorous charismatic and Pentecostal movements, which are expanding rapidly world-wide whilst the Protestant mainline churches are in world-wide decline. Thus the ecumenical scene is changing dramatically.[46]

The Pentecostals are not always easy dialogue partners. Some of them are very aggressive and proselytizing and, especially in Latin America, they cause great problems for the Catholic Church. With others we have been able to develop a positive and trustful dialogue.[47] They are very firm in their Trinitarian and Christological beliefs and their ethical convictions. In a word, they are serious Christians, but they lack a developed ecclesiology, especially a universal ecclesiology which transcends their respective local communities. The dialogue with these communities and the questions raised by them will be of great importance for the future of the ecumenical dialogue.[48]

The Second Vatican Council, too, brought a revival of the charismatic dimension of the Church.[49] The Council speaks not only of the activity of the Spirit through the bishops[50] but even

more of the understanding of faith of all believers,[51] of the Spirit
leading into the truth throughout the entire life of the Church.[52]
There should, therefore, not be any one-sided, top-down relationship between bishops and priests[53] or between lay people, priests
and bishops,[54] but rather a mutual relationship built on brotherhood and friendship.

A practical consequence of this was the charismatic movement,
through which the Pentecostal movement found its way into the
Catholic Church. In a certain sense one can even speak of a
'pentecostalization' of the Catholic Church in many parishes and
congregations, recognizable from the way in which they celebrate
their liturgy. However, in contrast to the Pentecostal movements
outside Catholicism, the Catholic charismatic movement remains
within the sacramental and institutional structure of the Church; it
is therefore able to have an invigorating effect on the Church.

This pneumatological approach can easily become part of a
renewed ecclesiology of communion, which in the last decades has
become more and more the key term of most of the ecumenical
dialogue documents.[55] Its central and fundamental idea is the
participation of all believers through the Holy Spirit in the life of
the triune God (1 John 1.3). The Holy Spirit gives his gifts in a
great variety (1 Cor. 12). This implies many questions of
ecclesiology, including the relation between the common priesthood of all the baptized and the hierarchical priesthood; the
relation of primacy and synodical or conciliar structures in the
Church; and the relations between bishops, priests and deacons
and between pastors and the entire people of God. But this
approach also opens many doors to less static and more dynamic
solutions to these problems.

Common participation in the life of the triune God signifies that
the Church is built in the image of the Holy Trinity.[56] The doctrine
of the Trinity is, in essence, the development of the statement from
the first letter of St John: 'God is love' (1 John 4.8, 16). God is, in
himself, the pure relationship of love; above all, the Holy Spirit is
love in person. A relational ontology follows from this, which is
fundamental for a renewed *communio*-ecclesiology. It can understand being only in terms of relations, as a mutual giving of space
and the mutual enabling of the relation. From this follows a
spirituality of *communio*, without which all discussions on
structures of communion become soulless and void.[57]

The freedom the Holy Spirit bestows is therefore not an individualistic freedom, but a communal freedom for others and with others; Christian freedom is essentially bound up with responsibility and finds its fulfilment in unselfish love and service for others. The apostle Paul in his Letter to the Galatians admonishes: 'You, my brothers, were called to be free. But do not use your freedom to indulge the sinful nature; rather, serve one another in love' (Gal. 5.13).

Luther, in his treatise *On Christian Freedom*, rightly took up this idea, but it was the renowned Tübingen theologian Johann Adam Möhler who splendidly captured the sense of this issue in the following words:

> Two extremes in Church life are possible, however, and they are both called egoism; they are: when *each person* or *one person* wants to be everything; in the latter case, the bond of unity becomes so tight and love so hot that suffocation cannot be averted; in the former case, everything falls apart to such an extent and it becomes so cold that you freeze; the one type of egoism generates the other; but there is no need for one person or each person to want to be everything; only everyone together can be everything and the unity of all only a whole. This is the idea of the Catholic Church.[58]

This leads us to envisage a church where the different roles and charismas co-operate in an open interplay, where, for example, the magisterium has its inalienable and irreplaceable role, but where also the sensus and the consensus of the faithful, the reception process, the function of the magisterium of theologians, and above all the testimony of liturgy, are not ruled out. In such an interplay the freedom of the Spirit works not beside but within and through the ecclesial communion, which is at the same time both institution and an ever-new charismatic event.[59]

Such a vision would maintain all the essential Catholic positions on ministry and magisterium and at the same time would respond to the criticisms of our separated brethren. Ultimately it leads us back to spiritual ecumenism. For we cannot 'make' or 'organize' this kind of communion. The prayer 'Veni Creator Spiritus' is the ultimate answer to how we can respond to the insistence of the one Spirit and overcome the scandal of division. Only in him are we able to implement our Lord's prayer on the eve of his death 'that all may be one' (John 17.22).

Notes

1   *Unitatis redintegratio* (UR) 1; *Ut unum sint* (UUS) 99.
2   UUS 3. For the 'Fruits of Dialogue' see UUS 41-9.
3   Cf. the declaration, *Dominus Iesus. On the Unicity and Salvific Universality of Jesus Christ and the Church*, 6 August 2000.
4   *Lumen gentium* (LG) 8.
5   LG 8; UR 3.
6   UUS 13.
7   LG 15; UR 3; UUS 48; *Dominus Iesus* 17.
8   UR 14.
9   UUS 34.
10 LG 8; UR 4; 6-8; UUS 15-17.
11 UR 4; *Dominus Iesus* 17.
12 UUS 28.
13 J. Ratzinger, *Gott und die Welt. Glauben und Leben in unserer Zeit*, Stuttgart-Munich 2000, 388f.
14 UR 7f.; UUS 21.
15 Published in important works by A. Grillmeier, A. de Halleux, L. Abramowski, etc.
16 Cf. *Wort und Wahrheit*, vol. 1/5, 1974/89; *Chalzedon und die Folgen* (FS Bischof Mesrob Kikorian), Pro Oriente, vol. 14, Innsbruck/Vienna 1992; D. Wendebourg, *Die eine Christenheit auf Erden*, Tübingen 2000, 116–46.
17 *Dokumente wachsender Übereinstimmung*, published by H. Meyer, H. J. Urban, L. Visher; vol. 1, Paderborn-Frankfurt a.M. 1983, 529–31; 533f.; 541f. (with the Copts); vol. 2 (1992), 571f. (with the Syrians); 575 (with the Copts); 578f. (with the Malankara Orthodox Syrian Church); *Growth in Agreement*, ed. J. Gros, H. Meyer, W. Rush; vol. 2, Geneva 2000, 707–8 (with the Armenian–Apostolic Church); 711–12 (with the Assyrian Church of the East).
18 *Tomos agapes*, Vatican-Phanar (1958–1970), Rome–Istanbul (1971); cf. J. Ratzinger, 'Rom und die Kirchen des Ostens nach der Aufhebung der Exkommunikationen von 1054,' in: *Theologische Prinzipienlehre*, München 1982, 214–39.
19 UR 14; 16.
20 Cf. Y. Congar, *Neuf cent ans après. Notes sur le schisme oriental*, Chevetogne 1957.

21 With regard to the international dialogue: *Documents on Increasing Agreement*, vol. 2, 531–41; 542–53; 556–7; the Balamand document, in: *Growth in Agreement*, ibid. 680–5; *Bilateral Dialogue: Orthodoxy in Dialogue*, ed. J. Bremer, D. Oeldemann, Stoltmann, Trier 1999; important North American dialogue: *The Quest for Unity*, ed. J. Borelli and J. H. Erickson, Crestwood-Washington 1996. In the meantime the North American dialogue was able to finalize a document on the *filioque* clause.

22 Cf. *Catechism of the Catholic Church* 246; *Les traditions grecque et latine concernant la procession du Saint-Esprit*, Vatican City 1996; *Vom Heiligen Geist. Der gemeinsame trinitarische Glaube und das Problem des Filioque*, Innsbruck-Wien 1998.

23 Paul VI, Address to the World Council of Churches in Geneva (12 June 1964) in: *Insegnamenti VII*, 1 (1984), 1686; John Paul II, Address to the Plenary of the PCPCU, in: *Information service*, 98 (1998), 118ff.; UUS 88.

24 UUS 95.

25 *Information Service* 2002/I–II, 29–42 (with extensive bibliography).

26 We shall mention only the international documents: with the Lutherans: *The Gospel and the Church* ('The Malta Report') (1972); *The Eucharist* (1978); *Ways to Community* (1980); *All Under One Christ* (1980); *The Ministry in the Church* (1981); *Martin Luther – Witness to Jesus Christ* (1983); *Facing Unity* (1984); *Church and Justification* (1994). With the Reformed: *The Presence of Christ in Church and World* (1977). Multilateral dialogues: *Baptism, Eucharist, Ministry, Convergence Declarations of the Faith and Order Commission of the World Council of Churches* (1982); *Confessing One Faith Together. An Ecumenical Interpretation of the Apostolic Credo as Known in the Profession of Faith of Nicea-Constantinople (381)*.

27 Especially *Justification by Faith. Lutherans and Catholics in Dialogue VII*, Minneapolis 1985; *Lehrverurteilungen – Kirchentrennend?* ed. K. Lehmann and W. Pannenberg, Freiburg i.br.-Göttingen 1986.

28 *Joint Declaration on the Doctrine of Justification. Official statement and appendix*. Frankfurt a.M.-Paderborn 1999.

29 Cf. H. Meyer, 'Einheit in versöhnter Verschiedenheit', in: the same, *Versöhnte Verschiedenheit. Aufsätze zur ökumenische Theologie*, vol. 1, Frankfurt a.m.-Paderborn 1998, 101–19; K. Lehmann, 'Was für ein Konsens wurde erreicht?' in: *StdZ* 124 (1999), 740–5; *Einheit – aber wie? Zur Tragfähigkeit der ökumenischen Formel von 'differenzierten Konsens'*, ed. by H. Wagner (*Quaestiones disputatae*, vol. 184), Freiburg i.Br. 2000.

30 M. Luther, *De captivitate Babylonica ecclesiae praeludium* (1520), in: WA 6, 561.

31 CA Art. 7 and 8 (BSELK 61f.); Schmalkaldische Artikel III, 10: *Von den Kirchen* (BSELK 459f.); *Grosser Katechismus* Art. 3 (BSELK 653-8); *Heidelberger Katechismus*, 54. Question (*Confessional Texts and Church Orders*, ed. W. Niesel, 43f.); *Barmener Erklärung*, Art. 3 (ibid. 335f.).

32 G. Gloege, Art. 'Gemeinde', in: *RGG* vol. 2, 3. 1958 edition, 1329.

33 Fundamental CA 28 (BSELK 120-34).

34 Cf. John Calvin, ibid. 714–24, in which Calvin excludes the episcopate from his doctrine on ministries.

35 *Baptism, Eucharist and Ministry* 38. Frankfurt-Paderborn 1982, 44.

36 Important above all is the last document of ARCIC: *The Gift of Authority – Authority in the Church* III, London-Toronto-New York 1999.

37 *The Porvoo Common Statement* (1992); *Called to Common Mission. An Agreement of Full Communion between the Episcopal Church of the USA and the Evangelical Lutheran Church in America* (1999); *Called to Full Communion. The Waterloo Declaration by the Anglican Church in Canada and the Evangelical Lutheran Church in Canada* (1999).

38 *Die Kirche Jesu Christi. Der reformatorische Beitrag zum ökumenischen Dialog über die kirchliche Einheit* (Leuenberg Texts, 1), Frankfurt a.M. 1995, 34; 56–9. Two recent German documents are *Leuenberg: Kirchengemeinschaft nach evangelischem Verständnis* (2001) and *Ökumene nach lutherischem Verständnis* (2004).

39 So today for example, W. Pannenberg, 'Reformation und Einheit der Kirche', in: *Kirche und Ökumene*, Göttingen 2000, 173–85; *The Catholicity of the Reformation*. ed. C. E.

Braaten and R. W. Jenson, Grand Rapids, Mich. 1996; *The Ecumenical Future. Background for In One Body through the Cross: The Princeton Proposal for Christian Unity*, ed. C. E. Braaten and R. W. Jenson, Grand Rapids, Mich. 2003.

40   *Grundkonsens – Grunddifferenz*, ed. A. Birmelé and H. Meyer, Frankfurt a.m.-Paderborn 1992; H. Meyer, *Ökumenische Zielvorstellungen*, Göttingen 1996, 159–62.

41   *The Nature and the Purpose of the Church. A stage on the way to a common statement*. Faith and Order Paper 181 (1998).

42   G. Ebeling, 'Der kontroverse Grund der Freiheit', in: *Lutherstudien* vol. 3, Tübingen 1985, 366–94.

43   This is the position of V. Lossky, *Théologie mystique de l'église d'Orient*, Paris 1944. This position was criticized by G. Florovsky, 'Christ and his Church, Suggestions and Comments', in: *L'Église et les Églises*, vol. 2, Chevetogne 1955.

44   Y. Congar, 'Pneumatologie et "christomonism" dans la tradition latine', in: *Ecclesia a Spiritu sancto edocta*, Gembloux 1970, 41–64; *Je crois en l'Esprit Saint*, vol. 1: *L'expérience de l'Esprit*, Paris 1979, 95–130; 207–17.

45   Y. Congar, *Je crois en l'Esprit Saint*, 191–8; R. Frieling, *Amt, Laie – Pfarrer – Priester – Bischof – Papst*, Göttingen 2002, 213f.

46   W. J. Hollenweger, *Pentecostalism*, Hendrickson 1997; C. M. Robeck, 'Pentecostals and Ecumenism in a Pluralistic World', in: *The Globalisation of Pentecostalism*, Oxford 1999.

47   On Catholic-Pentecostal dialogue: R. del Colle, 'The Holy Spirit and Christian Unity. A Case Study from Catholic/ Pentecostal Dialogue', in: P. Walter *et al.*, ibid. 290–305; C. M. Robeck, 'The Challenge Pentecostalism Poses to the Quest for Ecclesial Unity', in: ibid. 306–32.

48   Y. Congar, *Je crois en l'Esprit Saint*, vol. 2, Paris 1980, 193–270.

49   LG 4; 7; 12; 49; AA 3; AG 4; 29. Cf. Y. Congar, *Je crois en l'Esprit Saint*, vol. 1, Paris 1979, 227–35.

50   LG 21; 24f.; 27.

51   LG 12; 35.

52   DV 8.

53   LG 28; PO 7; CD 16; 28.

54   LG 37; PO 9; AA 25.
55   An extensive bibliography includes the following. Of funda-
     mental relevance: L. Hertling, *Communio und Primat. Kirche
     und Papsttum in der Antike* (Miscellanea Historiae Pontifi-
     ciae, Bd. 7), Rome 1943. For the Lutheran side: W.
     Elert, *Abendmahl und Kirchengemeinschaft in der alten Kirche
     hauptsächlich des Ostens*, Berlin 1954. For a biblical
     comparison: H. Seesemann, J. Hainz, P. C. Bori, K. Kertelge
     et al. For the period of the Council: H. de Lubac, Y. Congar, J.
     Hamer, M. J. Le Guillou *et al.* There is an extensive
     bibliography after the Council: A. Grillmeier, H. U. von
     Balthasar, O. Saier, J. Ratzinger, W. Kasper, J. M. R. Tillard,
     M. Kehl, G. Greshake, B. Forte, J. Hilberath *et al.*
     Importantly, the Festschrift for Bishop P. W. Scheele,
     Communio Sanctorum (1988), as well as for Archbishop O.
     Saier, *Gemeinsam Kirche sein. Theorie und Praxis der
     Communio* (1992).
56   LG 4; UR 3.
57   John Paul II, Apostolic Letter, *Novo millennio ineunte* (2001),
     43.
58   J. A. Möhler, *Unity in the Church*, § 70.
59   Elsewhere I have demonstrated how this vision corresponds to
     that of the first school of Tübingen as in J. S. Drey and J. A.
     Möhler.

3

The Nature and Purpose of Ecumenical Dialogue

A Burning Question

The twentieth century, which started with a strong impulse of faith in progress which is rather difficult to imagine nowadays, ended as one of the darkest and bloodiest centuries in the history of humankind. No other century has known as many violent deaths. But at least there is a small glimmer of light in this dark period: the birth of the ecumenical movement and ecumenical dialogues. After centuries of growing fragmentation of the *una sancta ecclesia* – the one, holy Church that we profess in our apostolic creed – into many divided churches and church communities, a new movement developed in the opposite direction. In deep sorrow and repentance, all churches realized that their situation of division was sinful, shameful, and contrary to the will of Christ.

The ecumenical movement had been prepared for by sporadic efforts since the seventeenth century, and especially by the Oxford Movement in the nineteenth century. It is significant that the new ecumenical awareness in the twentieth century developed in the context of the missionary movement. The World Missionary Conference at Edinburgh (1910) recognized that the division of the Church was a major obstacle to world mission. This is why, in the twentieth century, more or less all churches engaged in ecumenical dialogue, setting out to re-establish the visible unity of all Christians. The foundation of the World Council of Churches in Amsterdam in 1948 represented an important milestone on this ecumenical journey.

At the beginning the Catholic Church abstained. The encyclical letters *Satis cognitum* of Leo XIII (1896) and *Mortalium animos* of Pius XI (1928) even condemned the ecumenical movement, which seemed to relativize the claim of the Catholic Church to be the true Church of Jesus Christ. Yet Pius XII, albeit with caution, paved the way to a more open attitude in an Instruction of the Holy Office of 1949. However, only the initiative of John XXIII (1958–63) and the second Vatican Council (1962–65) brought about a shift. The conciliar Decree on Ecumenism, *Unitatis redintegratio*, stated that the ecumenical movement was a sign of the work of the Spirit in our time (UR 1; 4), opening the way for the ecumenical movement and highlighting the importance of dialogue with separated brothers and sisters and with separated churches and church communities (UR 4; 9; 11; 14; 18; 19; 21-23). Paul VI (1963–78) made the idea of dialogue central in his inaugural encyclical *Ecclesiam suam* (1963). This line was taken up in a document of the then Secretariat for Promoting Christian Unity, *Reflections and Suggestions Concerning Ecumenical Dialogue* (1970), then later in the *Ecumenical Directory* (1993) and finally in the great, important and even prophetic ecumenical encyclical of John Paul II, '*Ut unum sint*' (1995).

Nevertheless, the new beginning was not easy. From the outset, the first General Secretary of the World Council of Churches, Dr. Visser't Hooft, raised the question of whether the Catholic Church and the World Council of Churches understood ecumenism in the same way. This question was also related to the meaning of ecumenical dialogue, which the conciliar Decree on Ecumenism had proposed as a way of contributing towards unity.

The question arose again even more sharply when the Congregation for the Doctrine of the Faith issued the Document *Dominus Iesus* (2000) with the affirmation that the Church of Jesus Christ subsists fully only in the Roman Catholic Church and that the communities stemming from the Reformation of the sixteenth century are not churches in the proper sense. This statement angered many Protestant Christians, who perceived it as bold and offensive. The question arose: Is real dialogue possible for a church and with a church which claims to have the absolute truth in an infallible way? For dialogue presupposes openness towards other positions and an encounter of equals. So the question was, and for many still is: Is this document not a sign that the Catholic Church understands ecumenism only as simple return of the separated brethren into the fold of the Catholic Church and thus she withdraws from the spirit and the precepts of the Second

Vatican Council and relinquishes the concept of dialogue? An ecumenical cooling, a doubt and – as many see it – an ecumenical crisis ensued.

Here I want to take the questions raised by this document as an opportunity and even as a challenge to ask, more profoundly, what dialogue and especially ecumenical dialogue is all about. What is the Catholic understanding of dialogue and what can be its contribution to the wider ecumenical dialogue and to the one ecumenical movement? How can we overcome the ecumenical aporia and what many regard as the ecumenical crisis?

Basic Philosophical Presuppositions

Speaking about ecumenical dialogue and starting a dialogue on dialogue presupposes that we actually know what dialogue is. Dialogue is one of the most fundamental concepts of twentieth-century philosophy and is related to today's personalist way of thinking, epitomized in the writings of Martin Buber, Franz Rosenzweig, Ferdinand Ebner, Emmanuel Levinas and others. The young Polish professor Karol Wojtyla with his philosophy of love and responsibility was also influenced by this kind of personalist thinking. In the encyclical letter *Ut unum sint* (1995) (n. 28) that he later wrote as Pope he bore witness to this personalist under-standing of dialogue.

This new trend which emerged in the twentieth century and was characterized by dialogical philosophy marked the end of mono-logical thinking, and implied self–transcendence of the person towards the other. The starting-point and the fundamental principle of dialogical philosophy is: 'I don't be without thou'; 'We don't exist for ourselves'; 'We exist with and for each other'; 'We do not only have encounter, we *are* encounter, we *are* dialogue' . The other is not the limit of myself; the other is a part and an enrichment of my own existence. So dialogue is an indispensable step along the path towards human self-realization.

Dialogue therefore is not only dialogue consisting of words and conversations. Dialogue encompasses all dimensions of our being human; it implies a global, existential dimension and the human subject in his or her entirety. Of especially great importance is the field of symbolic interaction. So dialogue is communication in a comprehensive sense: it withstands and criticizes our Western individualistic way of life, and ultimately means living together and living in solidarity for each other.

Such dialogue is not only essential and necessary for individuals. Dialogue also concerns nations, cultures, religions. Every nation, culture and religion has its riches and its gifts. But it becomes narrow and evolves into ideology when it closes itself off and absolutizes itself. Then the other nation, culture and religion becomes the enemy. The 'clash of civilizations' (Huntington) will ensue. Dialogue is the only way to avoid such a disastrous clash. Today dialogue among cultures, religions and churches is a presupposition for peace in the world. It is necessary to pass from antagonism and conflict to a situation where each party recognizes and respects the other as a partner.

It is superfluous to say that in our present world situation such an intercultural and interreligious dialogue is especially necessary between Christianity and Islam, between the Western and the Arabic worlds. Medieval culture, philosophy and theology give a good example and show how fruitful such a dialogue can be for both sides. The *Summa* of Thomas Aquinas would not have been possible without the influence of and critical dialogue with Arabic philosophers such as Avicenna, Averroes and others.

In today's world of globalization there are two dangers to avoid. On the one hand, we must shun every kind of nationalism, racism, xenophobia and the oppression of people through other people, the claim of superiority and cultural hegemony. Nations, cultures and religions must open themselves and enter into dialogue. This presupposes mutual tolerance, mutual respect, mutual under-standing and acknowledgement of both one's own limits and the riches of the other, and it presupposes a willingness to learn from one another. On the other hand, this does not mean a uniform universal culture, where the identity of individual cultures is extinguished. On the contrary, dialogue presupposes partners which have, know and appreciate their identity. The aim of dialogue is neither an antagonistic pluralism nor a boring uniformity but a rich dialogue-unity of cultures, where cultural identities are preserved and recognized, but also purified from inherent limits and enriched by intercultural exchange.

Such dialogue-unity between cultures and religions is the only way to peace in an era of globalization. From a secular point of view the ecumenical movement can be seen as one important element within this ongoing world-wide process for peace and reconciliation. From a more ecclesiastical point of view one can say that in a globalized world ecumenical rapprochement is necessary in order that the voice of Christendom may become fully credible.

Theological Foundations

The dialogical vision of the human being and the whole of humankind is rooted in the biblical and Jewish tradition. God did not create us as isolated individual beings, but as man and woman, as social beings with a communitarian nature. Every human being, regardless of his or her sex, colour, culture, nation or religion is created in the image and likeness of God (Gen. 1.27); every human being has absolute value and dignity and requires not only tolerance but respect. The modern idea of the inalienable human rights of every human person can only be understood as a consequence of this fundamental biblical message.

The Bible expounds the golden rule, which in one form or another can be found in all world religions and which is the common heritage of all humankind: 'Do to others as you would have them do to you' (Luke 6.31; cf. Matt. 7.12). Here, attaining personal self-realization and turning one's attention to the other are intimately linked together. 'Love your neighbour as yourself' (Mark 10.30) is the great commandment of Jesus and the fulfilment of the law (Rom. 13.10). 'Man can fully discover his true self only in a sincere giving of himself' (*Gaudium et spes* 24).

Even revelation is a dialogical process. In revelation God addresses us and speaks to us as to his friends and moves among us in order to invite and receive us into his own company (*Dei verbum* 2). The highpoint of this dialogue is the Christ event itself. In Jesus Christ, who is true God and true man, we have the most intensive and totally unique dialogue between God and man. As the Gospel of John especially shows, the unity between Jesus as the unique son of God and his father is a dialogical one (John 10.30), a relation of intimate mutual knowledge and love (Matt. 12.25-27; John 10.15). At the same time he is the one who lives and gives his life for others (Mark 10.45); he is perfect pro-existence, existence for the other.

Christian faith claims that in Jesus Christ all human desires, longings, expectations and hopes are fulfilled. He is the fullness of time (Gal. 4.4) and the very aim of all creation and salvation history (Eph. 1.10). In him the ultimate truth of the dialogical human existence is revealed and realized. Jesus Christ is the way, the truth and the life (John 14.6). Following the New Testament, the early fathers of the Church affirmed that the logos radiating in all creation appeared in its fullness in Jesus Christ. The Second Vatican Council in its Pastoral Constitution *Gaudium et spes* expresses it in these words: 'The truth is that only in the mystery of the Incarnate Word does the mystery of man take on light. ... Christ, the final Adam, ... fully reveals man to man himself, and makes his supreme calling clear' (*Gaudium et spes* 22).

The confession that in Jesus Christ the fullness of time appeared once and for all is the fundamental Christian truth; it implies that concrete, firm and decisive affirmations are typical of Christian witness. The Christian message withstands every syncretism and relativization, especially relativization in the name of a wrongly understood dialogue. Dialogue does not produce truth, dialogue discovers the truth which is given to us once for all in Jesus Christ. 'Tolle assertiones et christianismum tulisti' wrote Martin Luther against Erasmus, whom he blamed for his scepticism.

However, this determination of Christian witness is fundamentally different from sectarian refusal to communicate and does not at all contradict dialogical openness. Jesus Christ is the fulfilment and fullness of dialogue, not its end or suppression. The Second Vatican Council states:

> The Catholic Church rejects nothing which is true and holy in these religions. She looks with sincere respect upon those ways of conduct and of life, those rules and teachings which, though differing in many particulars from what she holds and sets forth, nevertheless often reflect a ray of that Truth which enlightens all men.... The Church therefore has this exhortation for her sons: prudently and lovingly, through dialogue and collaboration with the followers of other religions, and inwitness of Christian faith and life, acknowledge, preserve, and promote the spiritual and moral goods found among these men, as well as the values in their society and culture. (*Nostra aetate* 2)

According to the Council's Declaration on Religious Freedom, *Dignitatis humanae*, the truth given once and for all cannot be imposed by violence; nobody can be forced to act contrary to their conscience. 'The truth cannot impose itself except by virtue of its own truth' (*Dignitatis humanae* 1).

Truth, however, is to be sought after in a manner proper to the dignity of the human person and his social nature. The inquiry is to be free, carried on with the aid of teaching or instruction, communication, and dialogue. ... in order thus to assist one another in the quest for truth. (*Dignitatis humanae* 3).

Reflections on religious freedom can be deepened by Christology when we consider the life of Jesus in concrete terms. The Gospels bear witness to Jesus Christ as the person for others. He, the Lord, did not come to dominate but to serve, and to give his life as a ransom 'for many' (Mark 10.45). He emptied himself even unto death, that is why he was raised high to be the Lord of the universe (Phil. 2.6-11). Through Jesus Christ, service which is self-consuming and self-sacrificing has become the new law of the world. It is not through power and force but by his kenosis that he manifests his Godhead. His absoluteness consists in his self-emptying, self-communicating, self-giving love.

Thus the Christian confession that Jesus Christ is the truth and the ultimate revelation that cannot be surpassed is no imperialistic thesis, and it neither constitutes nor allows an imperialistic understanding of mission; it has nothing to do with world conquest, even if, in the course of history, it was unfortunately sometimes misunderstood and misused as such. On the contrary, understood correctly, it establishes in its own way not only a kenotic relationship of tolerance and respect towards other religions but, over and above this, a kenotic relationship of dialogue and service.

So dialogue and mission are no opposites, they do not exclude each other. Through every dialogue I not only intend to impart something to somebody else, I also intend to impart what is most important and dearest to myself. I even wish the other one to share in it. Hence in a religious dialogue I intend to impart my belief to somebody else. Yet I can only do so by paying unconditional respect to his or her freedom. In a dialogue I do not want, and am not allowed, to impose anything on anybody against their will and conviction. It is the same with missionary activities. Since the beginning of Christianity it has been strictly forbidden to christen anybody against their will. This implies also the exclusion of material promises and gifts as a means of mission. Thus mission is different from proselytism and even excludes it. The Christian faith is, according to its inner nature, only possible as a free act. Mission that has a proper under-standing of itself is also a process of dialogue leading to a mutual exchange and enrichment.

Therefore the dialogue of Christianity with other religions is not a one-way street. No concrete historic form or formula of Christianity will ever be able adequately to exhaust its richness. For all our concepts are limited, and culturally and historically conditioned. Encounter and dialogue with other cultures can help us to discover new aspects of the truth, which is Jesus Christ. Dialogue helps us to know all the depth and dimensions of Jesus Christ. Only when we bring in all the riches of all cultures can we know the fullness of truth in its completeness. Consequently, in encountering the richness of other religions, Christianity may get to know its own richness in a better, more profound and more concrete way. In the encounter with other religions and in an exchange with them, a new historic form of Christianity may be found which adapts to new cultural surroundings.

Intercultural dialogue can thus be one way in which the Spirit guides us into all truth (John 16.13) and bestows upon us a deeper and wider understanding of our own faith. Intercultural and interreligious dialogue and, even more, ecumenical dialogue must be understood as a Spirit-guided spiritual process and as one way in which the Church grows in insight into the once and for all revealed truth, and advances towards a fuller understanding of divine truth (*Dei verbum* 8). Dialogue can be an impulse for the development of Christian doctrine.

Since the Second Vatican Council, the Church has been engaged in such a process of dialogue under the guidance of the Pontifical Council for Interreligious Dialogue in Rome. In this context, I want only to recall the two meetings of John Paul II with the representatives of all religions during the World Day of Prayer in Assisi (1986 and 2002), his visit to the Rome synagogue in 1986 (the first visit of a Pope to a synagogue), his visit to the famous Islamic university of al-Azhar in Cairo (2000), and the first visit of a Pope to a mosque, which took place in Damascus (2001). Since the Second Vatican Council, dialogue has replaced confrontation as a feature of the Catholic Church.

The Ecclesiological Foundation

What has been outlined up to this point has laid the foundation for a general dialogical understanding of the Catholic Church, especially within the actual context of interreligious dialogue. Ecumenical dialogue in the strict sense of the term differs from interreligious dialogue, because it is a dialogue between those who believe in Jesus Christ and are baptized in his name but belong to different churches or church communities which often contradict each other in matters of faith, church structures and morals. The central point of their disagreement and controversy, though not the only point, is their different understanding of the Church. The main aim of the ecumenical movement is therefore the re-establishment of the visible unity of the Church.

Notwithstanding all the ecclesiological controversies, there is one point of general agreement: faith in the one God and in the one Lord and Saviour Jesus Christ corresponds to confession of the one Church, which is not only a human social reality but the body of Christ, where Jesus Christ is present and works through the Holy Spirit. The controversial question arises only when one asks where this Church of Jesus Christ is present, where it can concretely be found. To this question the Catholic Church responds with her famous '*subsistit in*' and affirms that the Church of Jesus Christ subsists in the Roman Catholic Church (*Lumen gentium* 8). Or, as the declaration *Dominus Iesus* puts it in a much sharper way, the Church of Jesus Christ in the full sense subsists *only* in the Catholic Church. Whilst the Orthodox churches are recognized as true particular churches, the churches and ecclesial communities stemming from the Reformation are not – according to *Dominus Iesus* – churches in the proper sense. This harsh statement has become the focus of the ecumenical debate and is often seen as nurturing doubt in the ecumenical dialogue.

Progress in dialogue can only continue through a precise interpretation of this affirmation. This means interpreting it in the context in which it appears. For the Second Vatican Council says in the same context that outside the Catholic Church there are many and important ecclesial elements, especially baptism (LG 15; *Unitatis redintegratio* 3). We have more in common than what divides us. The Council adds that the Holy Spirit is at work outside the institutional boundaries of the Catholic Church (UR 3), where there are also saints and martyrs (UR 4; *Ut unum sint* 84). So outside the Catholic Church there is – as the encyclical *Ut unum sint* (13) affirms – no ecclesial vacuum. There is a church reality but, according to our Catholic understanding, not *the* Church in the proper sense, i.e. in the full sense in which the Catholic Church understands herself. But this does not exclude the possibility that there is church in an analogous way, or a different type of church.

This understanding implies not only deficiencies in the being church of the others, but also wounds in the being of the Catholic Church. In a state of division she cannot realize fully her own catholicity (UR 4). The Catholic Church, too, needs conversion and renewal (UR 5-8; UUS 15f.; 83f.); she needs dialogue and exchange with other churches and church communities; and also needs an exchange of gifts (UUS 28). Being catholic and being ecumenical are not contradictory but are the two faces of one and the same medal. So ecumenical dialogue – as John Paul II maintains – 'is not just some sort of "appendix" ' but 'an outright necessity, one of the Church's priorities' (UUS 20; 31). The Church is dialogical by her very nature.

This dialogical character of the Church is rooted in her very nature as communion. Communion implies communication. It means firstly communion and communication with God through Jesus Christ within the Holy Spirit; and, secondly, communion and communication among Christians themselves through word, sacraments and *diaconia* or service, but also through communication, information, prayer, exchange, co-operation, living together, mutual visits, friendship, celebrating and worshipping together, witnessing together and suffering together.

Such dialogue and such a spirituality of communion are essential and must be increasingly fostered within the Catholic Church herself. In order to become engaging and inviting for the so-called separated brothers and sisters, she must overcome her one-sided monolithic structure and develop more communal, collegial and synodical structures. Such dialogue *ad intra* and dialogical structures are a presupposition for the ecumenical dialogue *ad extra*. This is especially true of the invitation of Pope John Paul II to a brotherly dialogue on how to exercise the Petrine ministry in the new ecumenical situation (UUS 95f.). Thus dialogue is essential within the Catholic Church and with the churches and ecclesial communities with which we are not yet in full communion, but on a common way and pilgrimage to full visible communion. Ecumenical dialogue is essential for the identity and catholicity of the Catholic Church herself.

Consequences for Ecumenical Dialogue

The goal of ecumenical dialogue

The ultimate goal of ecumenical dialogue is the same as the goal of the ecumenical movement itself: not only the spiritual but the visible unity of the Church. On this, all churches engaged in the ecumenical movement agree. Since the Second Vatican Council the Catholic Church has understood this visible unity not as uniformity but as unity in plurality and as a communion of churches. The term communion, in the tradition of the patristic age and as the central ecclesiological concept of the Second Vatican Council, has increasingly replaced the term unity or, better, unity is increasingly interpreted as communion. According to a famous formula of the then Professor Joseph Ratzinger: the churches must become one Church while at the same time remaining churches.

However, we cannot reach this goal in one leap. There are intermediate goals: overcoming misunderstandings, eliminating words, judgements and actions which do not correspond to the conditions of the separated brethren, reaching greater mutual understanding and deepening what we already have in common, as well as each church's growth in its own faith and renewal, mutual enrichment and exchange of charismas, partial or differentiated consensus, human and Christian friendship. For Pope John Paul II, rediscovered brotherhood is one of the most important harvests already reaped in ecumenical dialogue (UUS 41f.).

In the last decades these steps have taken us to an intermediate phase. We are aware that through the one baptism we are members of the one body of Christ and already in a real and profound communion, while not yet in full communion; there are still doctrines which divide us. However, we can already live this still imperfect communion, praying together, sharing in common reading and study of the Bible, offering common witness to our faith and co-operating with each other, especially in the field of *diaconia*. For we have more in common than what divides us.

Nevertheless, the next step towards full communion will not be easy. To be honest, there are not only complementary opposites to be reconciled, there are still contradictions to be overcome. And unfortunately there is a danger that, in the face of the sociological changes emerging today, new contradictions in ethical questions may arise; or perhaps it would be better not to speak in terms of new contradictions but of new challenges which create new tensions. The most difficult problem is that our different ecclesiologies imply different understandings of how the goal of visible unity or full communion should be understood in concrete terms and what it actually implies.

Dimensions of ecumenical dialogue
The Council's Decree on Ecumenism presents three dimensions of ecumenical dialogue. Firstly, there is theological dialogue, where experts explain the beliefs of each individual church, so that their characteristics become clearer and better mutual understanding is fostered. The second dimension involves practical co-operation and especially common prayer, which represents the very heart of the ecumenical movement. This aspect of dialogue encompasses not only academic theological dialogue but the whole life of the Church and of all the faithful. The third dimension is renewal and reform of our own church so that she becomes more fully an authentic sign and witness of the gospel and an invitation for other Christians (UR 4). There cannot be ecumenism without personal conversion and institutional renewal (UR 15; 21; 34f.; 83f.).

Ecumenism *ad extra*, the dialogue with other churches and ecclesial communities, presupposes therefore ecumenism *ad intra*, learning from each other and self-reform. Full communion cannot be achieved by convergence alone but also, and perhaps even more, by conversion which implies repentance, forgiveness and renewal of heart. Such a conversion is also a gift of grace. So in the end it is not we who 'make' and create unity. The unity of the Church is the gift of God's Spirit which has been solemnly promised to us. Therefore theological ecumenism must be linked to spiritual ecumenism, which is the heart of ecumenism.

A distinction is often made between the dialogue of love and the dialogue in truth. Both are important, but neither can be separated; they belong together. Love without truth is void and dishonest; truth without love is hard and repelling. So we must seek the truth in love, bearing in mind that love can be authentic only when it is an expression of truth. This has certainly been my own experience in dealing with many dialogues. Even high-level academic dialogues function only if more than theological skills emerge; indeed, on the merely intellectual level anybody is capable of expounding an argument against what has been said by the other side. The very nature of academic dialogue embodies the continuity of discourse. Only when there is more – mutual trust and friendship, mutual understanding and sharing on a spiritual level, and common prayer – can ecumenical dialogue advance.

Structures of dialogue
Ecumenical dialogue should not be undertaken only on the universal level; it must also become a duty at individual and local levels. It needs to be realized in each Christian's personal life when he or she meets Christians of other churches, in families, particularly in mixed marriages, in local communities, in dioceses and at the level of Bishops' Conferences. Of particular importance is the ecumenical dialogue undertaken in theological faculties and institutes.

In the present situation councils of churches can be a helpful structure for ecumenical dialogue. They are by no means a super-church and they cannot take decisions on behalf of their member churches, to whom they are accountable. The member churches themselves have been and remain the main agents in the ecumenical movement. Nonetheless, the councils of churches are important instruments and forums for encounter, dialogue, sharing, common witness and action. Therefore they are recommended by the *Ecumenical Directory* (nos 166–71).

Methods of dialogue
It is not my intention here to present an entire methodology for ecumenical dialogue and a complete ecumenical hermeneutic; I only want to describe two aspects of ecumenical methodology.

Firstly, the Second Vatican Council admonishes us to pay attention to the hierarchy of truths (UR 11). When comparing doctrines theologians should bear in mind that Catholic teaching maintains the existence of a 'hierarchy' of truths, that is, an order or structure, since truths vary in their relationship to the foundation of the Christian faith in Jesus Christ. Thus Christian faith has a structure in which different degrees have different functions. Ultimately all doctrines refer to the mystery of Christ and the Trinity. This principle is not a principle of reduction or even elimination of certain so-called secondary truths, but it is a principle of interpreting the secondary truth in the light of the basic doctrines of the Trinity and Christology. This is important, for example, for the correct interpretation of Catholic Mariology, which can be understood and rightly interpreted only on the basis, in the context and under the criterion of christology. Correctly understood, Mariology in no way obscures, diminishes or even contradicts the unique mediation of Jesus Christ; rather, it reveals its power (*Lumen gentium* 60).

Another important hermeneutical principle is the distinction between the content of faith and its expression (*Gaudium et spes* 62). This formulation of the principle may be seen as over-simplistic because there cannot be a content without its expression through language. But there can be different formulations or linguistic approaches to the same content. Within the one Church there must be binding common formulations of basic truths, especially the creed, for Christians must be able to confess together and celebrate together. But in a communion-unity within diversity there can also be different formulations of the same faith regarding other less central aspects of Christian faith.

This has been proved true in the case, for example, of recent common declarations with the ancient Oriental churches. For centuries there have been Christological disputes with the Copts and Syrians, especially about the dogma of the Council of Chalcedon (two natures in one person). However, over time thorough historical research has made Christians aware that Chalcedonian and non-Chalcedonian churches have a quite different understanding of the terms 'nature' and 'person', and that in effect both churches, through different expressions, intend to confess the same faith in Jesus Christ as true God and true man. The same discovery was made with regard to the *filioque* clause in the creed, which is an expression of the Western (Latin and Augustinian) approach to the mystery of the holy Trinity; the Greeks – who do not have this clause – have a different approach but nevertheless have fundamentally the same faith. Similarly, the Joint Declaration on Justification is a consensus in basic truths, which is not destroyed by some still open questions due to different approaches, languages, theological elucidations, and emphasis in understanding. We are talking here of a differentiated consensus or reconciled diversity.

Personal presuppositions

The encyclical *Ut unum sint* in particular describes the essence and the personal presuppositions of dialogue. Since dialogue is more than an exchange of ideas and has a global and existential dimension, it presupposes more than theological expertise and also requires personal engagement. It presupposes a common quest for the truth which is Jesus Christ himself. Its soul is prayer. So dialogue has a vertical as well as a horizontal dimension; it cannot take place merely on the horizontal level of meetings, exchanges of points of view, or even sharing of gifts, but has a primarily vertical thrust directed towards the One who is himself our reconciliation. This is possible inasmuch as dialogue also serves as an examination of conscience and is a kind of dialogue of conscience permeated by the spirit of conversion.

This process involves the purification of memories and prayer for forgiveness of sins: not only personal sins but also social sins and sinful structures that have contributed and continue to contribute to division and to the reinforcement of division. On several occasions, especially at the liturgy of repentance on the first Sunday of Lent 2000, Pope John Paul II has provided a worthy and moving example of this purification of memories with an attitude of honesty, humility, conversion and prayer for forgiveness of sins.

Fundamental Questions

All churches more or less agree on all the points mentioned up to now. But problems remain. The main problem is whether the Catholic Church, through dialogue with other churches, can be open to criticism and change with regard to its binding tradition (dogmas). Here the Protestant churches and the Catholic Church have different convictions. While the Protestant tradition speaks of the '*ecclesia semper reformanda*', the Catholic Church maintains the infallibility and irreversibility of dogma. The question often arises here as to whether there can be true dialogue or whether dialogue for the Catholic Church is only a means of convincing and converting other Christians.

I will try to give a twofold answer. Firstly, *Lumen gentium* (8) speaks of the Church as '*ecclesia semper purificanda*'. This affirmation is not exactly the same as the Protestant '*ecclesia semper reformanda*', although there is a correspondence. For Catholic theology knows, especially since Johann Adam Möhler and John Henry Newman, the concept of doctrinal development. According to the conciliar constitution *Dei verbum*, the Holy Spirit leads us ever deeper into the once-for-all revealed truth (§ 8). The Joint Declaration on Justification is a good example of growth in a deeper understanding of truth. In the Joint Declaration Catholics did not give up the Council of Trent and Lutherans did not give up their confessional writings. Yet by studying the scriptures and both our traditions together we reached a new level of understanding and were able to see and interpret each tradition in a new light. We did not give up anything, but we were enriched. The Joint Declaration was not a victory of one side over the other; it was a victory for truth through a deeper understanding of the Gospel and of both our traditions.

My second response is immediately related to the concept of development of dogma and concerns the concept of the reception of dogma. In this situation reception – an important concept of the ancient Church – once again becomes an important theme. Yves Congar in particular affirmed with renewed clarity that reception is not a merely passive and obedient act of acceptance of a given doctrine, it is not a one-way process involving a mechanical take-over. It is a dynamic creative process which also implies interpretation, criticism and enrichment by new aspects.

Such a process took place in the Catholic Church herself after each council and between the councils, for example between Nicea and Constantinople, Ephesus and Chalcedon, Vatican I and Vatican II; with regard to Vatican II we find ourselves at present in the middle of such a reception process. The dogmas on papal primacy and infallibility, in particular, need re-reception and a reinterpretation with regard to the Oriental tradition. This leads us to the question of inter-church reception and to the reception required for documents of ecumenical dialogue. They are the work of ecumenical experts and do not speak on behalf of the churches themselves. These documents must become flesh in the churches. This is (or can be) a long and complicated process, involving not only the authorities in the churches, but also the life and hearts of the faithful. The new views must be mediated through traditional patterns. This process requires patience, which is, according to the New Testament, a fundamental attitude of Christian hope and, according to Péguy, the little sister of hope. Patience is the true strength of Christian faith.

There is therefore no reason for disillusion about our dialogues because they have not yet reached their final goal. What we have achieved after centuries of fruitless polemic is brotherhood, and that is really not nothing. There is therefore no reason to give up dialogue and effect a change of ecumenical paradigm towards a so-called secular ecumenism. On the contrary, there is no alternative to ecumenism, and there is therefore no alternative to ecumenical dialogue in love and truth which is essential to the nature of the Church. When we do what we can in faith, we can be sure that God's Spirit does its work too, leading us together as one flock under one shepherd (John 10.16).

4

Communio: *The Guiding Concept of Catholic Ecumenical Theology*

The Problem: Where Are We and Where Are We Going?

One question concerns us deeply: where are we today, more than 35 years after the Second Vatican Council, and after 35 years of ecumenical dialogue? From this arises a second question: What is the central idea that inspires us and leads us forward? And further: What is the ecumenical goal we are aiming for? Finally: How are we to continue in the new millennium? Is there a way forward at all?

If one considers the international dialogues of the last 35 years and study the two large volumes of *Growth in Agreement. Reports and Agreed Statements of Ecumenical Conversations on a World Level*, one surprising discovery emerges. Although all the dialogues are based on the Second Vatican Council and its Catholic principles on ecumenism (UR 2-4), they have never been held according to a preconceived plan. All the more astonishing is the fact that they converge in a surprising way. All the dialogues – with the Orthodox churches and the Anglican Communion, the Lutheran and Reformed ecclesial communities, the 'Free Churches' and the new Evangelical and Pentecostal communities – converge in the fact that they centre around the concept of *communio*. *Communio* really is the key concept for all bilateral and multilateral dialogues. All of them define the visible unity of all Christians as *communio*-unity, and agree in understanding it, by analogy with the original trinitarian model (LG 4; UR 2), not as uniformity but as unity in diversity and diversity in unity.

This *communio* is not a distant and future entity towards which ecumenical dialogue must aim. The *communio* is not something which has to be achieved ecumenically. Through the one baptism we have all been baptized into the one Body of Christ which is the Church (1 Cor. 12.13; Gal. 3.27). By baptism and faith all are already incorporated in Jesus Christ and have the right to be called Christians. The new and basic ecumenical insight, therefore, is that among the baptized there already exists a fundamental unity or *communio*, so that the distinction is not between full unity and no *communio* at all, but between full and incomplete *communio* (UR 3).

The ecumenical dialogues have concretely confirmed this insight in various ways. They have shown that incomplete *communio*, which links us with other churches and ecclesial communities, is not just a theory but a reality which can be experienced. We have found that what unites us is far more than what, sadly, still divides us. Everybody who has participated in ecumenical dialogue knows what an exhilarating and constantly surprising experience this is. This discovery represents a twentieth-century *novum* in church history. The separated churches and ecclesial communities no longer see themselves as hostile antagonists or at best indifferent neighbours. They see themselves as brothers and sisters who together have set out on the way to full communion. The encyclical letter *Ut unum sint* speaks about rediscovered brotherliness as the essential fruit of the ecumenical dialogue (UUS 41f.).

This new ecclesial reality fills us with gratitude, joy and hope; it is the fruit of the work of the Holy Spirit (UR 1; 4). But at the same time it also causes pain. For the closer we come to each other, the more painful is the experience that we are not yet in full communion. We are hurt by what still separates us and hinders us from gathering around the table of the Lord. We are increasingly dissatisfied with the ecumenical status quo, and ecumenical frustration and sometimes even opposition develops. Paradoxically, it is the same ecumenical progress which is also the cause of the ecumenical malaise. This gives increased urgency to the questions: How can we progress? How can we progress from the already existing incomplete communion to full *communio*, which is the ultimate goal of the ecumenical movement? (UR 3; UUS 14).

The answer is not easy because, as so often, there is no one answer. The present situation is complex and many-layered and there are many reasons why some people today have the impression that, although a lot is happening in ecumenical dialogue, no real progress is being made. One of the reasons (but by no means the only one) is that dialogue documents may show convergence about the concept of *communio* but, on closer inspection, different understandings are hidden behind the term. The common concept of *communio* has different meanings and thus calls forth different expectations and projected goals. This necessarily leads to misunderstandings on one's own side and with one's partners, raising expectations which the other cannot fulfil and thereby leading to frustration. Thus convergence about one and same concept is – apart from other factors – one cause for confusion. This is why we have to clarify first the concept of communion as the central idea and ultimate goal of the ecumenical movement.

Ideological Misunderstandings

The theological understanding of *communio* is often replaced or overlaid by an anthropological or sociological understanding. The secularized use of the word *communio* leads to a secular under-standing of ecumenism characterized by non-theological, general social criteria and interpretations.

In its secularized meaning, *communio* is understood in a 'horizontal' way as a community of people resulting from the individual's desire for community. *Communio* in this sense is the result of an association of partners who are in principal free and equal. This understanding is based on the idea of the social contract which developed during the period of the Enlightenment. Such an understanding of the Church can even become a battle-cry against the hierarchical structure of the Church. This conception views the Church 'from below', i.e. the 'base' church as opposed to the 'established' church. This understanding of the *communio* concept of the Church develops the idea of the equality and equal rights of all church members and demands the democratization of the Church, so that decisions are made in open, fearless dialogue, critical discourse, consensus-forming processes or by plebiscite.

Democracy may be considered the best of all bad possibilities. But democracy is far from being salvation. The experiences of the twentieth century, among others, have shown that majorities can be mobilized by populist agitation and often represent the sum of the highest number of private interests capable of forming a majority, at the expense of minorities which cannot mobilize sufficient voices. Democratically evolved majorities, if generally recognized, may have a pacifying influence; but the search for truth cannot be organized by majorities.

The neo-Romanticism of the early twentieth century tried to distance itself from the rational and utilitarian understanding of society and community. To the rational and interest-oriented, but cold and impersonal, civic society, it opposed the ideas of a naturally grown, personal community based on primary personal relations, and of personal nearness and warmth in a familiar and friendly atmosphere.

Often this *communio* idea is applied to the Church. Such a brotherly–sisterly understanding of the Church can model itself on the example of Jesus and the ideal picture of the early Church in Jerusalem. During the course of church history, there have been frequent attempts to realize this ideal in monastic communities and fraternities, as well as in some Free church and pietistic communities. Today it is often practised in small groups, in the base communities of the Church, and especially in the more recent spiritual communities.

There is no doubt that such communities have a beneficial effect on the renewal and revival of the Church. However, if the model of a fraternal ecclesiology is applied to the Church as a whole, it can lead to a 'cuddle in the corner' ecclesiology which chafes against the institutional reality of a large church instead of attempting to establish a constructive relation with it.

However, even sociologically these interpretations of community are unrealistic and do not stand up to rational reflection. Institutions not only carry the danger of personal alienation and suppression of personal freedom but also have a relieving and liberating function for the individual. They give independence from personal and communal arbitrariness and create security of behaviour, expectations and rights. If the Church is understood only as a community of discourse, it would be burdened by unending discussion and never free for its proper task, worshipping God together and bearing clear and unambiguous witness to Christ together before the whole world.

An institutional understanding of the Church can also lead to misunderstandings. It often leads to a concept of the Church as a *communio hierarchica*, in the sense that this term was usually understood in pre-conciliar theology: the Church as *societas perfecta inaequalis* or *inaequalium*. This understanding was developed as a defence against the egalitarian influences which came from the French Revolution and its spiritual fathers. Thus the statement of the Synod of Pistoia (1794) was deemed to be heretical because it claimed that the authority of the ministry and the leadership in the Church was passed to the shepherds by the community of the faithful, and was therefore democratically legitimized (DH 2603).

Attempts are occasionally made to justify this understanding of *communio* based on a unifying ministry. But the Council tried to overcome a one-sidedly hierarchical understanding of the Church and re-emphasized the biblical and early church doctrine of the priesthood of all the baptized, as well as the doctrine of the *sensus* and *consensus fidelium* which derives from it. Accordingly, the laity are not just the objects of acts of the official Church but active and co-responsible subjects in the Church. They have their own respective charisma and their own responsibility (LG 9-12; 30f.). This does not lead to a democratic understanding but to a participative concept of *communio* with graduated rights of co-operation.

The Church is therefore neither a democracy nor a monarchy, not even a constitutional monarchy. She is hierarchical in the original sense of the word, meaning 'of holy origin', i.e. she has to be understood on the basis of what is holy, by the gifts of salvation, by word and sacrament as authoritative signs and the means of the Holy Spirit's effectiveness. The Church exists and lives only out of the 'in advance' of God's salvific work through Jesus Christ in the Holy Spirit. The ministry is not a dominating power which oppresses people (cf. Matt. 20.25-27), but a gift and present from the Lord of the Church; it is an authoritative service for building up both the individuals and the whole (Eph. 4.7-12). This brings us to the original and authentic theological understanding of *communio*.

Theological Foundations

In its original sense the Greek word for *communio*, '*koinonia*', does not mean community but participation (*participatio*). The verb '*koinoneo*' means 'to share, to participate, to have something in common'.

In this sense, James and John are '*koinonoi*', participants, partners, companions on the way (Luke 5.11). According to the Acts of the Apostles, the early church in Jerusalem constituted a *koinonia* in the breaking of the bread and in prayer (Acts 2.42); they held everything in common (Acts 2.44; 4.23). The real theological meaning of *koinonia* is found in Paul and in the Johannine epistles. *Koinonia* with Jesus Christ (1 Cor. 1.9), with the Gospel (Phil. 1.5), in the Holy Spirit (2 Cor. 13.13), in the faith (Phm. 6), of suffering and comfort (2 Cor. 1.5,7; Phil. 3.10), of the glory to come (1 Pet. 5.1), of the divine nature (2 Pet. 1.4), with the Father and the Son and consequently among us (1 John 1.3). In the High Priestly Prayer, where Jesus prays that all may be one, the basis and measure of this unity is the communion-unity of Father and Son (John 17.21-23).

The sacramental basis of *communio* is the *communio* in the one baptism. For through the one baptism we have all been baptized into the one Body of Christ (1 Cor. 12.13; cf. Rom. 12.4f., Gal. 3.26-28; Eph. 4.3f.). Baptism is the sacrament of faith. So *communio* through baptism presupposes and implies *communio* in the common faith of the Church, i.e., communion in the Gospel. Both communion in faith and baptism are the foundations of *communio*.

The summit of *communio* is participation in the eucharist. In the history of theology, the most important text was to become 1 Cor. 10:16f.: 'Is not the cup of thanksgiving for which we give thanks a participation in the blood of Christ? Is not the bread we break a participation in the body of Christ? Because there is one loaf, we, who are many, are one body, for we all partake of the one loaf.' This text states that the *koinonia* in the one eucharistic bread is source and sign of the *koinonia* in the one body of the Church; the one eucharistic body of Christ is source and sign of the one ecclesial body of Christ.

Besides this sacramental basis of the *communio* in the one baptism and in the eucharist, it must also be remembered that the communion between the Apostles and between congregations (Gal. 2.9), the community of property of the early church in Jerusalem (Acts 2.44; 4.23) and Paul's collections for the church in Jerusalem all happen within the framework of the *koinonia* (Gal. 2.10; 2 Cor.

8-9). So communion with God through Jesus Christ in the Holy Spirit also affects communion among brothers and especially communion with the suffering. *Koinonia/communio* therefore has a theological and a communal and a social dimension. It would be wrong to limit the ecclesial significance of *koinonia/communio* to the area of sacraments and worship, or even just to the eucharist. There is, so to speak, both a vertical and a horizontal dimension of communion.

Even a trinitarian understanding of *communio* as participation in the life of the Trinity also implies a communal interpretation. For the trinitarian God is the self-giving and self-communication of Father and Son and of both in the Holy Spirit. So participation in the trinitarian life becomes the foundation and model of mutual communication, of communal and social behaviour, and of a spirituality of communion.

It would be interesting to follow in detail the subsequent history of the meaning of *communio* in the tradition, but this is not possible here. Instead, we will confine ourselves to a few reminders of the most important stages in this development.

The history of the meaning of *communio* is most closely linked with the confession of the '*communio sanctorum*' in the Apostles' Creed which is shared by all the churches of the Latin tradition, i.e. the ecclesial communities which emerged from the sixteenth-century Reformation as well as the Catholic Church, and therefore represents an essential ecumenical bridge of understanding, and is an important point of departure for ecumenical conversations.

In all probability *communio sanctorum* did not originally mean communion of the saints (*sancti*), but communion with the Holy (*sancta*); *communio sanctorum* meant the *communio* of the *sancta*, i.e. *communio sacramentorum*, especially *communio* in the eucharist. This meaning of *koinonia tōn hagiōn* was dominant particularly in the East (summed up by John of Damascus in his *Explanation of the Orthodox Faith* IV, 13; PG 94,1153). In the Latin tradition since Niketas of Remesiana (d. 414), in whose writings the addition of *communio sanctorum* to the Apostles' Creed is first found, there has been a significant and momentous change of meaning (*Explanatio symboli*, 23; PL 52, 87B). *Communio sanctorum* was increasingly understood to be the communion of the pilgrim (militant) and heavenly (triumphant) Church (Mary, the patriarchs and prophets, the apostles, martyrs and confessors, all the just and the angels), but also as the communion of the universal Church 'from the just Abel to the last of the chosen' (Augustine, *Sermo* 341, 9, 11; LG 2). Thus the so-called communal meaning became predominant.

Nevertheless, for the Latin fathers, especially for Augustine, the sacramental and eucharistic understanding of the Church, and the inner connection between eucharist and church, were still very important (*In Ioan* 26, 6, 13, etc.). As Henri de Lubac has pointed out, the change occurred only during the second eucharistic dispute around Berengarius of Tours in the eleventh century. The term '*corpus mysticum*', i.e. the mysterious sacramental body of the Lord, which until then had been usual for the eucharist, could now be misinterpreted in a purely spiritualist sense. In order to exclude this spiritualist misunderstanding, the eucharist now came to be called '*corpus verum*', and the expression '*corpus mysticum*' was reserved for the Church. Church and eucharist were therefore uncoupled.

This had far-reaching effects for the understanding both of the eucharist and of the Church. The eucharist or communion was largely understood individualistically as personal communion with Christ, leading to a deeply personal eucharistic devotion which was, however, more or less completely isolated from the aspect of church communion. On the other hand, as Yves Congar pointed out, in the follow–up to the Gregorian Reform the Church came to be understood as 'Christendom' and seen as a sociological and political entity, considered more in terms of the categories of law and power than in terms of the sacraments. There was a development from the communion of churches eucharistically assembled to an ecclesiology of the universal unity of the Church under the leadership of the Pope. In mitigation of medieval scholastic theology, however, it has to be added that theologians of the standing of Thomas Aquinas retained the relation between eucharist and church and emphasized it clearly. For Thomas the real presence of Jesus Christ in the eucharist is only an intermediate reality, the *res et sacramentum*; the *res sacramenti* itself is the unity of the Church (*Summa theol.* III, 73:1; 79:5).

The original basic meaning of *koinonia/communio* was first rediscovered in the Catholic Tübingen school, especially by Johann Adam Möhler; the real breakthrough came with the investigations by Henri de Lubac in his book *Corpus Mysticum* (1943). These

insights were made ecumenically fertile by Yves Congar. In
addition, a series of church history studies should be mentioned,
especially the contribution by Hertling. On the Protestant side,
Althaus, Bonhoeffer and Elert should be mentioned. A similar
rediscovery occurred in Orthodox theology following a new
patristic foundation of theology (Florovsky) and the influence of
sobornost philosophy (Chomjakow).

In the documents of the Second Vatican Council, at a first glance
other images and concepts seem to predominate in the description
of the nature of the Church: the Church as People of God, as Body
of Christ, as Temple of the Holy Spirit and as Sacrament, i.e. a sign
and instrument of unity. A detailed analysis, however, reveals that
these images and concepts are ultimately based on, and interpreted
through, the understanding of the Church as *communio*. Thus, the
statement by the extraordinary Synod of Bishops of 1985 is correct
and justified when it says that *communio*-ecclesiology is the
'central and basic idea of the Council documents' (II. C. 1). The
Council adopted the newer *communio*-ecclesiology centred on the
eucharist (SC 47; LG 3: 7; 11; 23; 26; UR 2; 15; AG 39).

In the Council's documents we find both the 'vertical'
sacramental, especially eucharistic, view and the 'horizontal' or
communal one. Both interpretations are justified and belong
together. This becomes clear particularly in the way the Council
considers the ecclesial *communio* to be based on, and pre-figured
in, the trinitarian *communio* of Father, Son and Holy Spirit (LG 4;
UR 2). The original trinitarian model understands *communio* as
self-communication between Father and Son, and of both in the
Holy Spirit; hence the Church, which is modelled on the image of
the Trinity, is also constituted by subjective communication. This
personal *communio* of Christians with each other and among
themselves is founded on the sacramental *communio*. Through
sharing in the one eucharistic body we become an ecclesial body;
but we cannot share the inter-eucharistic bread without also
sharing our daily bread.

Within the framework of this integral view of *communio*, we
must bear in mind the relation of the foundations of the different
aspects. The 'vertical' communion with God is the foundation and
support for the 'horizontal' communion among Christians in
churches and congregations. This *communio* does not come about
by gathering the members of the Church into a communion, but

individual Christians are incorporated into the sacramentally-given communion. According to Paul, one is baptized into the Body of Christ (1 Cor. 12:13). The sacraments are the foundation of the Church, and the sacramentally founded church celebrates the sacraments; and the sacramental communion expresses itself in communal and social behaviour.

However, different emphases can be placed on the different aspects of the one *communio* reality. Thus, different and sometimes even opposing *communio*-ecclesiologies can be derived from the one common basic term *koinonia/communio*. Notwithstanding an emerging ecumenical agreement on this concept, there are different confessional developments.

Different Confessional Developments

Since the Second Vatican Council, the Catholic Church has officially participated in the ecumenical movement. Thus it was confronted with the concepts of church and *communio* of both the Orthodox churches and the ecclesial communities which issued from the sixteenth-century Reformation.

The ecclesiology of the Orthodox churches claims to be faithful to the communion-ecclesiology of the fathers of the first millennium. The Orthodox churches are convinced that they are the true Church of Jesus Christ. They make reference to the binding canons of the ecumenical councils and to the church fathers, especially those of the Greek tradition. In principle they hold the position of Cyprian of Carthage, namely that outside the Church (that is, the Orthodox Church) there is no salvation. In this way they identify where the Church is, but they are not so clear on where the Church is not; that is to say, there is no consensus on the ecclesial and salvific character of the non-Orthodox churches and the validity of their baptism. The differentiation between full and incomplete communion, fundamental for Catholic ecumenism since the Second Vatican Council, does not belong to their official teaching.

According to the distinguished Russian theologian George Florovsky, Orthodox ecclesiology still finds itself in a pre-theological stage. The constructive but also critical ecumenical encounter of the last decades has occurred mainly in relation to eucharistic ecclesiology, developed in different ways by Afanessiev,

Schmemann, Zizioulas and others; it is centred on the eucharistic celebration of the locally gathered church. However, this eucharistic ecclesiology is not simply 'the' Orthodox position and it is not uncontroversial in inner Orthodox circles; ecumenically, however, it has become very influential.

The eucharistic view was adopted by some Catholic theologians, e.g. J. Tillard (*Église d'Églises. L'écclésiologie de communion*, 1987; *L'Église locale. Ecclésiologie de communion et catholicité*, Paris 1995); to some degree it is also found in the first document of the Joint International Theological Commission between the Orthodox churches and the Roman Catholic Church, *The Mystery of the Church and the Eucharist in the Light of the Mystery of the Holy Trinity* (Munich 1982).

In line with 1 Cor. 10.16f., the starting-point for eucharistic ecclesiology is the inner connection between ecclesial and eucharistic *communio*. It means that the Church is realized in the local church gathered for the eucharist. For most of these theologians the local church celebrating the eucharist is the church gathered around the bishop (this is different for Afanessiev, who represents a more presbyteral and congregational view). Since the one Christ and the one Church are present in every local church, no local church can be isolated; every local church is necessarily and essentially in *koinonia/communio* with all other local churches which are celebrating the eucharist. Since every local church is church in the fullest sense, there can be no ecclesial ministry or authority higher than that of the bishop.

Nevertheless, since earliest times, as witnessed by the first ecumenical councils, the metropolitan sees and the later patriarchal sees have held precedence. But their authority is synodically embedded. The Orthodox partners always refer to Canon 34 of the *Apostolic canones*, which states that the first of the bishop can only take important decisions in agreement with the other bishops, and these only in agreement with the first bishop. The universal Church is a *communio*-unity of such independent autonomous churches. In this sense Orthodox theologians sometimes take over the WCC's concept and speak of a conciliar fellowship or communion of churches (cf. below, p. 64).

The Orthodox churches can accept that Rome holds the 'primacy in love' (Ignatius of Antioch, *Ad Rom*, proem.) and that the Bishop of Rome is the first of the bishops; but in general they understand this as an honorary primacy and exclude any primacy of jurisdiction. They speak in terms of *primus inter pares*, but put the emphasis more on *pares*, in the sense of equality in episcopal consecration. The Petrine ministry is exercised by all the bishops, individually and in synodical communion. Therefore, in the opinion of the Orthodox churches, the problem of the primacy of Rome can only be considered in connection with the synodical or conciliar structure of the Church (cf. *Valamo Document*, 1988).

The Second Vatican Council reaffirmed the eucharistic conception of the Church (LG 2; 7; 11; 17; 26; UR 2; 15; CD 30), put a new emphasis on the local church (SC 41f.; LG 26; 29; CD 11; AG 19-22) and basically recognized the synodical church order which the churches of the East have had since early times (UR 16); the Council also made some attempts to revive the synodical or collegial structures which also exist in the Latin tradition. But the crucial point in ecumenical dialogue with the Eastern churches remains the charisma which is specific and proper to the Petrine ministry of the Bishop of Rome as successor of Peter, and which is therefore the visible centre and the principle of visible unity for the ecclesial *communio* (DH 3051; LG 18). The future task will be to reconcile the eucharistic *communio*-ecclesiology and its principle of conciliarity with the Petrine principle; this could help to throw greater light on the inter-Orthodox experience, often marked by ethnic or national tensions. There are highly regarded Orthodox theologians who consider the national autocephaly of the Orthodox churches as their greatest weakness (Meyendorff and others).

Starting from different and sometimes contradictory presuppositions, the ecclesiology of the ecclesial communities issuing from the Reformation arrives at a similar structural problem. In his early works, Luther is still very much aware of the connection between Holy Communion and the Church (*Ein Sermon von dem hochwürdigen Sakrament des heiligen Leichnams Christi und von den Bruderschaften*: WA 2, 742–58; cf. 26,493). But in Lutheran and Reformed theology the Church is generally understood as based on the proclamation of the word rather than on the sacraments, and defined as *creatura verbi* (*De captivitate Babylonica*: WA 6,551). This excludes an ecclesiology which understands the Church to be constituted 'from below', by an association of its members. According to Reformation understanding the Church is where the Word of God is preached in its purity and the holy sacraments are administered according to the Gospel (CA VII; *Apol.*7).

Thus the *communio sanctorum* becomes synonymous with the *congregatio fidelium* (ibid., *Great Catechism*: BSELK 653-8) – a term for the Church which was already usual in the Middle Ages (cf. also *Catechismus Romanus* I,10,2; UR 2; PO 4f.; AG 15). In this sense a basic agreement exists between the Catholic and the Reformation understanding of *communio* as founded not 'from below' by the association of the faithful but as constituted by word and sacrament. But the difference is also clear. For the Reformers, the Church becomes real in the worshipping community of the local congregation. Luther wants to replace the, for him, dark and obscure word 'church' with the word 'congregation' ('*Gemeine*' – *Von Konziliis und Kirchen*, WA 50,625). The Reformation understanding of the Church has its basis and centre of gravity in the congregation. The worshipping assembly of the local congregation is the visible realization and manifestation of the Church; it lacks nothing of what is constitutive for the Church.

The main difference concerns the understanding of church ministry. In the Catholic understanding, the ministry in the service of both word and sacrament is constitutive for the Church. This problem becomes especially urgent when one questions the episcopal ministry on the level beyond the local community. The concentration on the local congregation leads to criticism of the theological distinction between episcopate and pastorate, and especially of the 'papal monarchy' of the universal Church. According to the usually accepted Reformation understanding, the episcopate differs only functionally from the pastorate; it is the ministry of the pastor exercising a church leadership function. The text of the *Confessio Augustana XXVIII* in itself would really also allow for a 'more Catholic' interpretation. But in the main the view of the episcopate which prevails goes back to Jerome who, in contrast to the other fathers, founded the pre-eminence of the bishops 'magis consuetudine quam dispositionis dominicae veritate' (*Tit* 1,5). This position, that the difference between bishop and presbyter lies in an increased *potestas* but not in a universal sacramental authority, came, through Peter Lombard, to be widely held in medieval theology and was overcome definitively only by the Second Vatican Council (LG 21), basing itself on the overwhelming opinion of the patristic age.

The Council of Trent did not deal systematically with the arguments of Reformation ecclesiology, but only considered it under the aspect of the hierarchical understanding of the Church. The Council placed the denial of the hierarchical order of bishops, priests, and deacons under anathema (DH 1776; cf. 1768). The First Vatican Council additionally taught that the Pope's primacy of jurisdiction was *iure divino* and essential to the Church being the Church (DH 3050f.). According to Catholic understanding, episcopacy and Petrine ministry are therefore constitutive elements of the Church. But they are not the whole Church. Vatican II for the first time gave a magisterial presentation of the Catholic understanding of the Church as a whole and situated the episcopacy and the Petrine ministry within the whole people of God as well as within the college of bishops (cf. LG 22f.).

Within this general design, Vatican II retained the doctrine of the three 'perimeters' of the unity of the Church: unity in faith, the sacraments and leadership (LG 14; UR 2). The emphasis on unity in the episcopacy is not at all an anti-Reformation argument; it goes back to the basic decision of the early Church which opposed Gnosticism with the three bulwarks of Orthodoxy: the canon of scripture, the symbols of the faith, and the apostolic succession (cf. LG 19). We only have the biblical canon within the episcopally constituted Church. Thus the Reformation not only broke away from the later Tridentine tradition, but also from the fundamental decisions and tradition of the early Church. Because the Reformers did not maintain the church ministry, especially the apostolic succession in the episcopacy, the Catholic Church considers the communities issuing from the Reformation to be ecclesial communities but not churches in the proper sense (UR 19-23, esp. 22; *Dominus Iesus*, 17; cf. below).

But even regarding this difficult open question of episcopacy, some convergences on communion can be detected nowadays. Not even in Reformation times was it possible to maintain an approach which was exclusively centred on the local congregation; even then the question of *episkope* arose, of the ministry of supervision and oversight in the form of a ministry of visitation. However, the ministry of the *superintendentes* remained theologically insufficiently defined; usually it was considered simply *iure humano* as functionally a pastoral ministry, but exercising church leadership. Progress was made in the twentieth century, although no consensus was achieved (cf. BEM 19-25). It became clear that the Church realizes itself on different levels: the local, the regional and the universal. On each of these levels the 'with and over against' of ministry and congregation is constitutive. This raises anew the question of the quality of leadership ministries in the Church at regional and universal level. In the meantime, moreover, many of the ecclesial communities stemming from the Reformation have joined together to form world-wide confessional associations which are now on the way from federation to *communio*. With this new openness to a more universalist viewpoint, the question of the possibility of a universal ministry of unity has been raised in several dialogues (cf. below, p. 70).

At present, however, the approach centred on the local church and local congregation still prevails. The ecumenical goal accepted today by most of the ecclesial communities stemming from the Reformation is not institutional unity or organic union (New Delhi, 1961) but conciliar fellowship (Salamanca, 1973; Nairobi, 1975), or a communion of churches which remain independent but recognize each other as churches and agree to have altar and pulpit fellowship as well as mutually accepted ministries and services. This idea in particular is the basis of the Leuenberg Church Fellowship (1973) and is also behind the model of 'reconciled diversity' (LWF: Dar es Salaam, 1977) 'ordered in all its components in conciliar structures and actions' (LWF: Budapest, 1984).

So the question arises whether, and perhaps how, the Reformation model of unity as a network of local congregations and local churches, or nowadays of confessional families, is compatible with the Catholic ecclesiological approach and the Catholic understanding of communion. My thesis is that it is clear that some progress has been made here in formulating the problem, and that possible lines of convergence are beginning to appear. So far, however, a ecumenical consensus is not yet in sight.

The Catholic *Communio* Ecclesiology

For a systematic presentation of the Catholic *communio*-ecclesiology we start with the Dogmatic Constitution *Lumen gentium* of the Second Vatican Council. The first seven sections of Chapter I of this constitution, in which the *communio*-ecclesiology is touched upon occasionally, do not present any fundamental ecumenical problems; in principle, they are 'consensus-worthy'. Only in Section 8, which tries to define where the Church is really and concretely to be found, does the ecumenical question arise sharply with the famous '*subsistit in*'. The constitution states that the Church of Jesus Christ is concretely real in the Catholic Church, in communion with the successor of Peter and the bishops in communion with him.

The formula '*subsistit in*' replaces the earlier formula '*est*', which expressed a strict identity between the Catholic Church and the Church of Christ. The new formula has a twofold meaning. On the one hand, it states that the Church of Christ is really present and is to be found in the Roman Catholic Church. On the other hand, it takes seriously that outside her visible confines there are not only individual Christians but ecclesial elements or, as in the case of the churches of the East, even genuine particular churches. So it makes possible a greater ecumenical openness and flexibility, compared with the strict identification of the Roman Catholic Church with the Church of Jesus Christ which was expressed by the former '*est*'. This '*subsistit in*' is therefore the open ecumenical door; at the same time it represents the crux of the ecumenical dialogue. The declaration *Dominus Iesus* (2000) and the subsequent debate have shown very clearly that nerves here are raw and the pain threshold correspondingly low.

Therefore, first of all, the formula '*subsistit in*' needs to be correctly interpreted. The main drafter of *Lumen gentium*, the Belgian theologian G. Philips, foresaw that much ink would flow over this '*subsistit in*', and his prediction proved to be only too correct. The meaning of the word '*subsistit*' is controversial. Is it – as has been usually presumed – an idea serving more ecumenical flexibility; or is it to be understood in the sense of the scholastic concept of subsistence? The Council documents give no indications to support this last interpretation.

But it is not only a question of terminology; what is at stake is the ecumenically crucial question of how the two statements relate to each other: on the one hand, the one Church of Jesus Christ is concretely real and present in the Roman Catholic Church, and on the other hand, many essential elements of the Church of Jesus

Christ can be found outside the institutional boundaries of the Catholic Church (LG 8; 15; UR 3) and, in the case of the churches of the East, even genuine particular churches which are considered sister churches (UR 14).

The statement in *Dominus Iesus* goes beyond the Council's words and says that the Church of Jesus Christ is 'fully' realized 'only' in the Catholic Church. This statement only appears to be a sharpening of the Council's statement. In reality, it provides a hint for an appropriate answer. Logically and conclusively, it means that, although there is no full realization of the Church of Jesus Christ outside the Catholic Church, there still is an imperfect realization. Therefore there is no ecclesial vacuum outside the Catholic Church (UUS 13). There may not be 'the' Church, but there is a church reality. Consequently, *Dominus Iesus* does not say that the ecclesial communities which issued from the Reformation are not churches; it only maintains that they are not churches in the proper sense; which means, positively, that in an improper sense, analogous to the Catholic Church, they are church. Indeed, they have a different understanding of the Church; they do not want to be church in the Catholic sense.

If one asks further what actually constitutes the fullness of what is Catholic, the Council texts show that this fullness does not concern salvation or its subjective realization. The Spirit works also in the separated churches and ecclesial communities (UR 3); outside the Catholic Church there exist forms of holiness, even of martyrdom (LG 15; UR 4; UUS 12; 83). On the other hand, the Catholic Church is also a church of sinners; it needs purification and repentance (LG 8; UR 3f.; 6f.; UUS 34f.; 83f.). One can even speak about 'structures of sin' in the Church (UUS 34). The reality and fullness of what is Catholic does not refer to subjective holiness but to the sacramental and institutional means of salvation, the sacraments and ministries (UR 3; UUS 86). Only in this sacramental and institutional respect can the Council find a lack (*defectus*) in the ecclesial communities of the Reformation (UR 22). Both Catholic fullness and the *defectus* of the others are therefore sacramental and institutional, and not existential or even moral in nature; they are on the level of signs and instruments of grace, not on the level of the *res*, the grace of salvation itself.

Even if this understanding of '*subsistit*' does not resolve all the questions, it offers us a solid basis for ecumenical dialogue. The first consequence of the thesis that the one Church of Jesus Christ subsists in the Catholic Church is that unity is not simply given in fragments in the present, and therefore to be considered a future ecumenical goal. Rather, unity also subsists in the Catholic Church; it is already real in it (UR 4). This does not mean that full communion as the goal of the ecumenical way has to be understood simply as the return of separated brothers and churches to the bosom of the Catholic mother church. The Second Vatican Council overcame this ecumenism of return by an ecumenism of common return, or common conversion to Jesus Christ. In a situation of division, unity in the Catholic Church is not concretely realized in all its fullness; the divisions remain a wound for the Catholic Church too. Only the ecumenical endeavour to help the existing real but incomplete communion grow into full communion in truth and love will lead to the realization of catholicity in all its fullness (UR 4; UUS 14). In this sense the ecumenical endeavour is a common pilgrimage to the fullness of catholicity which Jesus Christ wants for his Church.

This ecumenical process is not a one-way street, in which only the others have to learn from us and ultimately join us. Ecumenism happens by way of a mutual exchange of gifts and mutual enrichment (UUS 28). Catholic theology can accept positively everything that the Orthodox *communio*-ecclesiology has to say because Catholic ecclesiology also maintains that, wherever the eucharist is celebrated, the Church of Jesus Christ is present. From Reformation theology it has learnt that the proclamation of the word of God also has the function of establishing church and *communio*. The Church lives by word and sacrament which in their turn depend on the authoritative service of the ministry (DV 21; AG 9). Where word and sacrament, especially the eucharist, are present through the service of the Church's ministry, the Church is a reality in the full sense, in every place.

Conversely the Catholic Church is convinced that its institutional 'elements' such as episcopacy and the Petrine ministry are gifts of the Spirit for all Christians; therefore it wants to offer them as a contribution, in a spiritually renewed form, to the fuller ecumenical unity. This does not mean the association or insertion of other Christians into a given 'system' but mutual enrichment and the fuller expression and realization of the one Church of Jesus Christ in all the churches and ecclesial communities. The closer we come to Christ in this way the closer we come to each other, in order at the end to be fully one in Christ.

The interpretation of *'subsistit'* and the ecumenical dialogue brings us to the Catholic understanding of the ecumenical goal of full communion. The interpretation of *'subsistit in'* points out that according to Catholic understanding unity is more than a network of local or confessional churches which recognize each other and share the communion of eucharist and pulpit. The Catholic understanding does not start with the differences in order to reach unity, but presupposes a given unity within the Catholic Church and its partial communion with the other churches and church communities in order to reach full communion with them. But this unity in the sense of full communion-unity does not mean uniformity but unity within diversity and diversity within unity. We could also say that the very essence of unity understood as full communion is catholicity not in its confessional but in its original and qualitative meaning as the full realization of all the gifts that the local and confessional churches have to contribute.

One of the main achievements of Vatican II was its revival of the theology of the local church, as it is found in the New Testament and in the tradition of the fathers (SC 41; LG 23; 26; CD 11). As a consequence, the Council stated that within the one Church there can exist a legitimate diversity of mentalities, customs, rites, disciplines, theologies and spiritualities (LG 13; UR 4; 16f.). Although every local church is fully church (LG 26; 28), it is not the whole Church. The one Church exists in and out of the local churches (LG 23), but the local churches also exist in and out of the one Church (*Communiones notio* 9), they are shaped in its image (LG 23). Thus local churches are not subdivisions, simple departments, emanations or provinces of the one Church, but neither is the one Church the sum of local churches, nor just the result of their association, their mutual recognition. The one Church is real in the *communio* of the local churches, it is a *communio ecclesiarum*, but unity does not grow out of communication, it is pre-given. Taking both together, this means that the one Church and the diversity of local churches are simultaneous; they are interior to each other (perichoretic).

Within this perichoresis the unity of the Church has priority over the diversity of the local churches. This thesis of the priority of unity with respect to diversity can be proved ontologically and biblically as well. For classical ontology the '*unum*' has, since the pre-Socratic philosophers and Plato and Aristotle, meant a transcendental qualification of being, which is the foundation of diversity. For the Bible the one Church corresponds to the one God, the one Christ, the one Spirit, the one baptism (cf. Eph. 4.5f.). The fact that unity has priority over all particular interests is obvious in the New Testament (1 Cor. 1.10ff.). Thus all churches confess in the creed their belief in the '*una sancta ecclesia*'. According to the model of the early church of Jerusalem (Acts 2.42), beyond all legitimate diversity she is one through preaching the one Gospel, the administration of the same sacraments and the one apostolic governing in love (LG 13; UR 2).

The thesis of the priority of a unity which does not exclude legitimate diversity but includes catholicity, is in opposition to the post-modern mentality of fundamental pluralism for which there is no longer one truth, but only truths. As a result, an ecumenically open Catholic position has difficulties at present in public debates. Catholic ecclesiology has, so to speak, to sail against the winds of the spirit of the age. That need not be a weakness, it can also be its strength.

This Catholic understanding of the *communio*-unity of the Church has its concrete expression in the Petrine ministry as sign and service to the unity of the episcopate and the local churches (DH 3050f.; LG 18). All other churches and ecclesial communities consider this position the greatest obstacle in the way of greater ecumenical unity. The problem is also emotionally heavily charged by 'certain painful memories' (UUS 88). For us, on the other hand, the Petrine ministry is a gift which serves to preserve both unity and the freedom of the Church from one-sided ties to certain nations, cultures or ethnic groups. Pope John Paul II has now seized the initiative and issued an invitation to a 'fraternal, patient dialogue' (UUS 96).

It would take too long here to deal with the whole difficult problem of the Petrine ministry. Only a few remarks are needed. The first and most basic is that we have to base the Petrine ministry on the biblical witness and the New Testament Petrine tradition, and therefore not understand it as a dominant power but as a service of love and as 'primacy in love' (UUS 61; 95). Secondly, in continuity with Vatican II, the Petrine ministry has to be integrated into the whole constellation of the Church and of all that is Christian, and interpreted as service to the *communio*, as '*servus servorum Dei*' (DH 306; UUS 88). It means a ministry of 'vigilance' (*episkopē*), 'a keeping watch (*episkopein*) "like a sentinel, so that, through the efforts of the pastors, the true voice of Christ the Shepherd may be heard in all the particular Churches"' (UUS 94). But such a responsibility would be illusory without effective authority (*exousia*). This means ultimately that the relative independence of the local churches and the synodical structures has to be strengthened, and that the principle of subsidiarity applies in an analogous sense. A balance is needed between the communal and synodical structures and the primatial Petrine structure. Therefore the three dimensions essential for every ministry in the Church could also be applied to the Petrine ministry: it has to be exercised in a personal, collegial and communal way (cf. BEM: Ministry, 26).

Encouraging progress and convergence on a universal ministry of leadership have been made in some of the dialogues (cf. Faith and Order, Santiago de Compostela, 1993; ARCIC II, *The Gift of Authority*, 1998; *Communio Sanctorum*, 2001) (cf. UUS 89, notes 148f.). But despite this new openness, a basic consensus is still not in view. The ecumenically open positions of the other churches may consider such a ministry of unity to be possible *iure humano*, or even desirable, but they do not recognize it as *iure divino* essential for the Church.

All these open questions are not only concerned with individual problems but with the basic relation between Jesus Christ and the Church, or between the Church of Jesus Christ and the concrete empirical churches. This relation is understood in different ways (*Nature and Purpose of the Church* 31). The aim of the expression 'subsistit in' is to indicate that there is a differentiated relation between Jesus Christ and the Church and of the Church of Jesus Christ with the Roman Catholic Church. They cannot be identified with each other or confused, but neither can they be separated from, or simply placed alongside, each other. The very essence of the Church has to be seen as analogous, not identical, to the incarnation; the divine and human dimensions are neither to be confused nor separated (LG 8). The Church is not the continuation of the incarnation, not the *Christus prolongatus*, the prolonged Christ, but Jesus Christ through and within the Spirit is sacramentally present and at work in the Church as his body and as the temple of the Spirit.

Only on this general basis and against the background of this incarnational understanding of the Church can in-depth discussions be held with the Reformation position. The Reformation view tends to overestimate the aspect of Jesus Christ as the head over the Church and to underestimate his presence within the Church. Starting from the analogy of their understanding of justification *sola fide* and *sola gratia*, they find it difficult to speak of church co-operation. This makes it difficult or even impossible for them to recognize the pope as the visible head of the Church, representing Jesus Christ as the invisible head. This becomes obvious too when reservations about the definitively binding character of ecclesial doctrines are registered on the basis of whether they are in accordance with scripture; the Protestant position, with its '*ecclesia semper reformanda*', tends to a certain revisionism. Though Catholic communion ecclesiology emphasizes the visible communion in faith, sacraments and church leadership as a sign and instrument for communion through Jesus Christ with God, Christ and church together make the 'whole Christ', the *totus Christus* (Augustine, *Enarratio in Psalmos*, Ps 90, Sermo 2,1; CCL 39,1266). In Catholic understanding the *solus Christus* is at the same time the *totus Christus, caput et membra*.

If we recognize the fundamental nature of these problems, we realize that despite encouraging progress, the way ahead still appears difficult and perhaps long (*Novo millennio ineunte* 12). It is therefore all the more important to ask: What can we do already, here and now? What are the next steps?

Interim Steps during the Transition Period

It is essential for the Church to acknowledge that she lives in an intermediate situation between the 'already' and the 'not yet'. Full communion in the complete sense can be only an eschatological hope. Here on earth the Church will always be a pilgrim church struggling with tensions, schisms and apostasy. As a church of sinners she cannot be a perfect church. But according to Johann Adam Möhler, who inspired Yves Congar, one of the fathers of Catholic ecumenical theology, we have to distinguish between tensions, which belong to life and are a sign of life, and contradictions, which make impossible and destroy communal life and lead to excommunication.

The ecumenical task therefore cannot be to remove all tensions but only to transform contradictory affirmations into complementary affirmations, i.e. to find a degree of substantial consensus which will permit us, though legitimate differences persist, to lift the excommunications. We reached this goal in the Christological agreements with the ancient Church of the East and in the Joint Declaration on Justification with the Lutheran World Federation. On other questions, particularly those regarding ministries in the Church, we have not yet been successful. We have made remarkable progress since the Second Vatican Council, but we have not yet reached the final ecumenical goal, which is not eschatological communion but full church communion as unity within a reconciled diversity. Thus we still live in a transition period, which will probably last some time.

We have to fill the interim stage that we have reached (of a real if not complete church *communio*) with real life. The 'ecumenism of love' and the 'ecumenism of truth', which both naturally remain very important, must be complemented by an 'ecumenism of life'. We have to apply all that we have achieved to the way we actually live. The churches did not diverge only through discussion, they diverged through alienation, i.e. the way they lived. Therefore they have to come closer to each other again in their lives; they must get accustomed to each other, pray together, work together and live together, bearing the pain of incomplete *communio* and of not yet being able to share eucharistic communion around the Lord's table. Thus this ecumenism of life is not to be understood in a static way; it is a process of healing and growing.

This interim stage must have its own ethos: renunciation of all kinds of open or hidden proselytism, awareness that all 'inside' decisions also touch our partners, healing the wounds of history (purification of memories). We need a larger reception of the ecumenical dialogues and the agreements already reached. Without danger to our faith or our conscience, we could already do much more together than we usually do: for example, common Bible study, exchange of spiritual experiences, gathering of liturgical texts, joint worship in services of the word, better understanding of the common tradition as well as of existing differences, co-operation in theology, mission and cultural and social witness, co-operation in the area of development and preservation of the environment, in the mass media etc. It is also particularly important for us to develop a 'spirituality of *communio*' (*Novo millennio ineunte*, 42f.), in our own church and between the churches. Only if we can restore the recently lost confidence in this way will further steps be possible.

We must find institutional forms and structures for the present interim stage and for the 'ecumenism of life'. This can be done particularly through councils of churches at regional and national level. They are not a super-church, and require none of the churches to abandon their own self-understanding. Responsibility for the way of ecumenism remains with the churches themselves. But the councils are an important instrument, a forum for co-operation between the churches and an instrument for promoting unity (cf. *Ecumenical Directory* 1993, 166–71).

After the substantial clarification of the central content of the faith (Christology, soteriology and the doctrine of justification), the question of the Church and her mission becomes central. It will be necessary to clarify the understanding of church and *communio* and to come to an agreement on the final goal of the ecumenical pilgrimage. In the present situation we have to explain anew the relation between the 'already givenness' of the Church, which is founded in the 'in advance' of God's redemption and grace in Jesus Christ, and the ecumenical goal of full communion that we search and pray for. All churches will have to do their homework in order to understand and better explain the nature and mission of the Church. In doing so we have to make plain our agreements and our differences; this is the only way to come to a clarification and, ultimately, to a consensus. False irenicism leads nowhere. The multilateral consultation process of the Commission for Faith and Order, '*The Nature and Purpose of the Church*' is therefore important even if it cannot yet lead to a full consensus.

Part of the discussion of the understanding of *communio* is a discussion of ministries in the Church. At present this is the crucial point of the ecumenical dialogue. The episcopate in apostolic succession and the Petrine ministry particularly require further clarification. We should make it more clear that both are a gift for the Church which we want to share in a spiritually renewed form for the good of all. But it is not only the others who can learn from us, we too can learn from the Orthodox and Reformation traditions, and consider further how best to integrate the episcopate and the Petrine ministry with synodical and collegial structures. Such an effort to strengthen and develop synodical and collegial structures in our own church, without giving up the essential aspect of the ministers' personal responsibility, is the only way in which an ecumenical consensus could be reached about the Petrine and episcopal ministries.

Finally, in this interim stage, two ways of ecumenism are important and interrelated: ecumenism *ad extra* through ecumenical encounters, dialogues and co-operation, and ecumenism *ad intra* through reform and renewal of the Catholic Church herself. There is no ecumenism without conversion (UR 6-8; UUS 15-17). From its very beginning the ecumenical movement was and will continue to be an impulse and a gift of the Holy Spirit (UR 1; 4). So the pre-eminent ecumenical activity is spiritual ecumenism, which is its very heart (UR 7-8; UUS 21-27).

Now, as we begin the new millennium, we need a new ecumenical enthusiasm. But this does not mean devising unrealistic utopias in the future. Patience is the little sister of Christian hope. Instead of staring at the impossible and chafing against it, we have to live the already given and possible *communio*, and do what is possible today. By advancing in this way, step by step, we can hope that, with the help of God's Spirit who is always ready with surprises, we shall find the way towards a better common future. In this sense, 'Duc in altum!' 'Put out into the deep!' (Luke 5:4)

5

Open Questions in the Ecclesiology of Sister Churches

Ever since the Second Vatican Council, the relationship with the Orthodox churches has experienced repeated ups and downs. Following the great hopes which accompanied the concept of sister churches in the 1980s, the radical political shift of 1989/90 gave rise to considerable difficulties relating to the issue of the Eastern churches in full communion with Rome, which the Orthodox churches designate as uniate churches and associate with the question of proselytism. If we leave aside the often highly emotive polemics, a closer examination reveals that important ecclesiological problems have been left unresolved on both sides of this discussion. The intention of this chapter is to deal with these questions in so far as they concern problems on the Catholic side. This does not in any way imply a claim to have already found the solution: the intention is rather to demonstrate the issues which need to be resolved, and simply to suggest a direction in which a solution may be found.

A New Language which Commands Attention

One of the positive ecumenical developments since the Second Vatican Council is the fact that the churches of the East and West, after 1000 years of separation, now recognize and designate one another as sister churches.[1] This term is relatively new. It has a certain basis in the second Epistle of John. There, one Christian congregation sends greetings to another congregation: 'The children of thy elect sister greet thee' (v. 13). The two congregations see one another as sister congregations. This terminology corresponds to the way in which the New Testament very often refers to the Church as a family, and especially to those passages where Christians are called brothers or describe themselves as such (Matt. 12.48f. and 18.15; 23.8; Acts 1.15; 10.23; 11.1f. *et al.*; Rom. 16.14; Cor. 16.20; 1 Thess. 5.26 *et al.*; 1 Pet. 2.17; 5.9), showing that they all belong to the one house and family of God.

This language borrowed from the conception of family life plays a fundamental role in the writings of the Fathers of the Church.[2] In later history the concept of 'sister church' occurs only in isolated instances. But in fact East and West have long understood themselves to be sisters. They have always been spoken of as the Church of the East and the Church of the West.[3] Even the Council of Florence spoke of the union of the oriental and the occidental churches in the foreword to its union decree *Laetentur caeli* (1419), and understood this union to be the restoration of sisterly love and peace.[4] Thus, long after the schism between East and West which is symbolically associated with the year 1054, they did not speak of churches of the East in the plural, but of the singular Church of the East. So the Eastern Church was seen as a relatively unified entity and – despite the difference on the primacy of Rome – ranked beside the Latin Church of the West.

The Second Vatican Council proclaimed its firm intention of reinstating the brotherly communion of East and West as it had existed in the first centuries. In this context the Council uses the concept 'sister churches'. It speaks of the family ties of the communion of faith and love which ought to exist between local churches as between sisters (UR 14). This rather circumlocutory formulation reveals that they were still treading on unsure ground and were therefore very cautious in formulating the phrase. Expressly, the concept of sister churches is applied only to the relationship between local churches. However, later in the text of *Unitatis redintegratio* the Eastern Church as a whole is addressed on the same footing as the Church of the West.

This concept of a 'sister church' is taken up 'after centuries of silence and expectation' in *Tomos agapis*, the correspondence between Pope Paul VI and the Patriarch Athenagoras.[5] The apostolic brief *Anno ineunte* (25 January 1967) is the first papal document to use this expression. Pope Paul VI speaks of the Church of the East and the West and their sisterly communion.[6] Subsequently, Pope John Paul has often used the concept of 'sister churches', above all in the encyclicals *Slavorum apostoli* (1985)

(27) and *Ut unum sint* (55f.; 60). In both encyclicals it is not only individual particular churches or particular church bodies which are called sister churches, but also the Church of the East and the West. The same turn of phrase is also found in the Joint Declarations of Pope John Paul II with Patriarch Dimitrios I on 7 December and with Patriarch Bartholomew on 29 June 1995.[7]

This new linguistic usage indicates a shift in the relationship of the Catholic Church to the Eastern Church. This had already been introduced by Pope Leo XIII, in particular in the encyclical *Orientalium dignitatis* (1894), and taken up and extended by Popes John XXIII and Paul VI. Pope John Paul II has made it his own and energetically taken it further. The Eastern churches are no longer referred to disparagingly as schismatic and heretical; the Latin Church no longer calls itself their mother but their sister. Correspondingly, we no longer speak of the *praestantia* of the Latin rite (Benedict XIV). Instead, we speak of the riches of the Eastern Church, which are considered a treasure of the universal Church (OE 1).[8]

Theological Foundations in a Eucharistic *Communio* Ecclesiology

The 'sister churches' ecclesiology of *Unitatis redintegratio* seems to go beyond the Dogmatic Constitution on the Church, *Lumen gentium*; but it brings into play a motif for which the constitution on the Church has indirectly laid the foundations. That expressly mentions 'ancient patriarchal churches' which have arisen 'through divine providence'. They owe their origin either to the apostles themselves or to immediate collaborators of the apostles; in the course of time they have joined together into an organically united communion. *Lumen gentium* says that '[while] preserving the unity of the unique and divine constitution of the universal Church [they] enjoy their own discipline, their own liturgical usage and ... theological and spiritual heritage' (LG 23). They are called ancestral mothers of the faith because they have as it were given birth to other daughter churches, and have remained linked with them 'by a close bond of charity' 'to our own time' (LG 23).

Unfortunately, the decree on the Eastern churches does not take these ideas any further; on the contrary, the chapter on the patriarchs is the weakest of the whole decree.[9] *Unitatis redintegratio*, on the other hand, repeats in detail the viewpoints cited in

Lumen gentium, expands on them and affirms them in summary form: East and West have taken up their common apostolic heritage in different forms and in different ways, and have from the beginning interpreted it differently (UR 14). On that basis the decree on ecumenism draws the conclusion: the Eastern churches 'have the power to govern themselves according to the disciplines proper to them' (UR 16). The Eastern churches have their own manner of being a church. They have not received their ecclesial being from the Latin church; on the contrary, the Latin Church owes much to them. The Latin church is therefore not the mother but the sister of the Oriental churches, the relationship between the two churches is not a dependent mother–daughter relationship, but a fraternal communion (UR 14).

The Council does not see the development of the early churches simply in terms of human sociological causes, but views it rather as the work of divine providence (LG 23). While the patriarchates are therefore not divinely instituted (*ius divinum*), neither are they merely a human creation which owes its existence to accidental historical constellations and interests (*ius humanum*). They are the work of the Church led by the Spirit (*ius ecclesiasticum*) and – with the support of the Spirit – of the decisive Ecumenical Councils of the as yet undivided Church (*ius conciliare*). The dignity and legitimacy of the patriarchate of the early Church is thus grounded in theology and not simply in sociology or mere human history. The decree on the Eastern churches expresses a similar view, which in the end occurs within the framework of the pneumatological *communio* ecclesiology familiar to the Eastern churches (OE 2).[10]

These statements relate expressly only to the five early patriarchates, with Rome consistently named in first place, followed by Constantinople, Alexandria, Antioch and Jerusalem. Since these patriarchates of the early Church are called the 'mothers of the faith', the status of the later patriarchates can also be derived from them. However, since they originated only after the separation of East and West, they are not accorded the same consensus of the universal Church. In addition, even some respected Orthodox theologians are of the opinion that the autocephalous national churches represent a weakness within Orthodoxy today.[11] The more recent development of autocephalous national churches and the concomitant tensions also give rise to the question whether it is possible to speak of an Orthodox

Church in the singular, or rather of Orthodox churches in the plural. This problem is intensified in the Diaspora, where various Orthodox hierarchies exist side by side within the same territory. Herein lies an unresolved problem for Orthodoxy; it is to be hoped that it will soon be resolved at some future pan-Orthodox synod.

In the Council texts, these historical and theological statements do not yet consolidate into a firm doctrine, but they do follow convergent lines and point in one specific direction. The more profound theological foundation arises indirectly from *Lumen gentium*. There the foundations are laid for a eucharistic *communio* ecclesiology (LG 3; 7; 11; 17; 26; UR 2; 15; CD 30) which has led to a rediscovery of the local church (SC 26; LG 23; CD 11).[12] In *Unitatis redintegratio* the concept of the local church is taken up and summarized in connection with the Eastern churches. The decree states that the Church of God is built up and grows in stature through the eucharist within these individual churches, and this communion becomes manifest in their concelebration (UR 16).

The fundamental principle of eucharistic ecclesiology shines through this statement: each local church is wholly church, but no local church is the whole Church; because each local church is the Church of Jesus Christ, and because there is only one Christ and one Church of Jesus Christ, each local church is in it innermost essence in *communio* with all other local churches. The one universal Church exists 'in and of/formed out of' local churches (LG 23), just as the local churches exist 'in and of/formed out of' the one universal Church.[13] This *communio* receives its highest expression in the eucharistic concelebration. This view is not based on the universalist, centralist and pyramidal concept of the Church which was typical of Latin ecclesiology in the second millennium, but on the communial understanding of church unity of the early and Eastern churches, which consists 'in and of' various local churches and local ecclesial communities or ritual communities.[14]

The fundamental equality of all local churches does not mean that no differences can and do exist between them. That would lead to an atomization of the particular churches. *Communio* between local churches presupposes communication structures. Such structures were already formed by common law in the first centuries; the first Ecumenical Council, the Council of Nicea (325), already presupposes and confirms in Canon 6 that certain metropoles are accorded precedence.[15]

The famous Canon 34 of the so-called *Apostolic Canons* (presumably late fourth century) – referred to again and again by the Orthodox churches – takes up this organic structure and sums it up in a concise formulation:

> The bishops of every nation must acknowledge him who is first among them and account him as their head and do nothing of consequence without his consent; but each may do those things only which concern his own parish and the country places belonging to it. But neither let him who is the first do anything without the consent of all, for so there will be unanimity and God will be glorified through the Lord in the Holy Spirit.[16]

The terminology of sister churches is thus more than a friendly turn of phrase with no objective substance. It not only signifies a turning-point in the definition of the relationship between East and West but also a turning-point in Latin ecclesiology as it frees itself from a one-sided universalist and centralist view, discovers the theology of local churches and from there arrives at a communial understanding of church unity. Thereby the Council laid the foundations of a new development; but this in itself is only the beginning of the beginning. The ecumenical consequences will only become apparent with time. Initially there are still many open historical and theological questions. The Council has prompted these questions rather than itself resolving them.[17]

Reservations of the Congregation for the Doctrine of Faith

Following the Council, the new usage of the 'sister churches' terminology threatened to become inflationary in some quarters. In some instances it was also applied to the ecclesial communities of the Reformation in the West. The main concern of the Congregation for the Doctrine of Faith was apparently that the 'sister churches' terminology was misunderstood to imply that the unity of the Church still remains to be sought by means of an ecumenical rapprochement between East and West, thus calling into question the fact that the one Church already 'subsists' in the Catholic Church. Therefore the Congregation for the Doctrine of the Faith saw a need for clarification. This took the form of a letter to the Presidents of the Bishops' Conferences (2000), that is, at a lower level within the exercise of its magisterium, and it restricted itself to regulating the usage of the terminology without dealing with the substantive issues as such.

The Congregation determined that the concept 'sister church' can only be applied to the relationship of churches with a valid episcopate, and is thus not applicable to the ecclesial communities of the Reformation. This amounts to an indirect affirmation that a valid eucharist is definitive for recognition as a church and thereby also as a sister church. In addition – and this is the major point of the document – the Congregation stressed that the terminology of sister churches can only be applied to the relationship between particular churches; it cannot be applied to the relationship of the universal Church to particular churches. The universal Church is not the sister but the mother of the particular churches (10).

These terminological clarifications are logical, easy to follow and theologically well-founded. But they are purely formal, and deliberately leave the actual underlying problem unanswered. The decisive issue is what is to be understood by the term 'universal Church', which particular churches are involved, and how the relationship between the two is to be determined.

According to this terminological regulation, it is clear that the church of Rome, just like the church of Milan or Cologne, is the sister church of, say, Alexandria or Antioch. But it is already less customary to call the Latin Roman Catholic Church a sister church of, for example, the Greek Catholic Church in the Ukraine. If that is possible, the question arises as to why the Roman Catholic (that is, Latin) Church cannot also be called the sister church of the Greek Orthodox or Russian Orthodox Church, which are recognized as true churches. This should be possible, because the Roman Catholic (Latin) Church is not identical with the universal catholic Church. In the sense of the first millennium and even of the Council of Florence, and more recently also of the Decree on Ecumenism and the apostolic brief *Anno ineunte*, the universal catholic Church is not identical with the Roman Catholic (Latin) Church. It too is a particular church and as such a sister church of the churches of the East.

Thus it can be said that the one Church of Jesus Christ exists in the Latin church and in the Oriental churches. The Oriental churches encompass both the Catholic Eastern churches which are in full communion with Rome and the Orthodox churches which are not in full communion with Rome but are nevertheless recognized as true churches. The full unity of the Church therefore will not be established in future by means of any kind of union; it already exists, though in the case of the Orthodox churches still in an imperfect (that is, only in an almost perfect[18]) manner. The goal of ecumenical dialogue is not union but the way from imperfect to full communion. If that is true, then we arrive at the most significant point of controversy standing between East and West, namely the question of the Bishop of Rome and the future exercise of the Petrine office.

The Pope: Patriarch of the West?

As a professor of theology, Joseph Ratzinger had convincingly demonstrated that the distinction between the primacy function of the pope as the Bishop of Rome and the successor of Peter within the universal Church and his function as the patriarch of the West is fundamental for the future structure of the Petrine office.[19] In the meantime, however, a different opinion has prevailed within the Congregation for the Doctrine of Faith. According to this view the Latin church has never seen itself as a patriarchate in the sense of the Eastern church, and the West has never shared the Eastern conception of the patriarchate or the pentarchy (i.e. the five original patriarchates). This thesis was developed historically above all by a then member of the Congregation, Adriano Garuti.[20]

Despite several queries, the Council itself deliberately refrained from expressing itself on this issue in the Constitution on the Church.[21] But the Decree on the Eastern Churches did designate the patriarchate as an institution of the whole Church, not only of the Eastern Church (OE 7).[22] Thus the thesis of Garuti is to be considered a personal historical thesis, one which is vigorously disputed by reputable historians.[23] So it is surprising that the Congregation for the Doctrine of Faith props up its argument so one-sidedly with the historically disputed theses of one of its former members, without taking into account the more comprehensive current research. The magisterial weight of such historical statements should be determined according to the general theological rules whereby purely historical expositions do not fall within the competence of the magisterium. Therefore it is not forbidden to represent another opinion on this issue or to consider the question open for further discussion among historians.

In this context we can leave open the question of whether the West saw itself as a patriarchate. To a certain extent it is a question of terminology. Even if the West did not see itself as a patriarchate, or did not see itself as a patriarchate in the same sense as the East, that does not alter the historical reality. Regardless of Rome's claim to primacy, the Eastern Church and the Western Church considered themselves as relatively autonomous entities; at the same time they were bound to one another in a brotherly or sisterly relationship, and they considered themselves obligated to restore such a fraternal relationship when it was endangered or temporarily interrupted. That is precisely the view which *Unitatis redintegratio* renewed.

The consequences of this view have been demonstrated by Ratzinger. The issue is to disentangle the functions which have accrued to the papacy in the course of time. The important thing is to distinguish the essential and therefore indispensable duties of Petrine ministry from those duties which pertain to the Pope as the first bishop (patriarch or primate) of the Latin church, or have accrued over time. Such a distinction could also lead to consequences (which do not fall within the scope of this paper) for the structuring of the Roman Catholic Church and the construction of intermediary authorities between the individual bishop, the bishops' conference and Rome.[24]

Nota Bene: a Hint from the Council

This is not the place to enter into a comprehensive theological hermeneutic of biblical and magisterial statements on the Petrine office; nor is it possible here to pursue the complex questions of the relationship between primacy and episcopate. Our concern here is one single but important viewpoint arising from this 'sister churches' ecclesiology and the fraternal designation of the Eastern and Western Churches urged by the Council.

In the third chapter of *Lumen gentium* the Council took an important step for the relationship of the Eastern and Western Churches. It attempted to overcome the traditional distinction between the powers of consecration and jurisdiction in order to tackle one of the most difficult problems in the legal and constitutional history of the Church.[25] In the Latin church prior to the Council this distinction had led to the widely-held theory that the consecrating powers of the bishop are transmitted through his consecration as a bishop, while his powers of jurisdiction are bestowed on him by the Pope. This theory arises out of the Western universalist, centralist and pyramidal concept of the Church in the Latin West in the second millennium. The Council attempted to perceive once more the unity of the powers of consecration and jurisdiction, and to anchor the pastoral powers in the consecration of the bishop, following the earlier tradition (LG 21f.).

It is a natural consequence of the concept of *communio* that the individual bishop can only exercise his authority in *communio* with all other bishops. This *communio* is not simply a vague matter of feeling but, according to the *communio* concept of the early Church, a legally tangible entity. In order to express this, the Council employs a neologism, stating that the bishop can exercise the authority which he has received through his consecration only in the '*communio hierarchica*', in hierarchical communion with the head and members of the college of bishops (LG 21f.). The neologism '*communio hierarchica*' gives full expression to the fact that *communio* is not a notional communion but represents a legally tangible entity.

The 'Nota praevia' to the constitution *Lumen gentium* takes up this statement and seeks to justify it on the basis that the pastoral office is exercised together with many others and therefore demands to be integrated into the *communio*, by which it is at the same time more precisely determined. Interestingly, the note also adds that the form and manner of this integration occur in accordance with the circumstances of the time, and is thus historically variable. Therefore a distinction is to be made between the essential, and therefore essentially binding, *communio* and its concrete canonistic structure. At the same time this implies that the form of canonical empowerment of bishops by the Pope, which has been customary in the Latin church for so long, is not the only possible way of making this legal determination.

The pre-conciliar distinction between consecration and jurisdiction was unknown to the early Church and is still unknown in the East (although titular bishops as well as auxiliary bishops and metropolitans who are not diocesan bishops do also exist in the East); the more recent theory of *communio hierarchica* is equally unknown in the East. In the past it was a matter of dispute within Catholic theology whether, and if so in what way, jurisdiction can be accorded to the bishops of the Eastern Church. In a 'Nota bene' attached to the 'Nota praevia' the Council leaves this question open for theological discussion. That is equivalent to a complete abstention from voting with regard to the ecclesiological problem of the Eastern churches.[26]

Indirectly, however, the Council presupposes that the Orthodox bishops are entitled to jurisdiction, otherwise the Decree on the Catholic Eastern Churches could not say that Catholic Christians can under certain circumstances receive the sacrament of penance in the Eastern churches (OE 27). That presupposes that the Orthodox bishops do possess their own jurisdiction. The Decree on Ecumenism goes one step further and expresses the principle that the Eastern churches are true churches and have the power to govern themselves according to their own disciplines (UR 16). Basically, the 'Nota bene' and (even more clearly) the two cited decrees give concrete expression to what the 'Nota praevia' says about the historically variable nature of the *communio hierarchica*. The ecclesiology of the Eastern churches is based as common law on earlier rights which have later been codified in detail by the canons of the early councils.[27]

That suggests the view that the concrete juridical form of the hierarchical communion, as it is provided for in the current Latin church (and in a different sense also in the Catholic Eastern churches), represents a legal discipline within the Latin church (and also the Catholic Eastern churches) which should not be canonized as such but remains fundamentally capable of change; in its present concrete form the pope seems to be acting as the head of the Latin church, while in the Eastern churches which are separated from Rome this function is by customary right accorded to the patriarch or metropolitan (together with their synods).

One can also draw the further conclusion that if the Eastern churches were to enter into full communion with Rome they would in principle not need to alter any of their legal discipline; it could be recognized as customary law which has evolved over time. The Council does not draw this conclusion but also does not exclude it, seeming rather to establish it by way of inclusion.

So the very concise 'Nota bene', which almost seems a coy afterthought, points toward a problem which *Lumen gentium* was not in a position to solve, but which in the light of *Unitatis redintegratio* suggests an ecumenically interesting and far-reaching solution. The 'Nota bene' of course only opens a very narrow crack in the door, but that shows that the door is in principle open. Post-conciliar 'sister churches' ecclesiology has opened this door wide; however, we can hardly claim to have actually passed through it. The present situation is no more than a finger pointing in a certain direction. The open questions which await us beyond this door relate not only to the issue – wrongly considered obsolete – of the place of Rome as patriarch of the West, but also to the closely connected and ecclesiologically and ecumenically significant question of the future structure and the future exercise of the Petrine office itself.

These theological questions already have practical consequences today, which are evident at each visit to Rome by a patriarch of the Eastern Orthodox church. As far as protocol is concerned these visits take place under the banner of the 'sister church' relationship; the Pope always reserves the place of honour on his right for these visitors. But in other situations the attitude is often different. Thus the Orthodox churches often complain that they are not treated as sister churches. They accuse our 'sister churches' rhetoric of dishonesty. The criticism has often been raised that individual symbolic gestures and words are not as yet grounded in a corresponding theology.[28] Therefore they are often lacking in didactic and practical consistency; the symbolic gestures arouse expectations that are not subsequently fulfilled, which can only lead to disappointment. This tension is not necessarily dishonest; it can also be understood as an anticipation of future solutions and thus as a provocation to further theological reflection.

The Thorny Problem of So-called Uniatism

The unsolved problems in 'sister church' ecclesiology also form the background to the conflict regarding so-called uniatism, i.e. the method of forming bridgeheads of a sort towards future union with the Eastern churches by way of particular unions with Rome. Here we are addressing an extremely complex and emotionally loaded problem. The Eastern Orthodox churches view the Catholic Eastern churches in full communion with Rome as anything but a bridge; for them they are rather a wall and a barrier, even an abomination. They accuse them of apostasy and treachery, and reproach them for stealing sheep from their own flock and plundering their own mother churches.

This emotion-laden problem cannot be discussed here in all its aspects, particularly not in its complex historical contexts.[29] Historically there is not just one uniatism as a single uniform phenomenon; and it is not only found on the side of the Catholic Church. The historical reasons for its development vary greatly between the individual Catholic Eastern churches. It is also historically incorrect to put all such unions down to proselytism without further ado. For example, the unions with the Ukrainians and the Ruthenians must be seen in connection with the Union Council of Florence; nor should one overlook the threat posed by the advance of the Reformation and the defensive post-Tridentine counter-Reformation mentality; that above all led to an exclusivist ecclesiology which saw the means of salvation as existing only within one's own church.

But however the individual particular unions may have come about historically, and whatever their theological foundation, they all have in common the fact that they have inflicted deep wounds on the Orthodox mother churches and aroused profound distrust regarding Rome's intentions. In the case of the Catholic Eastern churches they led to the formation of a type of church which was unknown in the previous tradition.

The dialogue of love and truth between Rome and the Orthodox churches which began on the basis of 'sister churches' ecclesiology after the Second Vatican Council was a hopeful new beginning; it was possible to lay the theological foundations for a new relationship.[30] But after the political shift in Eastern and Central Europe in 1989/90 the problem of uniatism once more settled like a frost on the dreams of budding blooms. The so-called uniate churches in the Ukraine and Romania, which had been banished underground and brutally persecuted by the Communist dictatorship, were able to take their place in public life once more. So it was psychologically inevitable that old wounds were reopened and new wounds were inflicted. In the eyes of the Orthodox churches, this so-called (to use their term) uniatism seemed to cast doubt on the honesty of Catholic ecumenism and the ecclesiology of sister churches. This led to a crisis within the ecumenical dialogue which has not yet been surmounted.

Following the difficult session of the Joint International Theological Commission in Freising in 1990, during and immediately after the political shift, the next meeting in Balamand (1993) was looking for an answer. The uniate churches were declared to have a right to exist (3). This recognition of the so-called uniate churches is distinct from uniatism as a method, which both Freising and Balamand dismissed as a way of achieving the unity of the Church both today and in the future (2; 12). Any form of proselytism was even more definitively rejected (18; 35). The exclusivist ecclesiology which attributes salvific significance only to one's own church was condemned (13). As a result, particular unions between churches should no longer be the definitive method and model; rather, the method of dialogue and the model of sister churches (12) should be taken as the basis for practical rules of reciprocal conduct.[31]

The Pope recognized this text as a significant step forward.[32] Understandably, it was not easy for the so-called uniate churches – which had suffered so much for their loyalty to Rome – to accept this declaration; some of them understood Balamand as a death sentence and saw themselves as victims of ecumenism. But in the end the vast majority of them endorsed it. On the Orthodox side the difficulties were and are just as great. Various Orthodox churches rejected the declaration of Balamand. They did not see themselves in a position to accept the 'sister churches' concept.

The Eastern Orthodox churches, no less than the Catholic Church, understand themselves to be the true Church of Jesus Christ.[33] They regard this as a strict statement of identity and, unlike the Second Vatican Council, they have not replaced this definition with the more open statement that the Church of Christ subsists in the Catholic Church (LG 8). Within Orthodoxy, therefore, no generally accepted answer has yet been found to the problem of how the Church of Jesus Christ can exist outside the borders of their own church; that definition would only be possible through a pan-Orthodox or ecumenical council. Thus many Orthodox churches even have difficulty acknowledging the Catholic Church, not to mention the Catholic Eastern churches, as sister churches. It is their conviction that the Catholic Eastern churches have been absorbed by the Latin church, and they have been placed in an 'abnormal situation'. The fact that the Catholic Eastern churches maintain the Eastern rite arouses Orthodox distrust rather than favourably predisposes them, because they suspect that the ulterior motive is proselytism.

Closer examination reveals that there are still unresolved ecclesiological questions on both sides. Although the Second Vatican Council adopted and published the Decree on the Eastern Churches and the Decree on Ecumenism on the same day, the two decrees embody differing ecclesiological approaches, and there is therefore a not inconsiderable tension between them. While the ecumenical decree sketches the outlines of the 'sister churches' ecclesiology, the Decree on the Eastern Churches maintains the line of the previous Latin conception of the Church.[34] It says that the uniate churches of the East have been entrusted to the pastoral leadership (*pastoralis gubernium*) of the Bishop of Rome (OE 3), who has the right to intervene in particular cases (OE 8). Individual authors go so far as to derive the authority of the patriarchs of the Catholic Eastern churches from the plenitude of power of the pope.

These differing ecclesiological conceptions of the Church present problems for ecumenical dialogue. It is clear that union with the Orthodox churches is not possible without union with the Catholic Eastern churches. The Council expressly exhorts them to ecumenical engagement (OE 34), and many of their bishops participate with zeal. But are the Catholic Eastern churches really a bridge towards the Orthodox churches?

There is no simple answer. The Catholic Eastern churches can and certainly should function as a bridge in the sense that they themselves keep alive the rich heritage of the Eastern Church and renew it when necessary; they keep alive both an awareness of this heritage within the Catholic Church and an awareness in the East of the urgency of communion with Rome. In short, they should keep us conscious of the anomaly of separation and stimulate our longing for unity. In this sense they can, precisely as a 'stumbling block' and a challenge, have a providential significance for ecumenism. But in their current state they cannot be a model for the anticipated future greater unity. Their current status – as the Decree on the Eastern Churches makes clear in its conclusion – is provisional. The Decree establishes that all their legal arrangements are valid only 'in view of present condition', 'until the Catholic Church and the separated Eastern churches unite together in the fullness of communion' (OE 30). The apostolic constitution *Sacri canones* (1990), which promulgated the new legal code of the Eastern churches, expressly reiterated this statement.

Towards a Solution: 'Neither Absorption nor Fusion'

The definitive resolution of the divisions within the ritual community can only by found through the resolution of the division between East and West on the basis of the renewed ecclesiology of *communio* and sister churches. According to this view each local church is wholly church, but not the whole Church. As a local church it exists 'in and of' the universal Church, as, vice versa, the universal Church exists 'in and of' the local churches (LG 23). Therefore each local church can regulate its affairs on its own responsibility; but it can only do this *in communio* with all other local churches as well as with the universal Church. The form and manner in which this occurs can vary historically and consequently can differ in the Latin church and in the Eastern churches. The important thing is that all decisions are made within the frame-work of the common faith, common sacraments and common episcopacy.

A solution on this basis opens up new terms of reference for an answer to the most contentious issue between East and West, the Petrine office. In order to make progress, the Pope has taken the initiative and invited the separated churches, in particular the Eastern churches, to enter into dialogue with him on the future exercise of the Petrine office.[35] We are as yet only in the initial stages of dealing with this question. Surveying historical develop-ments over the past 2000 years, it is obvious that the First and Second Vatican Councils left many more aspects of this question open than is generally assumed. While maintaining that which is essential and indispensable to the Petrine office, far-reaching developments are possible, although the results cannot be predicted in any detail.

In principle the goal of full *communio* for which we are to strive was defined in the conversations with the Anglicans at Malines (1921–26) between Cardinal Mercier and Lord Halifax, using the formula 'united but not absorbed'.[36] Pope John Paul II has made this formula his own and spoken of a full communion which is neither absorption nor fusion but an encounter in truth and love.[37] The document of Balamand reiterated this formula (14).

A reintegration of this kind which is neither fusion nor absorption means that the Catholic Eastern churches too cannot be absorbed or fused (which would in practice mean liquidation). They cannot, of course, simply remain as they are now, they must completely eliminate the traces of Latinization; but even if they return to their mother churches – and several of them have already expressed their willingness to do so – they will not simply disappear without trace; they have their own specific contribution to make to the *communio*. There will be different practical answers to how this can happen, including pragmatic transitional solutions; what is decisive is the *plena communio* itself.

The re-establishment of full unity between East and West can only be a pneumatological–charismatic process, and it is impossible to predetermine in detail what shape it will take. With human foresight, the solution of this complex problem will only be possible through many patient, individual steps. In order to arrive at a *communio ecclesiarum* we must first break the spiral of mistrust; that presupposes empathy, purification of historical memory, overcoming prejudices, acts of forgiveness, conversion and signs of fraternity. Many more theological dialogues will be necessary to build up mutual trust and mutual understanding. Above all it will demand repentance and prayer.[38]

Thankfulness for the steps which have been possible with the help of God over the past 40 years allows us at the same time to be full of hope that it is still meaningful to follow with courage and patience the path opened up by the 'sister churches' ecclesiology.

Notes

1 Cf. J. Meyendorff and E. Lanne, 'Églises-soeurs. Implications ecclésiologiques du Tomos Agapis' in: *Istina* 20, 1975, 35–46; 47–74; H. Meyer, *Ökumenische Zielvorstellungen* (Ökumenische Studienhefte, 4), Göttingen 1996, 135f.; E. C. Suttner, 'Schwesterkirchen in fast vollendeter Gemeinschaft', in: *Christlicher Osten* 47, 1992, 278–87; Suttner, *Die Christenheit aus Ost und West auf der Suche nach dem sichtbaren Ausdruck ihrer Einheit*, Würzburg 1999; the most recent publication from Z. Glaeser, *Ku eklezjologii kosciolow siostrzanych*, Opole 2000, was inaccessible to me due to language.

2 K. H. Schelkle, Art. 'Bruder', in: *RAC* 2, 1954, 639f.

3 V. Peri, 'Le vocabulaire des relations entre les Églises d'Occident et d'Orient jusqu'au 16e siècle', in: *Irénikon* 65, 1992, 194–9.

4 *Conciliorum oecumenicorum Decreta*, Freiburg i.Br. 1962, 499f.

5 *Tomos Agapis*. Vatican–Phanar 1958–70, Rome–Istanbul 1971, 112f. This concept is to be found for the first time in the letter of Patriarch Athenagoras to Cardinal Bea on 12 April 1962 (p. 40f.).

6 Ibid. 386–93

7 Quoted in: *Growth in Agreement II. Reports and Agreed Statements of Ecumenical Conversations on a World Level. 1982–1998*, ed. J. Gros, H. Meyer, W. G. Rusch, Geneva 2000, 669f.; 686f.

8 Also in the Apostolic letter *Orientale lumen* (1995), 1.

9 So the Melkite Patriarch Maximos IV, quoted in: *LThK Vat. II*, vol. 1, 373.

10 Cf. *LThK Vat. II*, vol. 1, 367.

11 J. Meyendorff, *Orthodoxy and Catholicity*, New York 1966, 41–4; *The Byzantine Legacy in the Orthodox Church*, New York 1982, 251–5.

12 Important for this rediscovery: H. de Lubac, *Corpus mysticum. L'Eucharistie et l'Église au Moyen Age*, 2nd edition, Paris 1949; *Méditation sur l'Église*, 3rd edition, Paris 1954. Taken up magisterially by Pope John Paul II in the encyclical *Ecclesia de eucharistia* (2003)

13 Document of the Congregation for the Doctrine of the Faith, *Communionis notio* (1992), 9.

14 Y. Congar, 'De la communion des Églises à une ecclésiologie universelle', in: *L'espiscopat de l'Église universelle*, Paris 1962, 227–60. On the two different conceptions cf. also J. Ratzinger, 'Die bischöfliche Kollegialität', in: G. Barauna (ed.), *De ecclesia*, vol. 2, Freiburg i. Br. 1966, 56–8.

15 *Conciliorum oecumenicorum Decreta*, 8. Cf. the Councils of Constantinople (381) can. 2f. (ibid. 27f.) and Chalcedon (451) can. 28 (ibid. 75f.).

16 Quoted from *Les constitutions apostoliques*, vol. 3 (Sources chrétiennes, 336), Paris 1987, 284f.

17 G. Philips, *L'Église et son mystère au Concile du Vatican*, vol. 1, Paris 1967, 315f.

18 The latter formulation is in the letter from Pope Paul VI to Patriarch Athenagoras of 8 February 1971, in: *Tomos agapis*, 614.

19 J. Ratzinger, Article 'Primat', in: *LThK VIII* (1963) 763; 'Primat und Episkopat', in: *Das neue Volk Gottes*, Düsseldorf 1969, 142.

20 A. Garuti, *Il Papa Patriarcha d'Occidente?* Bologna 1990; *Saggi di ecumenismo*, Rome 2003, 119–40.

21 G. Philips, *op. cit.* 315f. But for Philips' own opinion, ibid. 273.

22 See *LThK Vat. II*, vol. 1, 374.

23 Most importantly the works of W. de Vries, 'Die Entstehung der Patriarchate des Ostens und ihr Verhältnis zur päpstlichen Vollgewalt' in: *Scholastik* 37, 1962, 314–69; *Rom und die Patriarchate des Ostens*, Freiburg-München 1963; Y. Congar, 'Le Pape comme patriarche d'occident', in: *Istina* 28, 1983, 374–90. More recent and critical discussion of Garuti can be found in F. R. Gahbaur, Article 'Patriarchat I', in: *TRE* 26, 1996, 85–91; G. Nedungatt, 'The Patriarchal Ministry in the Church of the Third Millennium', in: *The Jurist* 61, 2001, 1–89. Nedungatt makes fun of Garuti by saying that such theses come from people who want to be more papist than the pope. Cf. J. Ratzinger, in: *LThK Vat. II*, vol. 1, 352–4; 'Die bischöfliche Kollegialität', 47–53; 61–5; G. Philips, op. cit., 254–7; 282f.; 289f.

24 G. Greshake, 'Die Stellung des Protos in der Sicht der römisch-katholischen Theologie', in: *Kanon* 9, 1989, 17–50.

25 Cf. J. Ratzinger, in: *LThK Vat. II*, vol. 1, 352–4; 'Die bischöfliche Kollegialität', 47–53; 61–5; G. Philips, op. cit., 254–7; 282f.; 289f.

26 *LThK Vat II*, vol. 1, 219–21; 357–9; J. Ratzinger, 'Die bischöfliche Kollegialität', 67f.; G. Philips, op. cit., 254–63; A. de Halleux, 'Fraterna *communio*', in: *Irénikon* 58, 1985, 291–310.

27 G. Philips, op.cit., 273. Y. Congar, *Mon journal du Concile*, vol. 2, Paris 2002, 99; 279; 291; 388.

28 Y. Congar, *Mon journal du Concile*, vol. 2, Paris 2002, 99; 279; 291; 388.

29 A selection of the rich literature: A. de Halleux, 'Uniatism et communion', in: *Revue Théologique de Louvain* 22, 1999; V. Peri, 'Considerazioni sull'uniatismo', in: *Lo scambio fraterno fra le Chiese*, Città del Vaticano 1993, 365–94; *Orientalis varietas. Roma e le Chiese d'Oriente*, Roma 1994; E. Ch. Suttner, esp.: *Die Christenheit aus Ost und West auf der Suche nach dem sichtbaren Ausdruck für ihre Einheit*, Würzburg 1999; R. F. Taft, 'The Problem of "Uniatism" and the "Healing of Memories": Anamnesis not Anamnesia', in: *Logos* 41–42, 2000/01, 155–96; A. Garuti, *Saggi di ecumenismo*, 17–118.

30 The previously published dialogue documents together with a historical introduction can be found in: *Growth in Agreement II. Reports and Agreed Statements of Ecumenical Conversations on a World Level. 1982–1998*, 647–85; *The Quest for Unity: Orthodox and Catholics in Dialogue. Documents of the Joint International Commission and Official Dialogues in the United States. 1965–1995*, ed. J. Borelli and J. H. Erickson, New York–Washington DC 1996.

31 Even though the document of Balamand must be regarded as a important step forward, some formulations are not fully matured. Greater ecclesiological depth is no doubt necessary. For example, proselytism is not clearly distinguished from missionary activity, which is part of the essence and duty of the Church, although it cannot of course be directed at Christians of another church (12). The important volume issued by the Comité mixte Catholique – Orthodoxe en France 'Catholiques et Orthodoxes: les enjeux de l'uniatisme. Dans le sillage de Balamand', Paris 2004, was published after the competition of this manuscript and could not be taken into consideration.

32 UUS 60.

33 J. Meyendorff, *The Orthodox Church*, New York 1981, 225: 'As opposed to Protestantism and Roman Catholicism, the Orthodox Church claims to be the true Church of Christ from which Western Christians have separated. Its claims are as exclusive and categorical as those of Rome, but they are put forth in the name of a different conception of the Church.'

34 E. Lanne, 'Églises unies ou églises soeurs: un choix inéluctable', in: *Irénikon* 48, 1975, 322–42

35 UUS 95; with reference to the Catholic Eastern churches the address to the members of the Plenary of the Congregation for the Oriental Churches, in: *Insegnamenti*, XXI/1611. An overview of the current discussion is in: *Information Service* 2002/I–II, 29–42

36 Lord Halifax, *The Conversations at Malines: Original Documents*, London 1930.

37 Encyclical *Slavorum apostoli* 27

38 With great empathy, M. van Parys, 'Les Églises orientales catholiques et l'oecuménisme', in: *Irénikon* 64, 1991, 323–31; F. Bowen, 'Les relations œcuméniques au Moyen-Orient : pour une évaluation théologique', *Proche Orient Chrétien* 52 (2002), 1–2, 92–111.

6

The Renewal of Pneumatology in Contemporary Catholic Life and Theology: Towards a Rapprochement between East and West

According to the Holy Scriptures and in the tradition of the Church the Holy Spirit is the spirit of unity, the bond of love. In the New Testament we find the famous formula: κοινωνια του Α'γιου Πνευματος (*koinōnia tou Hagiou Pneumatos*), 'communion in the Holy Spirit' (2 Cor. 13.13). This means: The Holy Spirit constitutes the communion of the Church. Consequently, the renewal of church life since the Second Vatican Council has been ultimately a spiritual renewal based on a renewed pneumatology. This is especially true and important with regard to the ecumenical movement.[1]

Ecumenically, we find ourselves in a rather paradoxical situation. The Spirit unites, but East and West have been at odds over the doctrine of the Holy Spirit for a thousand years. The difference is reflected in the liturgical creed at the very centre of church life, in the celebration of the eucharist. Though Western liturgical tradition confesses that the Holy Spirit proceeds from the Father and the Son (*filioque*), the Oriental churches do not have this *filioque* clause in their creed; on the contrary, it is for them a major cause of dissent from the Latin tradition.

It would be too easy to say that this is a mere quarrel among theologians that need not be of interest to the 'simple' Christian. Leading Orthodox theologians refer the cause of the (real or supposed) ecclesiological deformations in the West to the *filioque* because, in their view, the *filioque* constitutes subordination, or a one-sided attachment of the Spirit to the Son.[2] They trace the (real or supposed) subordination of the charisma to the institution, of personal freedom to Church authority, of the prophetic to the juridical, of mysticism to scholasticism, of joint priesthood to hierarchic priesthood and, finally, of episcopal collegiality to the primacy of Rome, back to this very Christomonism and, in their conviction, the resulting oblivion of the Spirit. Similar questions and critiques arise within the church communities issuing from the Reformation, all of whom lament that in the Catholic Church there is not enough room for the freedom of the Spirit; it seems to them enchained by the Church and her institutions. So this dispute is by no means a mere theoretical and speculative problem; rather, it concerns questions that shape the life of the Church in a positive or negative way.

Rather than beginning with such controversial issues, I would like to start from our common heritage, before demonstrating the constraints found in modern Western theology, and then illustrating the new approaches and developments in both Catholic theology and the life of the Church. It is only against this background that the old, thorny and painful controversy surrounding the *filioque* can, I hope, be guided towards a solution, paving the way for a *communio*-ecclesiology and leading us one day, hopefully, to full communion in the Holy Spirit.

A Brief Look Back at Tradition

The common heritage in the holy scriptures, church fathers and scholasticism

Any deliberation on the subject of the relationship between the Holy Spirit and the Church will proceed from the account in the Acts of the Apostles of the outpouring of the Holy Spirit on the first Pentecost, when the Church appeared publicly for the first time (Acts 2.1-13). According to the witness of the Acts of the Apostles, the further path of the Church, particularly her mission, was directed by the Holy Spirit. It was the Spirit that brought about the 'unanimity' of the disciples of Christ, the 'trade mark' of the Church (Acts 1.14; 2.46; 4.24; and other references). Paul can thus describe the Church as a temple or building in the Holy Spirit (1

Cor. 3.16f.; cf. 2 Cor. 6.16; Eph. 2.21), while the first letter of St Peter adds that it is a building made of living, not dead, stones (1 Pet. 2.4f.). The diversity and richness of the spiritual gifts is an expression of this life in the Spirit (1 Cor. 12.4-31; Rom. 12.4-8; Eph. 4.3).

This pneumatological view of the Church is reflected in the creed. Both the Niceno-Constantinopolitan creed and the Apostles' Creed refer to the 'una sancta ecclesia' not in the second, christological part but rather in the third, pneumatological part of the creed. The creed thus deals with ecclesiology within the context of pneumatology, and it speaks of the Spirit as a reality within the Church.

While it would be interesting to examine all the statements made by the church fathers about the Holy Spirit and his work in the Church, this is not possible in the present context.[3] I will confine myself to one single witness, that of the martyr Bishop Irenaeus of Lyons, in which we find that the pneumatology of the fathers was already very well expressed in the third century. 'Wherever the Church is, there is also the spirit of God; and wherever the spirit of God is, there is the Church and all Grace' (Adv. haer. III, 24, 1). According to this statement, the Church is the place and home of the Holy Spirit; it gives life, inspires, stimulates and preserves the Church. The Council of Constantinople (381) summarizes this conviction in its confession of the Holy Spirit as 'the Lord and Giver of Life'. This is the common heritage of all churches in both the East and the West.

The pneumatology of the church fathers continued to have a considerable effect on the theology, spirituality and mysticism of the Middle Ages. Again, for reasons of space I would like to refer to just one – certainly representative – theologian of medieval scholasticism, Thomas Aquinas.[4]

According to Thomas, the Spirit acts not only in the Church; he leads and brings to life all that is created and is at work in the whole of creation (Summa theol. I 45, 6 ad 3; Summa contra gentiles IV 20-22). The Spirit brings the body of the Church to life in a special way (Summa theol. II/II 183, 2 ad 31; III 8, 1 ad 3); he unites the Church and shares the gifts of one with the other (Summa theol. III 68, 9 ad 2; 82, 6 ad 3). Thomas goes a step further in a quaestio concerning the essence of the New Covenant, which has no parallel elsewhere in scholasticism, affirming that the *lex evangelica* is not an external but rather an internal law, i.e. the 'gratia Spiritus Sancti, quae datur per fidem Christi. Et ideo principaliter lex nova est ipsa gratia Spiritus sancti, quae datur Christi fidelibus' (*Summa theol.* I/II 106, 1). This is an interesting and astonishing statement, since it implies that everything associated with the Church as an institution should take second place; its only purpose is to lead to (*dispositiva*) and teach the correct use and application (*ordinativa*) of what is given by the Spirit. What is essential is only the Holy Spirit itself.

Individual aspects of the pneumatology of Aquinas are undoubtedly open to criticism,[5] but these few references to Thomas show that there can be no question of any oblivion of the Holy Spirit in medieval theology. The great theologians and mystics of the Middle Ages had much more to say about the work of the Spirit in the Church, and with much greater profundity, than appeared in the later manuals of dogmatic theology.

Modern constraints

Modern Catholic theology has not been able to maintain this high level of theological thought. Luther's opponents in the sixteenth century quite rightly refer, contrary to the reformer, to the guiding of the Church by the Holy Spirit. While the reformers attributed the interpretation of the Gospel to the Holy Spirit, Catholics ascribed it to the Church guided by the Spirit; thus, in practical terms, they made the doctrine of the Church the living Gospel. The teaching authority of the Church, which invokes the Holy Spirit, then becomes the guarantor of the doctrine and the unity of the Church. The Church itself became the '*fons fidei*'; and could even be referred to as '*Ecclesia sibi ipsi est fons*'.[6]

In the encyclical *Divinum illud* (1897), devoted to the Holy Spirit, Leo XIII wrote: 'One sentence suffices: Christ is the Head of the Church, the Holy Spirit her soul.' Pius XII repeated this sentence verbatim in the encyclical entitled *Mystici corporis* (1943). Both popes refer to Saint Augustine, but the reference is not precise, since Augustine says: 'The Holy Spirit works in the Church the same way as the soul in the body; the soul plays the same role for the body as the Holy Spirit for the Body of Christ, the Church' (*Sermo* 267, 4). What was a 'functional' relationship for Augustine thus became an ontological affirmation, in danger of leading to an ecclesiological monophysitism which underestimated the human and historical side of the Church. Only the Second Vatican Council returned to its original meaning (LG 7).[7]

Traditional Catholic ecclesiology cannot therefore be accused of forgetting the Spirit. Fault can, however, be found in the fact that traditional ecclesiology did not adequately illustrate the hypostasis, and thus the freedom, of the Holy Spirit; consequently it ran the risk of domesticating and monopolizing the Spirit of God in ecclesiological terms. Here the Second Vatican Council brought about a new departure.

A new departure through Vatican II
When Pope John XXIII opened the Second Vatican Council (1962–65), he expressed the hope of a new Pentecost. Yet after its closure, the Council was reproached for Christomonism and a one-sided, Christocentric ecclesiology. It is true that the doctrine of the Council was Christocentric and remained within the framework of the Latin tradition of pneumatology. The council documents do, however, show that the council fathers endeavoured to break away from a constricted and one-sided Christocentricism, without sinking into the opposite extreme of pure pneumatocentricism, which is also to be excluded because, according to the scriptures, the Spirit is the Spirit of Christ (1 Cor. 12.3; Rom. 3.9; Rom. 8.9; Gal. 4.6).

This is made particularly clear by the fact that Vatican II did not take up the doctrine, disseminated in the first half of the twentieth century, of the Church as the continuation of the incarnation; rather, it carefully differentiated and corrected this teaching. This is evident in the way the Council describes the Church in *Lumen gentium* 8. It states that the Church is 'one interlocked reality which is comprised of a divine and a human element'. For this reason,

> by an excellent analogy, this reality is compared to the mystery of the incarnate Word. Just as the assumed nature inseparably united to the divine Word serves Him as a living instrument of salvation, so, in a similar way, does the communal structure of the Church serve Christ's Spirit, who vivifies it by way of building up the body.

The effectiveness of the Spirit is classified under the effectiveness of the Logos in this context but not simply subordinated to it. By an 'excellent analogy' the two are almost parallel.

A conclusion arising from this concept is found in *Lumen gentium* 14, which deals with the question of membership of the Church. There it states that: 'They are fully incorporated into the society of the Church who, possessing the Spirit of Christ, accept her entire system and all the means of salvation given to her.' Any purely christocentric and, in particular, purely institutional view is thus refuted. As Y. Congar puts it: 'C'est le début du dépassement d'un "christocentrisme". Le début seulement. Cela va continuer.'[8]

Current Discussion and Present Church Life

The economics of the Holy Spirit and pneuma-Christology

In a first important and fundamental approach, the Council took up an idea from Irenaeus of Lyons, according to which the Church participates in the anointing of Christ through the Spirit (SC 5; LG 7; 9; PO 2; 5). Reference is thus made to the baptism of Jesus in the River Jordan and the origin of the Holy Spirit which then rested on him (Mark 1.10) and – as Jesus himself said – anointed him (Luke 4.18). This means that the Holy Spirit not only follows the life and work of Jesus by bringing it to fruition, but also enters into the saving work of Jesus and is actively present in it. By participating in the anointing of Jesus by the Spirit, we share not only in his individual words and the institutions he established, but also in his Spirit.

With the reference to Irenaeus, the Council forged a link with the theological developments of the previous decades and the attempts at a Christology of the Spirit.[9] They proceed from the statements of Holy Scripture concerning the work of the Holy Spirit and seek to relate the salvation economics of the Spirit to the salvation economics of the Logos.

This renewed view corresponds to the witness of the scriptures. For, according to the scriptures, the Spirit of God is present and effective as the breath of life in the whole of creation and history, which it leads towards their eschatological goal. It reaches this goal by enabling the incarnation of the Son of God (cf. Luke 1.35), in his anointing (Luke 4.18) and, finally, in the cross and resurrection (Rom. 1.4). The entire life and work of Jesus is brought about and accompanied by the Spirit. The risen Lord acts in the Church and in history through the Spirit. This is the sense of the famous sentence: 'The Lord is the Spirit' (2 Cor. 3.17). The function of the

Spirit is to bring what happened in Jesus Christ once and for all to fulfilment in the Church and in world history. He does this by enabling those who believe in Christ to participate in the anointing of Jesus through the Spirit. He makes present the work of Christ not in a legalistic but in a spiritual way.[10]

A new definition of the relationship between the economics of Christ and those of the Holy Spirit is therefore undertaken in the christology of the Spirit. The christology of the Spirit – unlike the view of many enthusiasts – does not assert an economy of the Holy Spirit independent of the economics of the Logos. The Spirit is the Spirit of Jesus Christ (Rom. 3.9; Rom. 8.9) and the Spirit of the Son (Gal. 4.6). However, the Spirit does not simply follow the work of Christ; he goes before it, supporting and enabling it. He is the Spirit of the Son but not (as stated by the Pneumatomachi) his servant. He is not a slavish administrator of the word and work of Christ; he is a sovereign and life-giving Spirit ('*Dominum et vivificantem*') who interprets spiritually the person, word and work of Christ with relative freedom, in the freedom of the Spirit. 'Where the Spirit of the Lord is, there is freedom' (2 Cor. 3.17). Thus the Holy Spirit is always good for a surprise.[11]

This inner relationship of the economy of Christ, the economy of the Spirit and the freedom of the Spirit within the one divine economy of salvation has consequences for the nature of the Church. This was already clear in the foundation of the Church, which was initiated in life, by the cross and the resurrection of Jesus, but completed by the outpouring of the Spirit at Pentecost (LG 3); in this sense the Spirit can be called the co-founder of the Church, as the Church is at the same time both the institution and the event of the Spirit. A one-sided, enthusiastic understanding of the Church, and in particular a subjective, individualistic, emancipatory understanding of liberty, are alien to her nature, as is the opposite extreme: a mere legal understanding. In the Holy Spirit, church tradition is – as J. A. Möhler and J. H. Newman argued – a living tradition (DV 7f.).

Thus the church fathers' spiritual interpretation of the scriptures was rediscovered and renewed both before and after the Council.[12] Similarly, it has been shown that it is the *epikeia* rather than a legal understanding of objective norms that is the greater righteousness, a virtue, not a cunning circumvention of the law.[13] It calls for compassionate, not rigorous, application of church laws, related to specific situations. A theory for the practical application of church norms has been developed from this.[14] Such theories are in line with the Eastern Church's principle of οἰκονομία (economy), which is founded on the freedom of the Spirit in the Church.[15]

In this sense the Council knew that the Spirit leads to an unexpected and new spiritual awakening. It knew from the Acts of the Apostles (10.44-47; 11.15; 15.8), for example, that the Spirit on occasions precedes the work of the apostles (AG 4). It attributed the *aggiornamento* of the Church (LG 9; 21; 43; PO 22), the liturgical movement (SC 43) and the ecumenical movement (UR 1; 4) to the momentum of the Holy Spirit.

The Spirit and the charismatic dimension of the Church
The Council made it clear in many places and in different ways that the unity given by the Spirit is not a uniform monotony but rather a unity of great diversity. Catholicity implies an 'abundance of unity' in the variety of peoples and cultures, offices, ministries and positions, as well as the many local churches (LG 13). The theology of the local churches, in particular, was revived once again by the Council (LG 26; CD 11). In some ways, unity in diversity extends beyond what is visible in the Catholic Church; the Spirit of God is also at work in the non-Catholic churches and church communities (LG 15; UR 3f.).

The Council was serious about this charismatic structure of the Church. So, it did not only speak of the effect of the Spirit through the bishops (LG 21; 24; 27), particularly through the teaching authority of the Church (LG 25), but also of the sense of faith of all believers (LG 12; 35) and the Spirit leading into truth throughout the entire life of the Church (DV 8). There should, therefore, not be any one-sided, top–down relationship between bishops and priests (LG 28; PO 7; CD 16; 28), or between lay people, priests and bishops (LG 37; PO 9; AA 25), but rather a mutual relationship built on brotherhood and friendship.

These impulses were taken up and continued in the period after the Council. From the many different aspects, particular mention should be made of the revival of the charismatic dimension of the Church (LG 4; 12; 49; AA 3; AG 4; 29). The most detailed treatment is to be found in *Lumen gentium* 7, where the Council refers to 1 Cor. 12.1-11, and says the following:

There is only one Spirit who, according to His own richness and the needs of the ministries distributes His different gifts for the welfare of the Church. ... Giving the body unity through Himself and through His power and through the internal cohesion of its members, this same Spirit produces and urges love among the believers. Consequently, if one member suffers anything, all the members suffer it too, and if one member is honoured, all the members rejoice together (cf. 1 Cor. 12.26).

A practical consequence was the charismatic movement, through which the Pentecostal movement found its way into the Catholic Church. In contrast to the free Pentecostal movements outside Catholicism, the Catholic charismatic movement has remained within the sacramental and institutional structure of the Church; it therefore has the potential to invigorate the Church. The emphasis on the charismatic dimension of the Church goes far beyond the charismatic movement itself. Worthy of particular mention in this context are the spiritual movements characteristic of post-conciliar Catholicism, which constitute a hope for the universal Church.[16] Finally, it should be remembered that the real charismatics are not those who clap their hands during worship, play a guitar or sing rhythmic songs; rather, they are the saints. The charismatic dimension of the Church is above all realized in the sanctification of personal life, to which – as the Council reminded us – not only the chosen few but all Christians are called (LG 39-42).

We can summarize the character of this renewed charismatic perspective by saying that the rediscovery of the charismatic dimension has not led to any denial of the special charisma bestowed sacramentally upon the ecclesiastical ministry (1 Tim. 4. 14). On the contrary, since the Church is no longer seen as officially structured as a one-sided, pyramid-type hierarchy, but more as a collegial 'interaction' of all charismata, the ecclesiastical ministry is also assured of its place and particular mission. Conversely, however, the ecclesiastical ministry must also listen to the other charismata, pay heed to them and grant them the freedom and space due to them. The Catholic Church sees itself as a whole (καθολον (katholon)) in which each Christian has his/her charisma (1 Cor. 7.7) and, consequently, neither one nor each can be all. In the final analysis, this is what is meant by the ecclesiology of the people of God, renewed by the Second Vatican Council.

The work of the Holy Spirit through the word of the holy scriptures
The Spirit acts objectively in the Church through the word and sacraments. In this context, the Council spoke of the two tables, the table of the word and the table of the eucharist (DV 21). Let us therefore speak firstly about the work of the Spirit through the word of the holy scriptures.

The holy scriptures are the word of God inspired by the Spirit of God (DV 11). Revealed in them is 'the marvellous condescension of eternal wisdom ... that we may learn the gentle kindness of God, which words cannot express' (DV 13). Therefore the Council admonishes: 'all the preaching of the Church must be nourished and ruled by sacred scripture' (DV 21). 'Easy access' to it must be provided for the faithful (DV 22). However, scripture must be read and interpreted according to the same Spirit by whom it was written (DV 12). The reading of scripture should therefore be accompanied by prayer (DV 25), so that reading the holy scriptures becomes God the Father speaking to his children (DV 21; 25). In particular, as words cannot be separated from breath, so the word of God cannot be isolated from the breath of the Holy Spirit. 'Pupil of the Holy Spirit', the Church itself must penetrate ever more deeply into understanding of the scriptures in order to 'unceasingly feed her sons with the divine words' (DV 23).

With these words, the Council revived the old tradition of *lectio divina*, which goes back as far as the Old Testament and Jewish tradition and has influenced the liturgical and monastic traditions. In this tradition, there was an awareness that only the Holy Spirit can disclose the word of God and that he alone can cause the word of God to find its way into the human heart.[17] The ecumenical importance of the revival of the spiritual reading of scripture cannot be overestimated, and within the Catholic Church itself it has been a veritable 'well of living water' (John 4.11). Over time, it has refreshed and stimulated the life of the Church as well as many communities and individual Christians. The encounter with the holy scriptures has helped the revival of many old orders and the emergence of new religious communities and movements. For them and for many grass-roots communities in the Third World, reading scripture together is an essential feature of spiritual life and a source of inspiration and motivation for them. The ecumenical movement thrives, not least of all, on the joint encounter with the word of God in the holy scriptures. Hardly anything has changed the face of the Catholic Church over the past few decades as much as the revival of biblical spirituality.

The work of the Holy Spirit in the sacraments of the Church
The Church is the Church of the word and the Church of the sacraments. The Council stated that the entire celebration of the paschal mystery takes place in the power of the Holy Spirit (SC 6). Unfortunately, the Constitution of the Liturgy only made reference to this fundamental aspect, without delineating its practical adaptation. However, the post-conciliar liturgical renewal has since given gave clear expression to the pneumatological dimension of the sacraments.

The work of the Holy Spirit at baptism is attested in a quite special way in the holy scriptures (John 1.33; 1 Cor. 6.11; 12, 13; Tit. 3.5). Baptism together with confirmation forms the one initiation (SC 71). Confirmation has always been regarded as the sacrament of the Holy Spirit. In the post-Council liturgy reform, the administering formula of confirmation was changed accordingly and aligned with the form of the Eastern Church from the fourth and fifth centuries. Its wording is: 'Be sealed by the gift of God, the Holy Spirit'.

The other sacramental formulae of administration also have pneumatological characteristics. The reformed formula of absolution in the sacrament of penance is as follows: 'God, the Merciful Father, reconciled the world with itself through the death and resurrection of His Son and sent the Holy Spirit to forgive our sins. Through the service of the Church may it give you forgiveness and peace.' The words of the prayer during the anointing of the sick are: 'May the Lord help you in His abundant mercy through this unction and stand by you with the strength of the Holy Spirit.' Finally, the words spoken during the consecration of bishops are also worth mentioning in this context: 'Father, exude over this chosen one the strength that emanates from You, Your Spirit of direction and guidance which You gave Your Beloved Son, Jesus Christ, and which He passed on to the Holy Disciples...'

What is most important from the ecumenical aspect is the liturgical post-conciliar renewal of the eucharistic *epiclesis*, i.e. the invocation of the Holy Spirit upon the eucharistic gifts of bread and wine. Such an *epiclesis* is to be found in all new eucharistic prayers.

This epicletic structure of the eucharist is expressed at a very early stage in the call '*Maranatha!*' (*Didache* 10, 6; cf. Rev. 22.20). Explicit *epiclesis* of the Spirit is found in the *Traditio apostolica* of Hippolytus (4), while a consecratory effect is first attributed to it in the *Mystagogical catechises* of Cyril of Jerusalem (5, 6). The *epiclesis* of consecration has to be distinguished from the *epiclesis* of the communion, which asks for fruitful spiritual receiving of the communion. While the latter has been preserved in a large number of post-communion prayers in the Roman liturgy, the *epiclesis* of the consecration is contained in the Roman canon only in a rudimentary fashion, in the prayer '*Quam oblationem*' which precedes the words of institution. In contrast, it is of fundamental importance in the Eastern liturgies, where the *epiclesis* follows the words of institution.

The differing development in the East and West has been the subject of many controversies. While the Western tradition since the time of Ambrose has understood the words of institution as words of consecration, Orthodox theology attributes the consecration to the *epiclesis*. This gave rise to a controversial debate concerning the precise moment of consecration. In general terms, these discussions are now a thing of the past, since the eucharistic prayer is a whole and, as a whole, is epicletic by nature. It was all the more important that an explicit *epiclesis* should have been reintroduced into the new eucharistic prayers in the post-conciliar reform of the liturgy.

P. Evdokimov, a well-known Orthodox theologian, commented that the renewal of the *epiclesis* in the new eucharistic prayers of the Roman liturgy is important for contemporary ecumenical dialogue on the *filioque* question, and that it helps to reposition the *filioque* in the light of the *epiclesis*.[18] The renewal of the *epiclesis* is also of great importance in the ecumenical discussions with the churches of the Reformed tradition.[19] L. Vischer, former chairman of the Commission on Faith and Order, referred to the *epiclesis* as a symbol of unity, a pledge for the renewal of the churches and the breakthrough of ecumenism.

The renewal of the *epiclesis* in the eucharist is far more than the change of a rite; it says something about the nature of the Church and the sacraments. The sacraments are not simply an extension of the person and work of Jesus Christ in the sphere of the Church; the Church must, rather, ask for the Spirit so as to recall Jesus

Christ and his saving work. In overall terms the Church has an epicletic structure.[20] It does not 'have' the Holy Spirit nor is the Holy Spirit at the disposal of the Church; however, it can and may ask for the coming of the Holy Spirit and can be certain that this plea will be heard.

What applies to the *epiclesis* of the consecration applies in a similar way to the *epiclesis* of the communion, i.e. a plea for the Spirit to ensure the worthy and fruitful receiving of the sacrament of the eucharist. This is found in many post-communion prayers in the eucharist and follows the teaching on the *manducatio spiritualis*, spiritual communion, i.e. both the bodily and spiritual nourishment of the sacrament. Anyone remotely familiar with the Reformed doctrine of the eucharist going back to Calvin will recognize the ecumenical significance of that teaching. It has deep roots in the tradition.[21] In the end, it goes back to the great speech on the eucharist in John 6.32-59: 'It is the spirit that gives life, the flesh is useless' (6.63).

The Question of the *Filioque*

The problem

We have already ventured into the sphere of controversy with the question of the *epiclesis*. The real controversy does not, of course, relate to the *epiclesis* but rather to the addition of the *filioque* in the Latin form of the creed. Historically, alongside the question of Roman primacy, this is the most strained distinction in doctrine between East and West. Because the churches of the Reformation have adopted the Latin tradition, this issue concerns not only the relationship between Rome and the East but also the relationship between the churches of the Reformation and the churches of the East.[22]

It is, of course, not possible to deal satisfactorily here with a question that is historically so complicated and in speculative terms so complex. For this reason, I shall confine myself to commenting on the latest position in the ecumenical debate, based on the document drawn up by the Pontifical Council for Promoting Christian Unity entitled *The Greek and Latin Traditions Regarding the Procession of the Holy Spirit* (Rome 1996). In 1998, the Pro Oriente Foundation in Vienna organized a symposium where this document was discussed in detail.[23] A whole series of other dialogues should, of course, also be referred to, but I cannot go into these in this context.[24]

Historical review

The common ecumenical starting point is the creed of the 150 fathers of the Council of Constantinople (381). This states that the Holy Spirit emanates from the Father (ἐκπορευόμενον (*ekporeuo-menon*)) (DH 150). With this concept, the Council adopted the wording of John 15.26 (ἐκπορεύεται (*ekporeuetai*)). This creed was adopted by the East and the West through the Council of Chalcedon (451) and remained the common normative basis of profession during the first millennium. It would appear, however, that it was adopted differently in the East and West from the very beginning, i.e. in the sense of their own respective theological traditions.

Already at the time of the Council of Chalcedon East and West had developed different theologoumena. As early as Origen and then, in particular, with Basil, Eastern theology proceeds from the Father as the origin and source (ἀρχῇ και πηγη (*archē kai pēgē*), the origin without origin; its concern is the μοναρχια (*monarchia*) of the Father. Western theology, since the time of Tertullian, has thought more in terms of God as a being. However, even on the basis of this assumption, the Western tradition has abided by the concept that the Spirit *principaliter* emanates from the Father (Augustine, *De Trin.* XV, 25, 47). The East often spoke of a ἐκπορευσις δια του Υιου (*ekporeusis dia tou Huiou*), which did not arouse any suspicion whatsoever in the West. In addition, the East was also familiar with the formula of Epiphanius of Salamis and John of Damascus, which is sometimes drawn on again today; according to this, the Holy Spirit emanates from the Father and rests on the Son. Other formulae similar to the Western *filioque* were found in Alexandrian theology and Cyril of Alexandria. Different formulae have been and are also common among the old Oriental churches. In the West Ambrose was the first to use the *filioque* formula; it was adopted by Augustine and Pope Leo the Great and did not cause any offence at all in the East at that time. Thus, by the time of the Council of Chalcedon the creed of 381 was already understood differently in the East and in the West.

Thomas Aquinas and the Council of Florence were also in agreement with the '*per filium*' formula, even though they interpreted it from the viewpoint of their Western doctrine of the Trinity. For as the Son owes everything he is not to himself but entirely to the Father, he is also indebted to him for the breathing of the Spirit. Thus the Father and the Son are not, for example, two parallel, independent principles for the origin of the Spirit. Rather, because the Son breathes the Spirit in the strength of the Father, it can also be said within Latin theology that the Spirit *principaliter* emanates from the Father through the Son (Thomas Aquinas *Summa theol.* I, 36, 3)

In the first millennium, therefore, there was one common creed which did not contain the *filioque*; there were, however, different theologoumena for determining the relationship of the Son and the Spirit. Nonetheless, the East and the West coexisted peacefully. In the seventh century, for example, Maximus the Confessor was able to defend the Latin way of speaking and demonstrate that it reconcilable with the Greek position on this matter. When a theological controversy occurred in the ninth century with Photius, this was less an expression of insuperable dogmatic antitheses than mutual estrangement; the two churches did not understand each other any more and used different theologoumena as an opportunity for polemic.

The theologoumena for the *filioque* first became the subject of church doctrine in the '*Quicunque*' creed (the so-called Athanasian creed) (DH 75) and then in a series of Spanish provincial synods in the sixth and seventh centuries (DH 470; 485; 490; 527; 568). These were, however, particularist ecclesiastical statements which left the common wording of the creed itself untouched. The Spanish synods were concerned with a different problem to that of 381. In contrast to the Arianism and Priscillianism still widespread in Spain, the intention was to emphasize the equal importance of the Son and the Father. This motif was in line with the creed of 381 and the view of the East in this matter, though the problem no longer existed there and so there was no cause for corresponding observations.

Thus the *filioque* did not originally represent any change in the common creed or have any anti-Greek intention. It was located in the context of a specifically Western problem, but was also recognized by the East in its objective concern.

The *filioque* first became a problem between the churches of the East and West when it was inserted into the common creed of 381 in the eleventh century. This first occurred at particularist Franconian synods. Initially, Pope Leo III opposed the suggestion of Charlemagne to include the *filioque* in the creed at the eucharist. However, the crowning of Charlemagne as emperor by the Pope in 800 was regarded in Byzantium as a betrayal and led to further alienation between East and West. When Pope Benedict VIII eventually gave way to the insistence of Emperor Henry III at his coronation in 1014 and incorporated the *filioque* into the creed, this was seen by the East as a unilateral schismatic action and an irregular act that violated canon 7 of the Council of Ephesus (431), which had forbidden the drawing up of a different creed (ἑτερα πιστις (*hetera pistis*)). The reaction to this was that the name of the Pope was deleted from the diptych in Byzantium.

Besides the question of content, the insertion of the *filioque* into the common creed also raised canonical issues concerning the *communio* of the Church. The unilateral addition had turned the creed, which was a symbol of unity in 381, into a symbol of division.

East and West henceforth went their separate ways, which led them even further apart. Two general synods of the West, the Fourth Lateran Council (1215) (DH 805) and the Second Council of Lyons (1274) (DH 850; 853), declared the *filioque* to be binding doctrine. Lyons rejected the misconception that there were two points of departure in the Trinity, which would jeopardize the unity of the Trinity, and condemned all those that would not accept the *filioque*. This sealed the division on the part of the West.

The Council of Union of Florence (1439–45) attempted to mediate. It referred to the Father as '*principium sine principio*' (DH 1331) and recognized the legitimacy of the '*per filium*' formula while at the same time seeking to interpret this in the sense of the Latin *filioque* and impose it as such on the Greeks (DH 1300-1302; cp.1330-1332). When the Greeks subsequently rejected this demand as unreasonable, the Latin scholars saw the fall of Constantinople (1453) as just punishment.

The basic problem of Florence lay in the fact that, to reconcile East and West, the Council interpreted the creed of 381 in the light of the subsequent *filioque*, instead of starting from the creed of 381, which was normative for both sides, and demonstrating that the *filioque* was not inconsistent with that common creed and could, when interpreted in the light of such a creed, be regarded as legitimate in objective terms. Such a reversal of the issue and the burden of proof was not possible until the twentieth century and the relaxed new climate of dialogue in the ecumenical movement. This is precisely what forms the new approach set out in the document drawn up by the Pontifical Council for Promoting Christian Unity.

The present status of the debate
The current status of the debate, from the official Catholic standpoint, was expressed by Pope John Paul II in a homily delivered on the occasion of the visit to Rome by the Ecumenical Patriarch Bartholomew I in 1995.[25] The Pope started from the basis of the common faith, as set out in the creed of 381, and stated that it is in this context that the sense and meaning of the differing traditional modes of expression regarding the eternal procession of the Holy Spirit in the Trinity have to be interpreted.

This affirmation established an important hermeneutic principle: differences should be interpreted in the light of the common creed. The consequence of this is that, on the Catholic side, the *filioque* as it exists in the liturgical tradition of the Latin creed has to be emphasized in terms of its complete harmony with the creed of the Ecumenical Council of Constantinople. The fundamental matter of concern in 381 was the monarchy of the Father as the origin without origin, i.e. the Father as the source of the entire Trinity, the origin of both the Son and the Holy Spirit. The homily of the Pope affirms that the Catholic Church abides by this common conviction.

The document drawn up by the Council for Promoting Christian Unity sought to fulfil a twofold task, which can be summarized in two points. (1) The Church of Rome acknowledges the legitimacy and normative nature of the original wording of the Council of 381. No other declaration or profession may contradict this. In particular, the monarchy or the Father as the origin without origin must be preserved. (2) The document maintains that although the *filioque* can give rise to misunderstandings, it is not inconsistent with the creed of 381. For this reason, it attempts to interpret the *filioque* in the light of the original common creed.

According to this conception, it is not a case of the Catholic side abandoning the *filioque* as such for the sake of unity but, rather, interpreting it in the light of the original common and normative tradition and fully safeguarding the monarchy of the Father. Conversely, the Orthodox side would not have to adopt the *filioque* but accept that it is not heretical and can be interpreted in the light of the common creed.[26] These two approaches lead to the conclusion that the Eastern and Western traditions, rather than being contradictory, are complementary. Such complementarity was acknowledged on the Catholic side in the *Catechism of the Catholic Church* (§ 248). The Ecumenical Patriarch Bartholomew I welcomed this type of approach,[27] which establishes a good basis for further ecumenical steps.

How to proceed?

While there is agreement today on the dogmatic normativeness and meaning of the creed of 381 as well as on the essential questions of historical development, although opinions may always differ with regard to many matters of historical detail, there are a number of fundamental theological issues that still have to be clarified.[28] Such questions are raised, in particular, by Orthodox theologians.[29] The basic problem is the relationship of the Trinity in terms of economics and immanence.[30] While Orthodox theology questions any kind of unity of the immanent Trinity and the Trinity within salvation economics, Reformed theologians (as well as Catholic theologians to a great extent)[31] continue to abide by this concept. Within the Trinity they want to adhere to the *filioque* because in salvation economics the Spirit is always the Spirit of the Father and the Son.[32]

This unity of the Trinity in terms of economics and salvation history is vehemently disputed by neo-Palamitic Orthodox theologians in particular. In the fourteenth century, Gregory Palamas[33] further developed the positions of the Eastern fathers and distinguished between the hidden being of the trinitarian divinity and the uncreated divine energies revealed to us. The correlation between the Trinity in terms of immanence and salvation economics was thus abandoned. For this reason, according to these theologians, the conclusion that the Spirit is the Spirit of Jesus Christ in salvation economics cannot be applied to the inner-Trinity relationship of the Son and the Spirit. This leads to fierce rejection of the *filioque* as heretical, a characterization that can be found up to the present day among a number of representatives of neo-Palamitic theology (e.g. V. Lossky). This neo-Palamitic background and the fundamental problem raised by it are mostly overlooked by Western theology.

Both sides would, of course, have to be prepared to regard their own individual traditions self-critically, since neither the Orthodox 'through the Son' nor the Catholic 'filioque' is able to provide a satisfactory answer to the open question of the creed of 381, the relationship between the Holy Spirit and the Son. Both positions thus have their weak points and their difficulties.[34] It therefore does not make any sense to continue the sterile polemic or attempt to impose one's own solution on the other. Fundamental theological questions need to be clarified and the unresolved problems on both sides tackled. The tiresome thousand-year polemic is not simply founded on a personal argumentative disposition; it has also had a specific place in the life of the churches.

It is certainly not imperative for all theological issues to be resolved prior to ecclesiastical declarations of consensus. Much can be left to subsequent theology. So in principle it would be possible for the Catholic Church to abide by the factual legitimacy of the filioque while at the same time returning to the original creed in its liturgy for the sake of peace and unity,[35] since the councils of the Middle Ages did not stipulate the insertion of the filioque into the creed as a binding dogma, but only as the profession of faith. In formal terms, the Catholic Church would not, therefore, offend against any council by returning to the original wording in liturgical usage.

However, changing a thousand-year-old liturgical creed concerns the spiritual identity of a church. This is only possible after thorough pastoral preparation. The easiest solution at the moment would probably be to insert into the Latin Missal for ecumenical use the Latin version of the creed as proclaimed by the Council of Chalcedon (451), i.e. the creed without the filioque, beside the Latin creed of the second millennium with the filioque. The equivalence of both formulae would thereby become evident and the situation of the first millennium, where different formulae co-existed, would be restored.

The much more important problem lies in finding a language for preaching and developing a doctrine of the Trinity from the basis of the common creed and the clarifications already reached, which can, existentially, provide for a greater understanding of this fundamental mystery of the Christian faith in modern language.

Approaches to such a renewed theology of the Trinity and to such a pneumatology, taking up both Eastern and Western concerns, exist already in the theology of all the churches and should be further developed.[36]

Ecclesiological consequence: a spiritual communio-*ecclesiology*
More recent approaches to the doctrine of the Trinity in Catholic, Orthodox and Protestant theology make it clear that the issue of the *filioque* is not simply a matter of speculation, but also a matter of elementary importance for the life and unity of the Church. It comprises a renewed theology of the Trinity as well as a renewed view of the Church which, according to the teaching of the fathers as renewed by the Second Vatican Council, is shaped to the archetype of the Trinity (LG 4; UR 3).

This theological renewal gave rise to a renewed *communio*-ecclesiology.[37] *Communio* became the key term for most of the ecumenical documents. The aim of the ecumenical movement, the full visible unity of the divided churches, is seen today as full communion. What is originally meant by the *communio sanctorum* of the Apostles' creed is joint participation in the sacred (*sancta*).[38] This coincides with the κοινωνια του Ἁγιου Πνευματος (*koinōnia tou Hagiou Pneumatos*) of which Paul speaks (2 Cor. 13.13). In this perspective the Church can be seen as communion nourished and structured by the Holy Spirit and as temple of the Holy Spirit (1 Cor. 3.16-17; 2 Cor. 6.16; Eph. 2.21).

The most profound justification for such a *communio*-ecclesiology is the eternal trinitarian communion (κοινωνια; *communio*) of the Father, Son and Holy Spirit. The doctrine of the Trinity is, in essence, the development of the statement from the first letter of St John: 'God is love' (1 John 4.8, 16). God is, in himself, the pure relationship of love; above all, the Holy Spirit is love in person. A relational ontology follows from this, which is fundamental for a renewed *communio*-ecclesiology. It can understand being only as being in a relational sense, as a mutual giving of space and the mutual enabling of relations.

This implies many structural questions of ecclesiology, including the relation between the common priesthood of all baptized and hierarchical priesthood; the relation between primacy and the synodical or conciliar structures in the Church; the relation between bishops, priests and deacons; between pastors and the entire people of God, between clergy and religious, between associations and ecclesial movements. These relations, together with the operational model of Bishops' Conferences, Councils of Priests and Pastoral Councils, must all be characterized by communion.

Pope John Paul II, in the apostolic letter entitled *Novo millennio ineunte* (2001) (43f.), pointed out that a *communio*-spirituality does not move in an unworldly vacuum, so to speak; rather, it has consequences for the understanding and practice of collegiality at all levels of church life, and also for the exercising of the Petrine ministry. But rather than bring up only structural questions, a *communio*-ecclesiology – first of all and to a much greater extent – raises spiritual questions. *Communio*-ecclesiology calls out for *communio*-spirituality.

The Pope gives a marvellous description of this spirituality of communion:

> A spirituality of communion means an ability of think of our brothers and sisters in faith within the profound unity of the Mystical Body, and therefore as 'those who are a part of me'. This makes us able to share their joys and sufferings, to sense their desires and attend to their needs, to offer them deep and genuine friendship. A spirituality of communion implies also the ability to see what is positive in others, to welcome it and prize it as a gift from God: not only a gift for the brother or sister, who has received it directly, but also as a 'gift for me'. A spirituality of communion means, finally, to know how to 'make room' for our brothers and sisters, bearing 'each other's burdens (Gal. 6.2) and resisting the selfish temptations which constantly beset us and provoke competition, careerism, distrust and jealousy. (43)

The Pope concludes: 'Let us have no illusions: unless we follow this spiritual path, external structures of communion will serve very little purpose. They would became mechanism without a soul, "masks" of communion rather than its means of expression and growth.'[39]

An ecclesiology devised under the influence of pneumatology according to the archetype of the Trinity leads us right to the heart of a large number of concrete issues which affect not only the Catholic Church but all churches. But at the same time it tells us that these questions cannot be resolved through structural debates alone; rather, they require a renewed pneumatology and a renewed ecumenical spirituality. In the same way as a theology of the Holy

Spirit is only possible 'in the Spirit', i.e. only spiritually, ecumenical theology and the ecumenical movement are, in the end, a spiritual task that can only be undertaken in the Holy Spirit. Only the spiritual person grasps what the Spirit is (cf. 1 Cor. 2.10-15). Johann Adam Möhler captured the sense of this issue splendidly in the following words:

> Two extremes in Church life are possible, however, and they are both called egoism; they are: when *each person* or *one person* wants to be everything; in the latter case, the bond of unity becomes so tight and love so hot that asphyxia cannot be averted; in the former case, everything falls apart to such an extent and it becomes so cold that you freeze; the one type of egoism generates the other; but there is no need for one person or each person to want to be everything; only everyone together can be everything and the unity of all only a whole. This is the idea of the Catholic Church.[40]

Thus, through a renewed pneumatology we are confronted with the task and challenge to reconsider the κοινωνια του Ἁγιου Πνευματος, the communion of the Holy Spirit, more profoundly and develop a *communio*-ecclesiology from a *communio*-spirituality, which will lead us to the full *communio* of the churches in the one Spirit of the one and common Lord Jesus Christ, who is the way to the one God, the Father of all. We cannot 'make' or 'organize' this communion, because it is – as we were told – of epicletical structure. So the prayer 'Veni Creator Spiritus' is the ultimate answer to how to fulfil the insistence of the Spirit, to overcome the scandal of division and to build up communion in the one Holy Spirit.

Notes

1 Second Vatican Council, Decree on Ecumenism, *Unitatis redintegratio* 1.

2 Especially V. Lossky, *Théologie mystique de l'Église d'Orient*, Paris 1944. The position was criticized by G. Florovsky, 'Christ and his Church', in: *L'Église et les Églises*, vol. 2, Chevetogne 1955, 159–70.

3 See Y. Congar, *Der Heilige Geist*, Freiburg i. Br., 82, 75–99.

4 For others, see Y. Congar, *op. cit.*, 107–18.

5 Cf. G. Greshake, *Der dreieinige Gott*, Freiburg i. Br. 1997, 116–26.

6 Y. Congar, *op. cit.*, 143. Cf. W. Kasper, *Die Tradition in der Römischen Schule*, Freiburg i.Br. 1962.

7 Y. Congar, *op. cit.*, 144.

8 Y. Congar, *Le Concile de Vatican II*, Paris 1984, 169. Important in this regard is the encyclical of Pope John Paul II, *Dominum et vivifantem* (1986).

9 Overview in Y. Congar, *op. cit.*, 433–8; H. U. von Balthasar, *Theologik III*, Einsiedeln 1987, 45–53.

10 Cf. W. Kasper, *Jesus der Christus*, Mainz 1974, 301–22.

11 Cf. H. U. von Balthasar, *Theologik III*, 26.

12 H. de Lubac, *Exégèse médiévale*, Paris 1959–64; *L'Écriture dans la tradition*, Paris 1966 (German: *Typologie, Allegorie, Geistlicher Sinn*, Einsiedeln 1999).

13 Thomas Aquinas, *Summa theol.* II/II 120; cf. G. Viert, *Epikie – verantwortlicher Umgang mit Normen*, Mainz 1983.

14 W. Kasper, 'Gerechtigkeit und Barmherzigkeit. Überlegungen zu einer Applikationstheorie kirchen-rechtlicher Normen', in: *Theologie und Kirche* II, Mainz 1999, 183–91.

15 Y. Congar, 'Quelques concepts orientaux intéressants notres questions', in: *Diversités et communion*, Paris 1982, 80–102.

16 M. Camisaca and M. Vitali, *I Movimenti nella Chiesa*, Milano 1981; P. J. Cordes, *Mitten in unserer Welt*, Freiburg i. Br. 1987; *Den Geist nicht auslöschen*, Freiburg i. Br. 1990; encyclical *Christifideles laici* (1988).

17 Y. Congar, *op. cit.*, 492–4; E. Bianchi, *Pregare la Parola. Introduzione alla 'Lectio divina'*, Milano 2002.

18 P. Evdokimor, *L'Ésprit Saint dans la tradition orthodoxe*, Paris 1969, 101.

19 J. J. van Allmen, *Prophétisme sacramentel*, Neuchâtel-Paris, 1964, 300; L.Vischer, *Ökum. Skizzen*, Frankfurt 1972, 46–57; 'Groupe de Dombes', *L'Esprit Saint, l'Église et les sacrements*, § 113f.

20 Y. Congar, *op. cit.* 488–95

21 H. R. Schlette, *Komunikation und Sakrament*, Freiburg i. Br. 1959.

22 On the theological discussion: Y. Congar, 361–70; 439–53; W. Kasper, *Der Gott Jesu Christi*, Mainz 1982, 264–73; H. U. von Balthasar, *Theologik III*, 189–200; J. Moltmann, *Trinität und Reich Gottes*, Munich 1980, 194–206; R. Slenzka, in: *Glaubensbekenntnis und Kirchengemeinschaft*, 82–99; W.

Pannenberg, *Systematische Theologie I*, Göttingen 1988, 344–7; *LThK III*, 1995, 1279–81.

23 *Vom Heiligen Geist. Der gemeinsame trinitarische Glaube und das Problem des Filioque*, Innsbruck-Vienna 1998.

24 Cf. *Dokumente wachsender Übereinstimmung II*, 26f.; 112f.; 123; 532f.; 676f.; *Geist Gottes – Geist Christi*, ed. L. Vischer, Freiburg 1981 [Klingenthal Conference of the Commission on Faith and Church Constitution]; *Gemeinsam den einen Glauben bekennen*, Frankfurt a.M.-Paderborn 1991 [Study document on Faith and Church Constitution]; Joint declaration of the Working Group of Protestant and Catholic theologians, in: *Glaubensbekenntnis und Kirchengemeinschaft*, edited by K. Lehmann and W. Pannenberg, Freiburg i. Br.-Göttingen 1982, 122f.; good overview in *RGG III*, 2000, 120f. The agreed statement of the North American Orthodox–Catholic Theological Consultation; 'The Filioque: A Church-dividing issue,' issued on 5 October 2003 and offering valuable theological and practical recommendations, became available only after the completion of this manuscript.

25 *Information Service* 1995/IV, 120–22.

26 P. Evdokimov, *L'Ortodossia Bologna* 1965, 198 note 61 shows to what extent this could be possible for Orthodoxy.

27 'Un entretien avec Bartholomee Ier, patriarch oecuménique, à propos du Nouveau Catechism Catholique: Convergences et Divergences entre Catholiques et Orthodoxes', in: *Service Orthodoxe de Presse* 178, 1993, 24.

28 Cf. the summary of the discussion in the final Symposium report, *op. cit.*

29 The issues are clearly and respectfully formulated by J. Zizioulas in: *Vom Hl. Geist*, 141–9; his own conception is found in his work entitled *Being as Communion*, New York 1995. The position of V. Lossky and a number of Greek theologians is much harsher (cf. R. Slenzka, *op. cit.* 89–92). There are also Orthodox theologians who, although they do not view the *filioque* as possible dogma or as heresy, regard it as an objectively possible theologoumenon. Cf. V. Bolotov, 'Thesen über das Filioque', in: *Rev. intern. de Théol.* 6, 1898, 681–712, and S. Bulgakov, *Il Paraclito*, Bologna 1987, 274–304; Evdokimov, *L'Esprit Saint dans la tradition orthodoxe*, Paris 1946.

30   See R. Slenzka, B. Forte, D. Ritschl.

31   In fundamental terms, K. Rahner, 'Bemerkungen zum dogmatischen Traktat "De Trinitate"', in: *Schriften IV*, 115ff. With a differing view: W. Kasper, *Der Gott Jesu Christi*, 333–7.

32   Especially K. Barth, *Kirchliche Dogmatik*, I/1, 500–11; I/2, 273. In the Lutheran tradition, the Spirit and the Word essentially belong together, directed against the enthusiasts. An open stance critical of the *filioque* is taken, on the other hand, by J. Moltmann and W. Pannenberg, amongst others, as well as the results of the Klingenthal Conference.

33   See D. Wendenburg, *Geist oder Energie*, München 1980; G. Podalsky, Art. 'Gregorios Palamas': TRE XIV, 1985, 200–6. Podalsky, following R. Flogaus, *Theiosis bei Palamas und Luther*, Göttingen 1997, pointed out that there is no fundamental contradiction between Augustine and the Eastern tradition, as is often assumed (cf. *Vom Hl. Geist*, 171).

34   After S. Bulgakov, this was convincingly illustrated by, in particular, H. U. von Balthasar, *Theologik III*, 189–200. So both East and West sit in glass houses and have no reason to throw stones at each other.

35   This had already been suggested by Congar (*op. cit.* 449–53) and others. Back in 1742 and 1755, Pope Benedict XIV decided that the Eastern churches united with Rome should be allowed to use the unchanged creed of 381. In ecumenical worship, the creed is also spoken in the original form of 381 by the Pope.

36   Fundamental for Catholic theology is the essay by K. Rahner, *Theos im Neuen Testament, Schriften I*, Einsiedeln 1954, 61–167, which starts with the Father in the sense of the biblical and Eastern tradition. Other theologians proceed in this personal direction, including J. Moltmann and W. Kasper, thus coming very close to more recent Russian Orthodox approaches like those of Soloewjev, Berdajev, Bulgakov, Evdokimov and Schmemann. Cf. M. A. Meerson, *The Trinity of Love in Modern Russian Theology*, Quincy IL 1998. Other Catholic authors: H. Mühlen, *Der Hl. Geist als Person*, Münster 1963; B. Forte, *Trinità come storia*, Milano 1985; B. J. Hilberath, *Pneumatologie*, Düsseldorf 1994; G. Greshake, *Der dreieine Gott*, Freiburg, i. Br. 1997, 171.

37 Cf. I. Hertling, 'Communio und Primat', in: *Una Sancta* 17, 1962, 91–125; Y. Congar, *Ministères et communion ecclesiale*, Paris 1971; O. Saier, 'Communio' in *der Lehre des II. Vatikabnischen Konzils*, München 1973; W. Kasper, 'Kirche als communio', in: *Theologie und Kirche* I, Mainz 1987, 272–289; J. M. R. Tillard, *L'Église d'èglises*, Paris 1987; J. Ratzinger, *Zur Gemeinschaft berufen*, Freiburg i. Br. 1991; G. Greshake, 'Communio – Schlüsselbegriff der Dogmatik', in: *Gemeinsam Kirche sein*, FS O. Saier, Freiburg i. Br. 1992, 20–121; M. Kehl, *Kirche*, Würzburg, 1992; J. Hilberath, 'Kirche als Communio', in: *ThQ* 17, 1994, 45–64; J. Drumm, Art, 'Communio': *LThK II*, 1994, 1280–3. R. Schäfer, Art. 'Communio', in: *RGG* II. 1999, 235–437.

38 For the original meaning of *communio sanctorum* see P.-T. Camelot, 'Die Lehre von der Kirche', in: *Handb.d. Dogmengeschichte* II/3b, Freiburg i.B.r. 1970, 60.

39 Apostolic letter *Novo millennio ineunte*, n. 43.

40 J. A. Möhler, *Unity in the Church*, § 70.

7

The Joint Declaration on the Doctrine of Justification

The Ecumenical Impulse

With the Second Vatican Council and its Decree on Ecumenism, *Unitatis redintegratio*, the Catholic Church officially declared its irreversible commitment to ecumenism. Since then she has entered into dialogue with almost all the Christian churches and ecclesial communities of both East and West. Together with the Anglican Communion, the Lutheran World Federation was the first to initiate dialogue immediately after the Council. In this dialogue the doctrine of justification was prominent from the very beginning, because it was this doctrine which stood at the centre of the controversy in the sixteenth century. For Martin Luther this was the centre of the Gospel, the teaching by which the Church stands or falls, the point on which one cannot give in.

Ultimately this was not just a theoretical problem for Luther; it was an existential question about the core, the centre, the heart of Christian existence. His question focused on the search for God's mercy and the concept of a merciful God. After a difficult inner struggle, Luther concluded that we cannot merit God's mercy by our own abilities and that we are not righteous before God on account of our good works. Rather, we are righteous because God declares us righteous by his sovereign mercy and accepts us as sinners. Thus we are '*simul iustus et peccator*', righteous and at the same time sinners. Justification is not a matter of our own righteousness, a righteousness we do not possess as our own, but of the righteousness of God that, unmerited by us, God bestows because of Christ's merits alone, as grace alone and on the basis of faith alone (*sola gratia, sola fide*).

The Council of Trent also condemned the Pelagian doctrine that a person can save himself by good works. The question at issue, however, was not about justification by grace or by good works; rather, it was whether and to what extent God's action enables and stimulates the co-operation of the human person. The Council of Trent concluded that we can co-operate in our justification, not by our own strength but animated and empowered by grace. The Council also wanted to make clear that God does not merely declare us to be righteous but truly makes us righteous; he makes us new within so that we are a new creation and can live as new human beings. Faith must become effective in love and loving deeds. Thus, whereas Luther's concern was the sovereignty of grace, the Council was concerned about the effective power of grace, which transforms us and makes us righteous.

These doctrines have divided us for more than 400 years, bringing great suffering to individuals and to many of the peoples of Europe. Through our missionary work we exported our differences to other continents. It was only in the twentieth century that Christians in all churches became ashamed of their divisions. It is noteworthy that the ecumenical movement started with the experience in mission lands, where Christianity's credibility is called into question whenever Christians are at loggerheads. Only a reconciled Church can carry forward its mission of reconciliation. This problem takes on even greater relevance in the religious situation of Europe, where people speak about a drying-up of faith. Faced with such a crisis we cannot afford to continue with the old controversies.

Especially in their common resistance to the inhumane, unChristian system of the Nazis, in the concentration camps and trenches of the Second World War, many Catholics and evangelical Christians discovered that they were not as far apart as they had seemed. United in opposing an inhuman and unChristian system, they discovered that there was more uniting than dividing them. Ecumenical theology after 1945 was able to make use of these experiences. We could mention a whole host of theologians from both sides who prepared the way for what has now been achieved: Karl Barth, Karl Rahner, Hans Urs von Balthasar. We are like dwarfs on the shoulders of these giants. I could also mention Hans Küng, Harding Meyer, George Lindbeck, Wolfhart Pannenberg, Eberhard Jüngel, Carl Peter, Otto Hermann Pesch and many others.

When the official dialogue was started after the Second Vatican Council it was already able to draw on the results of theological research. The very first document from the dialogue, the so-called 'Malta Report' of 1971, outlined a wide-ranging consensus on the doctrine of justification. The question was taken up once more and deepened by the dialogue in the United States, published under the title *Justification by Faith* (1985), again with the same results. It was also treated later, when a joint commission, after the first papal visit to Germany, examined all the doctrinal condemnations of the sixteenth century. The results are presented in the book *Lehrverurteilungen – Kirchentrennend?* (*The Condemnations of the Reformation Era: Do They Still Divide?*) (1986). Finally, the last document of the international Roman Catholic–Evangelical Lutheran dialogue remains to be mentioned, namely *Church and Justification* (1994), which concluded once again that there were no longer any church-dividing differences over this issue.

So the first thing we should note is that what is said in the Joint Declaration on Justification solemnly signed on 31 October 1999 in Augsburg did not drop out of the sky; it was prepared for by decades of specialized international theological work and ecumenical dialogue under the auspices of the churches. Serious and distinguished theologians from both sides were involved; the results were made public and so from the very beginning were open to discussion. All the more painful and difficult to understand, therefore, has been the surprised critical reaction of some theologians after the Joint Declaration; they had obviously slept through the international ecumenical debate over the preceding two decades.

What have we Reached?

It should firstly be stated that in this dialogue there has been no question of easy short-cuts or false irenicism, relativism, or liberalism. On the contrary, § 14 of the Joint Declaration, where the common understanding of justification is expressed, commences with the statement: 'The Lutheran churches and the Roman Catholic Church have together listened to the good news proclaimed in Holy Scripture. This common listening, together with the theological conversations of recent years, has led to a shared understanding of justification.' We studied the sources of our faith together and immersed ourselves in the sacred scriptures and our respective traditions. This gave us new insights, which shed new light on the statements of the sixteenth century. Neither church can give up the doctrinal statements of that time or disown its own tradition, but we were enabled to understand them afresh and in a deeper way.

Thus we neither discovered a new Gospel nor rejected what our fathers and forefathers believed to be the expression of the revealed Gospel. What we did discover anew was that this once and for all revealed Gospel is so deep and so rich that nobody, no council and no theologian, can ever exhaust it. It was by the gift of the Holy Spirit that we were able to deepen our understanding, so we could recognise and re-receive our respective traditions. In the richness of the other we discovered our own richness. This new perception and re-reception is a gift of the Holy Spirit, who leads us into the whole truth (John 16.13). There was at stake a Spirit-guided development of dogma and understanding of dogma. So the event of Augsburg was not only, or primarily, a formal signing of a document, but above all a celebration of joyful thanksgiving to God in the presence of his people.

A second point is that although the previous documents mentioned above were produced by theologians and commissions which had been officially appointed, their results had no official status for the two churches. They were the documents of theological commissions. Thus, after these fundamental theological preparations, it was time for the churches themselves to take up the question and deal with the results of the theological dialogue. Accordingly, the Lutheran World Federation and the Pontifical Council for Promoting Christian Unity decided to attempt a Joint Declaration on the Doctrine of Justification.

This was a new attempt and we had no guiding experience. It was thoroughly acknowledged that it would not be easy. Not only are the decision-making processes and respective institutions in both churches quite different, there is also a quite different understanding of the magisterium and its authority in the Church. On the Lutheran side the Declaration had to pass the synods of all 130 member churches of the Lutheran World Federation. The Lutheran World Federation itself, after obtaining the approval of about 80 per cent of the member churches, had the role of stating and declaring a 'magnus consensus'. On the Catholic side, the Joint

Declaration was approved, after some difficulties and discussions, by the Congregation for the Doctrine of the Faith and the Pontifical Council for Promoting Christian Unity. Immediately after the signing, the Pope publicly expressed his approval and joy, which has been reiterated publicly on several occasions since. Of course, this was no infallible statement, where the Pope speaks with his full and highest authority, but to reduce the signing to a more or less private and personal act of the President of the Pontifical Council for Promoting Christian Unity is a more than fantastic idea.

There were problems on both sides. But what counts is the result. The problems could be dealt with in the Official Common Statement and its Annex, which drew out and confirmed the main result of the Joint Declaration. This Official Common Statement could finally be signed in Augsburg and through it the Joint Declaration was recognized by both churches.

People who know a bit about the history of dogma and confessional writings are familiar with such problems; they are neither surprising nor extraordinary. Of course, it was not possible that in such a statement of agreement every theologian should find all his or her own concerns and theories. The fact that compromises must be found in order to reach consensus on the formulation of such a text is also known from the whole history of dogma and confessional writings. But not every compromise is bad; there are wise compromises too, which hold what is essential and leave other aspects open for further discussion. Such wise compromises can be found – as every church historian knows well – in almost all dogmas and confessional writings, not least in the documents of the Second Vatican Council.

The crucial thing is that through the Joint Declaration the churches themselves, rather than just theologians or even groups of theologians, have reached a substantial and fundamental consensus. It is this that makes the Joint Declaration something new. It is a document of the churches and, even more, a church event.

It is true that the Joint Declaration did not deal expressly with the problem of ecclesiology and our differences about this issue. Nevertheless it is wrong to say that Augsburg did not say anything on the issue of ecclesiology. The event itself was ecclesiological. The Joint Declaration is not only a theoretical doctrinal statement; its signing was an event. In Augsburg and since Augsburg there has been a living experience, and the relationship between Catholics and Lutherans has reached a new quality and intensity. We held out our hands to each other as churches and we do not wish to let go ever again. Or let me put it in this way: the Joint Declaration does not entail a statement on the Church, but it entails and promotes a church reality which now can inspire reflection on the Church. As in every other context, life precedes reflection and reflection presupposes life.

Obviously this agreement is not meant to exclude any other church or church community or the fellowship in the larger ecumenical movement. It is open for all and an invitation to the other churches to join us. With the Anglican Communion there is already a substantial consensus with the document from the Anglican–Roman Catholic dialogue, *Salvation and the Church* (1986). Since Augsburg we have extended an invitation especially to the Reformed churches and the Methodist World Federation. We are happy that the latter has responded in an open and positive way and initiated a process of reception in its member churches. Thus there is a promising 'growth in agreement' among the churches.

Thirdly, when considering the content of the Joint Declaration we have to distinguish different levels of affirmation. The basic content is stated in § 15 of the Joint Declaration:

> In faith we together hold the conviction that justification is the work of the triune God. The Father sent his Son into the world to save sinners. The foundation and presupposition of justification is the incarnation, death and resurrection of Christ. Justification thus means that Christ himself is our righteousness, in which we share through the Holy Spirit in accord with the will of the Father. Together we confess: By grace alone, in faith in Christ's saving work and not because of any merit on our part, we are accepted by God and receive the Holy Spirit, who renews our hearts while equipping and calling us to good works.

I think that this is a very wide consensus, involving not only justification, but justification in the framework and on the foundation of the christological and trinitarian confessions of the undivided Church of the first centuries, a consensus on the centre and focus of the Gospel. Without such an agreement on the christological and trinitarian basis the agreement on justification would collapse. On this basis it was possible to integrate both concerns, the Lutheran one of the sovereignty of grace and the Catholic one of the effective power of grace, enabling us to bring forth the fruits of good works. This fundamental consensus on the core of the Gospel is not simply theoretical; it enables us to bear common witness to the Gospel to a world in need of this message of grace and mercy. At the same time this consensus is the basis for the solution of all the other questions dividing both church communities.

Beyond this fundamental consensus there remain several problems on which we were not able to reach such a full consensus. Mention should be made of the question of the '*simul iustus et peccator*', the question of co-operation, the question of how to speak about merits, and, particularly, the question of the central normativity of the doctrine of justification. On these and other questions it was possible to rule out formal contradictions; we were able to understand the concerns of our partner and to see convergences. But there remained different languages, different accents and emphases, different concerns, so that a full consensus was not reached. We had to refer these problems to further theological dialogue between the churches.

In the light of the fundamental consensus and the still open questions (§§ 40 and 41 of the Joint Declaration), we can come to a twofold conclusion. (1) There is a consensus between Lutherans and Catholics on some basic truths (not *the* basic truths) of the doctrine of justification. In the light of this consensus the remaining differences of language, theological elaboration and emphasis in the understanding of justification are acceptable. Therefore, the Lutheran and the Catholic explanations of justification are open to one another in their difference and do not destroy the consensus regarding the basic truths. (2) The condemnations of the sixteenth century, in so far as they relate to the doctrine of justification, appear in a new light. The teaching of the Lutheran churches presented in this declaration does not fall under the condemnation of the Council of Trent. The condemnations in the Lutheran confessions do not apply to the teaching of the Roman Catholic Church presented in this declaration. The mutual condemnations no longer apply today if each partner stands by what is agreed in the Joint Declaration. But nothing is thereby taken away from the seriousness of the condemnations relating to the doctrine of justification. Some were not simply pointless. They remain for us 'salutary warnings' to which we must attend in our teaching and practice.

So we are dealing with a differentiated consensus rather than total agreement. There exists full consensus about key fundamental issues, in the exposition of which various starting-points, different thought-forms and expressions, and different emphases and statements are possible. Thus the Joint Declaration does not repeal the Council of Trent. For Catholics it remains just as valid as it was before. But it can be interpreted according to our present understanding of the faith in such a way that Luther's doctrine, as set forth in the Joint Declaration, is no longer ruled out as opposed to the Council and thus church-dividing. The differences that remain are not contradictory statements; they complement and complete each other.

Assessing the Joint Declaration all depends on where you stand regarding such a differentiated consensus. This concept goes back to Johann Adam Möhler, the best-known representative of the Catholic Tübingen School in the nineteenth century and one of the fathers and forerunners of contemporary ecumenical theology. In his early work *Die Einheit in der Kirche* (1825) Möhler distinguished between acceptable and even necessary internal oppositions (*Gegensätze*) as mutually complementary, and heretical contradictions (*Widersprüche*) as incompatible with the faith of the Church. Whereas complementary oppositions belong to life and are therefore signs of a living church which is on the way, contradictions isolate themselves from the whole of church doctrine; they deny complementary opposition, becoming one-sided and fruitless. In order to regain their worth as fruitful living opposition, they have to be reintegrated into the whole of church life and doctrine.

These insights were taken up in the ecumenical theology of the twentieth century; they became fundamental to an understanding of what differentiated consensus is all about. Differentiated consensus definitively excludes contradictions, but it includes complementary oppositions. To demand a full consensus would make unity an eschatological affair. In this world only a differentiated consensus is possible and this means that the one, holy, catholic and apostolic Church is an organic whole of complementary opposites. Or to put it another way: the Church is modelled as the image of the triune God who is oneness in diversity.

In the background lies a certain image of the unity of the Church for which we are striving: a unity which does not mean uniformity but a unity in diversity, or (as Lutheran theologians above all say today) a unity in reconciled diversity. The Official Common Statement expressly takes up this model and has thus given it official confirmation by the Church. This is another remarkable result of the Joint Declaration which has been too little noticed. Behind the declaration there is an ecumenical model for the unity we are seeking, not only between Catholics and Lutherans but among all the disciples of Christ. So the Joint Declaration points the way forward and opens up a wider perspective.

What Has Still to be Done: New Tasks and Challenges

The Pope has described the Joint Declaration as a 'milestone'. The image fits the situation exactly: we have reached an important staging post but are not yet at the final goal. The Joint Declaration is important even though it has limits. Its greatness lies in the fact that we can now give joint witness to what is at the heart of our faith, and with this common witness we enter a new century and a new millennium together. Our ever more secularized world needs such common witness. Its greatness is also that it does not disguise its limits but openly names the issues that remain between us. So, clearly, the signing does not mean that everything has been done. Rather, we have to ask how the ecumenical movement is to go forward now that the signing is over.

Ecumenism is a multi-layered process which has to involve the whole Church. We have to distinguish between the tasks on the ground, at the level of parish or diocese, and those pertaining to the universal Church. Therefore, on the Catholic side it would be wrong to wait for Rome for everything. There is firstly the task of the reception of what has already been undertaken, which takes place above all at the local church level. The Joint Declaration should not remain a piece of paper and a dead letter; it must become known and lived out; it must become a reality in the body of the Church. Much has already been done, but there is still a lot to do in catechesis, the continuing formation of adults and clergy, and theological education at the academic level. Nevertheless, here I shall limit myself to the level of the universal Church, and in particular to what the Pontifical Council for Promoting Christian Unity can do.

First of all, we shall have to review the questions about the doctrine of justification that have been left open after the Joint Declaration; for example, the particular contents of certain doctrinal questions, such as clarifying further the issue of '*simul iustus et peccator*' or the criteriological significance of the doctrine of justification. Several issues connected with the question of justification remain to be clarified, for example the question of indulgences, issues tracing their origin to the beginning of the Reformation and still today shaping the collective memory on both sides. Although the issue of indulgences is not a central concept, and in the hierarchy of truths not one of priority, it is intimately linked with the theme of penance, which is central for Christian existence even if today it is unfortunately often forgotten. It has thus been a common concern since Augsburg to take up these questions through symposiums and different dialogue groups and to widen the agreement already reached.

This first consideration of future tasks brings me to a second reflection. We have to strengthen a fundamental understanding of the doctrine of justification. Further biblical research is a priority in this perspective. The Bible, for both our church communities, is the fundamental document of our faith and I have the impression that we can make further fundamental progress by involving scripture study more fully in dogmatic questions. This is self-evident for Lutherans theologians, but it has also been the official Roman response, which from the outset has called for a deeper biblical understanding. It is important to reflect further, for example, on the fact that as well as justification the Bible uses manifold images and terms to describe the reality which justification signifies: kingdom of God, life, reconciliation, peace, redemption, grace and many others. These images and terms interpret each other and only all together give a full picture of the biblical message.

Particularly from a biblical perspective, the message and doctrine of justification is rooted in the christological message of the Bible and of our common tradition as expressed in the creed. The Joint Declaration speaks clearly of this foundation in its fundamental agreement. But it would be an illusion to think that this christological and trinitarian foundation is accepted today more or less as it used to be in the sixteenth century. In the meantime the problem has become aggravated and has become a new common challenge for both church communities. But justification tells us what Jesus Christ is for me and for us; it is, so to speak, the subjective aspect of christology. Without the christological foundation it hangs in the air and becomes an ideological affirmation. Only in this light can we understand why the Catholic side insisted so strongly that justification can only be the criterion of all church doctrine and practice when it is coupled with what is central in the New Testament: the message of Jesus Christ.

Thirdly, mention should be made of the important questions still at issue between us, beyond the doctrine of justification. From the Catholic point of view there is above all the ecclesiological question, i.e. the 'Nature and purpose of the Church', as it was put by the Faith and Order Commission of the World Council of Churches. Intimately connected with this question is the sacramental dimension of the Church, for justification by faith is linked with baptism as the sacrament of faith and, with the eucharist, the centre and focus of Christian and church life. These questions come to a head in the issue of church ministry, i.e., the priesthood of all believers and the ordained, the ministry of bishops in apostolic succession, and the Petrine ministry. The Joint Dialogue Commission between the Lutheran World Federation and the Catholic Church has already taken up some of these questions and begun working on them again.

To be sure, the solution to all these questions cannot be deduced directly from the doctrine of justification; but the doctrine of justification points to the horizon, the point at which such a solution is possible, and shows us why and how sacraments and ministries in the Church are constituted and should be exercised. These are not ends in themselves but instruments and witnesses of God's gracious and merciful justification.

A fourth and final, but a very important and urgent, point. Many Christians today no longer understand the formulations of the sixteenth century. That is especially true of us Catholics. Speaking about justification is not part of our normal catechetical language. We prefer to speak about salvation, grace, new life, forgiveness and reconciliation. However, the real reason why many Catholics (and Protestants as well) no longer understand the term justification lies at a deeper level. We no longer feel the burden of guilt and sin as

Luther did, we no longer live in the fear of God's judgement; we have all become too deistic, seeing God as quite withdrawn from our world and our everyday existence. Hence the question of a merciful God, which moved Luther so deeply, leaves us somewhat cold. The question of justification seems to be at odds with our modern experience; we welcome the fact that the churches were finally able to solve the problem, but it is no longer an existential problem for us.

Thus we have to translate both the questions and the answers of the past into contemporary language and dialectic, so that our words will touch and make an impression on our deepest experiences, anxieties and hopes and stir us as much today as in the past. This is not only a matter of language and the translation of a few dogmatic statements, even less of lapsing into trendy jargon. It is ultimately a question of a new opening up and interpretation of our experience of hopelessness and our desire for meaning and mercy. So the problem of justification raises deep anthropological and theological questions and is linked with the overall question of evangelization.

Thus in order to discover anew the profound meaning of justification we must delve more deeply and ask: What does God mean? What does it mean to believe in a merciful God? What does Jesus Christ mean for us today? What does it mean to believe that we are saved and redeemed by his cross and resurrection? What does this imply for our personal and our common life? The question of justification brings us back to the centre of the Gospel and to the basic questions of our human existence.

Since Augsburg, some work has been done to open our eyes to the deeper actual meaning of justification and to disseminate its proclamation in the modern context. It has been made clear that the doctrine of justification wants to say to us that we neither can nor should 'make' our own life or its fulfilment: we cannot accomplish this by our own efforts. Our value as persons does not depend on our good or bad achievements. Before we ourselves do anything, we have been accepted and affirmed. Our life stands under the horizon of mercy and is ruled by a merciful God, who through everything and despite everything holds us in his kind hands. We are able to live by God's mercy. This frees us from fear, gives us hope and courage and fills us with the joy of the children of God.

Understood in this way, justification is not only good news for our individual life. While it enables us to live as individuals, at the same time it opens us to our fellow human beings. Just as we live by God's mercy, so we can and should be gracious and merciful towards our fellow men and women. Thus, justification enables and even compels us to work for justice and peace, the recognition of human dignity and human rights. Because we all live by God's mercy and love, justification enables us to interact with our community and give ourselves to social concerns. For that reason we can bring hope to a world which is suffering because of injustice, lack of mercy and cynicism, a world which is disoriented and above all lacks hope – which has, indeed, become nihilistic.

Conclusion: Courage in Ecumenism

Many think that the process of ecumenical rapprochement is going too slowly. They even say we are making no headway in ecumenism. It is certainly laborious and needs patience and a great deal of staying power. However, the Joint Declaration has shown that progress is possible. This can give us new ecumenical confidence and momentum.

We should be more grateful for what we have already achieved. At the beginning of the twentieth century, nobody would have expected us to be where we are now. It has been a successful journey from isolation, hostility and competition to tolerance, respect, mutual co-operation and even friendship. We have discovered our already existing communion in Jesus Christ, which is real and deep even if not yet full. The Joint Declaration enlarged and deepened this communion.

The next step to achieving full communion will not be easy. To be honest, there are not only complementary oppositions, there are still contradictions to overcome, not least the danger that today's sociological changes will give rise to new contradictions in ethical questions – though perhaps it would be better to speak not of new contradictions but rather of new challenges. In any case, full communion will not be achieved by convergence alone, but even more by conversion, which implies repentance, forgiveness and renewal of the heart. Such conversion is a gift of grace too – *sola gratia, sola fide*.

One day the gift of unity will take us by surprise, just like an event we witnessed just over ten years ago. If you had asked passers-by in West Berlin on the morning of 9 November 1989, 'How much longer do you think the wall will remain standing?', the majority would surely have replied, 'We would be happy if our grandchildren could pass through the Brandenburg Gate some day.' On the evening of that memorable day the world saw something totally unexpected in Berlin. It is my firm conviction that one day we too will rub our eyes in amazement that God's Spirit has broken through the seemingly insurmountable walls that divide us and given us new ways through to each other and to a new communion. Hopefully we won't have to wait another 400 years.

8

A Discussion on the Petrine Ministry

An Emotional Question

The issue of the primacy of the Bishop of Rome is one of the most difficult ecumenical questions. Indeed, when discussion turns to the pope, the question becomes much more than a very complex, theoretical and theological problem. More than any other, the papacy issue stirs emotions, both positive and negative; it meets with enthusiastic approval as well as prejudice and – even today – anti-Roman feeling even among Catholics.[1] The acceptance of the primacy of the Bishop of Rome is a very hallmark of Catholic identity, just as anti-Roman feeling can only lead to the self-destruction of the Catholic Church. Likewise, the refusal of this primacy is often a determining feature of the very identity of Protestant and Orthodox Christians.

The criticism of the Reformers is well known. They saw the pope as the eschatological fiend described in apocalyptic terms in 2 Thess. 2.1-12 and as the beast referred to in Rev. 13.1-10, and after some initial hesitation they labelled him as the Antichrist. The use of this image was nothing new. In antiquity it was attributed to Nero and the Roman Empire, and it also played an important role in the criticism of the Church in the late Middle Ages.[2] But, with the Reformers, it entered into confessional writings and poisoned the relationship between the communities for centuries.

The Middle Ages, however, also gave rise to a different tradition: the nostalgia for a *Papa angelicus*, an angel-like pope who could reform the Church and be the guide of a pure and renewed Church. Gioacchino da Fiore foresaw the coming of a third epoch, which would divest itself of the hierarchical Church and be a time of the Spirit. These expectations also influenced the prophecies of

Malachias (c. 1590), which stirred the spirits every time there was a papal election.[3] There is a kind of papal veneration that can take on touching dimensions, but also, unfortunately, tasteless features. Hence the question of papal primacy can evoke not only feelings of refusal, disappointment and even hatred, but also great hopes and extraordinary expectations.

This is why we have to admit with honesty that the primacy of the pope, which understands itself as a service to unity, can paradoxically be seen – today as in the past – as the greatest obstacle to broader ecumenical unity. Both Pope Paul VI and John Paul II were long-sighted enough to speak openly about this paradox.[4]

A Changing Atmosphere

With the development of the ecumenical movement, and in an increasingly globalized and unified world, the question of a ministry of unity has resurfaced and a heated debate on the papal or, better, Petrine ministry has developed.[5] This question has been raised in different ecumenical documents and has been widely discussed, generally in a positive way.[6] The newly awoken interest in the biblical figure of Peter in academic studies of the New Testament is a particularly important element. His special position among the Twelve, his role as representative and speaker on behalf of the other apostles, the special task entrusted to him by Jesus, his leading role in the primitive Christian community, and the Petrine tradition which developed in the New Testament after his death, have been clearly underlined.[7]

This does not mean that papal primacy and the infallibility of the pope, as they were defined in the First and Second Vatican Councils and (even less) as they are concretely exercised, have become acceptable to the other churches and church communions. Such a consensus does not exist. Recognition of the special task and role of the historical Peter does not lead directly to recognition of a permanent Petrine ministry in the Church. And even where this is accepted as a possibility, the difference between a biblical Petrine service and the Petrine ministry as it was defined by the First and Second Vatican Councils seems for many to be impossible to reconcile from a biblical and theological perspective.

Most of the answers to this question are therefore a kind of 'Yes, but ...'. A ministry of unity, yes – or maybe – but not as it is defined and practised by the Catholic Church; rather, a papal ministry like that of the first millennium, a pope like Peter, who had been contradicted by Paul. Hence the documents of the Lutheran–Catholic Dialogue focus only on the possibility of a Petrine ministry under specific conditions; they underline further the need for a theological reinterpretation and practical reshaping – whatever this may mean in detail.

However, it is clear that the old controversy has been replaced by a new openness. The conviction that today, in the face of an increasingly globalized world, there should somehow be a ministry of unity in the Church is developing ecumenically. This is why the pope, as Bishop of Rome and, according to an old church tradition, the first of the bishops, enjoys a high esteem and moral authority not only within the Catholic Church. At the same time, on the Catholic side, there is a growing conviction that a spiritual and institutional renewal, which does not relinquish the very essence of the Church but on the contrary is rooted in it, is fundamental for any future ecumenical understanding. These are the new pre-requisites for a theological discussion on the question of the Petrine ministry.

A Revolutionary Invitation and a New Debate

In order to respond to this new situation, Pope John Paul II made a revolutionary step for a pope in his encyclical letter *Ut unum sint* (1995). He affirmed that he was aware that 'the Catholic Church's conviction that in the ministry of the Bishop of Rome she has preserved ... the visible sign and guarantor of unity, constitutes a difficulty for most other Christians, whose memory is marked by certain painful recollections'. He also added: 'To the extent that we are responsible for these, I join my Predecessor Paul VI in asking forgiveness.'[8]

Being aware of his 'particular responsibility' for Christian unity, the Pope affirmed that he is willing to 'find a way of exercising the primacy which, while in no way renouncing what is essential to its mission, is nonetheless open to a new situation'. He prayed 'the Holy Spirit to shine his light upon us, enlightening all the Pastors and theologians of our Churches, that we may seek – together, of course – the forms in which this ministry may accomplish a service of love recognized by all concerned'.[9] Finally, the Pope invited church leaders and theologians to engage with him in 'a patient and fraternal dialogue on this subject'.[10] The Pope has repeated this invitation on many occasions, underlining that we have no time to lose.

Clearly, the Pope does not want to bring into question the Petrine ministry and the dogma of primacy and infallibility. He wants to look for new forms of exercising this ministry without renouncing its essence. Thus the encyclical letter distinguishes between this unchangeable essence and its changeable forms. But this very distinction is a problem, because non–Catholic churches often deny that there is a Petrine ministry at all, or disagree on the question of its essence and the type of its changeable forms. Hence the question is not purely practical or pragmatic, but theological. It is a question of understanding what for the Catholic Church is this essence which cannot be renounced without losing its identity, and whether the other churches and church Communions are capable of accepting it without renouncing their own identity.

The answer involves a series of difficult and complex theological problems, such as the biblical foundation, the historical development in the first and second century, the interpretation of the doctrine of the First and Second Vatican Councils, and the practical implementation of new insights.

Despite such difficulties, the ecumenical dialogue is back on track on the question of Petrine ministry, fostered by the invitation of the Holy Father himself. There have been official replies from some churches (e.g. the Church of England and the Church of Sweden) and a wide range of theological contributions in books, magazines, conferences and symposia.[11] Furthermore, a short time after the encyclical, the Congregation for the Doctrine of the Faith and the Pontifical Council for Promoting Christian Unity organized symposia on the question and published their findings.[12] The question of the Petrine ministry has also been dealt with in several of our dialogues with other churches and church communions. Of particular interest is a theological symposium held by the Pontifical Council for Promoting Christian Unity, with representatives of all the Orthodox Patriarchates; its proceedings are being prepared for publication.

With the help of the Johann Adam Möhler Institute in Paderborn (Germany), the Pontifical Council gathered all these contributions and undertook an overview of the issue, presenting and discussing it during its Plenary Assembly in November 2001, sending it to all the churches involved, and finally publishing its results.[13] With this overview we wanted to initiate a second phase of the discussion.

How can the debate proceed in its second phase? Many doubt that it can go on at all. The Catholic Church is dogmatically bound by the First and Second Vatican Councils, which she cannot relinquish; similarly, our ecumenical partners are de facto bound by their confessional writings, as well as their traditional critique and opposition to these dogmas. Where is the room for manoeuvre, then? Can there be an honest solution?

I would like to offer an answer from the Catholic perspective. It is obvious that Catholic theology has to take dogma seriously. It must be borne in mind, however, that dogmas should be interpreted in the sense in which the Church once declared them.[14] In the Catholic view, this does not imply an irrational and fundamentalist compliance with a formula. Nothing would contradict the Catholic understanding more than to make a dead petrification out of a dogma, instead of a living truth. In fact, according to the First Vatican Council, faith and understanding belong together. Catholic teaching therefore recognizes an evolution in the deepening of our understanding of the truth that was revealed once and for all.[15] There is a history of dogma in the sense of a history of understanding and interpretation, and there are theological rules for its interpretation.[16]

In this context, Ratzinger speaks of the need for a rereading,[17] while Congar and others speak of a re-reception of the First Vatican Council.[18] Rereading and re-reception are not an evasion. These concepts involve interpreting the teaching of the First Vatican Council on the primacy and infallibility of the Pope according to the 'normal' and common rules of dogmatic hermeneutics. Thus, according to the Catholic view, such a rereading and re-reception does not call into question the validity of the definitions of the Council, but is concerned with their interpretation. Reception does not mean an automatic, merely passive, acceptance, but a lively and creative evolution of appropriation and integration.[19]

Four Hermeneutical Principles

Integration within the whole context of ecclesiology

A first rule for such a rereading is the integration of the primacy within the whole context of ecclesiology. This rule was formulated by the First Vatican Council itself. It affirmed that the mysteries of faith are to be interpreted '*e mysterium ipsorum nexu inter se*', that is, according to the internal connection binding them together.[20] The Second Vatican Council expressed the same idea with the help of the doctrine of the hierarchy of truths.[21] Therefore, no dogma should be considered in isolation but should be interpreted taking into account the whole doctrine of the faith. In particular, it should be interpreted on the basis, in the context, and in the light of, the basic Christian dogmas of christology and the Holy Trinity.

This integration of the primacy within the whole of ecclesiology had already been suggested by the First Vatican Council. The Council describes the meaning of primacy in the Prooemium to the Constitution *Pastor aeternus*, affirming that, according to God's will, all the faithful should be kept together in the Church through the bond of faith and love. It then mentions the famous quotation which is the basis of today's ecumenical commitment: '*ut omnes unum essent*'. Finally, it refers to Bishop Cyprian: 'Ut episcopatus ipse unus et indivisus esset', Peter was called to be 'perpetuum utriusque unitatis principium ac visibile fundamentum.'[22] An article published by the Congregation for the Doctrine of the Faith presents this formulation as fundamentally important for a *theological* interpretation of the *juridical* declarations on the doctrine of primacy.[23] Thus the unity of the Church is the *raison d'être* and the context of interpretation of the Petrine ministry.

Due to the outbreak of the Franco-German war, the Council was not able to proceed with the integration of primacy into the whole ecclesiological context. This process remained uncompleted, since the Council only managed to define the primacy and infallibility of the pope. This led later to unbalanced interpretations. But already the First Vatican Council affirmed that the primacy does not cancel but, rather, confirms, strengthens and defends the direct power of the bishops.[24] Pope Pius IX explicitly underlined this when he confirmed the declaration of the German bishops against Bismarck's dispatch. Thus, Pius IX warded off extreme interpretations and defended the position of the bishop as ordinary pastor of his diocese.[25]

The Second Vatican Council took up the question and made a second important step towards the integration of primacy into the whole doctrine of the Church, especially into the whole collegiality of the episcopal ministry. This council was the first to explain, in the Dogmatic Constitution *Lumen gentium*, the whole Catholic doctrine of the Church; in this wider context it reaffirmed the doctrine of the First Vatican Council, although it also affirmed the sacramental understanding of the episcopal ministry, which is not to be seen as derived from the pope and only representative of the Pope;[26] the Council further affirmed the dignity of the lay ministry, the importance of the local church and, above all, the understanding of the Church as *communio*. This has revived synodical elements, especially at the level of synods and Bishops' Conferences.

Nevertheless, the Second Vatican Council was not fully able to reconcile the new elements – which in reality correspond to the oldest tradition – with the statements of the First Vatican Council. Many issues have remained unconnected. So some people find two different ecclesiologies in the texts of the Second Vatican Council. This may be an exaggeration but the compromise character of many affirmations is obvious. This led, after the Second Vatican Council, to the controversy on interpretation, which to some degree still remains open today. In this sense, not only the First Vatican Council but also the Second Vatican Council have remained uncompleted. The integration of the Petrine ministry within the whole of ecclesiology, the relation between primacy and collegiality, the relation between the universal and the local church, the interpretation of the direct jurisdiction of the pope in all local churches, the question of the applicability of the principle of subsidiarity and other issues raise theological and practical questions which remain open.

H. U. von Balthasar went a step further still in his attempt to integrate the Petrine ministry. He spoke about an integration in the whole constellation of the Church: the Christological, the Mariological and the Pauline dimensions.[27] Thus there is still room for a further process of interpretation and reception.

If we thus take seriously that the Petrine ministry is constitutive within the Church and yet recognize that communion with it does not deny that others have their own sacramental roots and are not derived from it, then we can overcome a one-sided, pyramidal conception of the Church and a communal one will emerge, in which the different institutions and instances have their respective and irreplaceable roles in interplay with each other. Such a communal view, which leaves room for the freedom of the Spirit, could be the result of a fuller reception of the Second Vatican Council.[28]

Integration into the whole tradition
The second principle of dogmatic hermeneutics concerns a rereading of the First Vatican Council in the light of the whole tradition, and its integration in it. This way was already indicated in the texts of the First Vatican Council itself, and was described in the Introduction to the Dogmatic Constitution *Pastor aeternus* as the intention to interpret this teaching 'secundum antiquam atque constantem universalis Ecclesiae fidem' and to defend it against mistaken views.[29] Clear mention was made of the declarations of former popes and the ancient councils.[30] The First Vatican Council even appealed to the consensus between the Church in the East and the Church in the West.[31] The Second Vatican Council especially reinforced this last point when it affirmed the legitimacy of the particular tradition of the Oriental churches[32] and recognized their juridical self-determination.[33]

Such indications express an important concept, valid for all councils: the Church is the same in all centuries and in all councils; this is why each council is to be interpreted in the light of the whole tradition and of all councils. For the Holy Spirit guiding the Church, especially the councils, cannot work in contradiction. What was true in the first millennium cannot be untrue in the second. Therefore the older tradition should not simply be considered as the first phase of a further development. The other way round is also true: the later developments should be interpreted in the light of the older tradition. Thus, the ecclesiology of *communio* of the first millennium, reaffirmed by the Second Vatican Council, constitutes the hermeneutical framework for the First Vatican Council and helps to integrate it into the context of the whole ecclesiological tradition.

In the meantime, especially after Cardinal Ratzinger's well-known conference in Graz, the normative importance of the first millennium has also been widely recognized in Catholic theology.[34] What was recognized as corresponding to the very nature of the Church and the Gospel, what was vigorous for centuries, cannot be wrong today. This applies especially to the relative autonomy of the Eastern patriarchates in the first millennium.[35] Cardinal Ratzinger emphasized the importance for an ecumenical rereading of primacy of the distinction between the function of the pope as patriarch and his Petrine ministry.[36] Indeed, the Second Vatican Council recognized anew the treasures and the independence of the spiritual, liturgical, theological and canonical traditions of the Eastern churches and their power to govern themselves according to their own discipline.[37]

But it is essential to understand this principle correctly. It is clear that it is not a question of going back to the first millennium or reverting to an 'ecumenism of return'.[38] Such a return to the first millennium is impossible for purely historical reasons; different views existed already in the first millennium, and it cannot offer us, therefore, any miraculous solution. Moreover, significant developments took place not only in the Catholic Church but also in the Oriental churches in the second millennium.[39] Why should we suppose that the Spirit guided the Church only in the first millennium? And are there not already in the first millennium the foundations of what developed in the second, which can also be found in the Eastern tradition?[40]

Thus, on the eve of the third millennium, we cannot turn back the clock of history, but we can interpret the dogmatic developments of the second millennium in the light and the context of the first one, in order to open the door to the third millennium. This could open our eyes to the possibility of different forms of the exercise of the Petrine ministry throughout history; history did not come to an end with the First Vatican Council but continues in the third millennium.

The Second Vatican Council has already started to interpret the First Vatican Council in the wider horizon of the ecclesiology of *communio*. A corresponding reception on behalf of the churches in the East is only just beginning. Such a reception does not imply a mechanical acceptance or a submission of the East to the Latin tradition; it would entail a lively and creative process of appropriation into their own tradition. This would enrich the tradition of the Eastern churches and give them a greater degree of unity and independence, which they now lack. The Latin tradition would also be freed from the constraints in which it found itself in the second millennium. The Church as a whole – as the Pope has expressed many times – would start breathing with both her lungs again. This implies integrating each other's respective traditions and could lead to different forms and expressions in the exercise of the Petrine ministry, as the first millennium has testified and as the Oriental churches in full communion with Rome continue to testify today.

Historical interpretation
We come now to a third hermeneutical principle: the historical interpretation. According to this principle, all dogmas have to be interpreted in the sense that they were declared.[41] This implies taking into account the historical context of a dogma and the historical meaning of the concepts used by it. Thus for all dogmas, including those of the First Vatican Council, it is fundamental to make a distinction between their unchangeable binding content and their changeable historical forms. This principle was clearly expressed by the Second Vatican Council: 'the deposit and the truths of faith are one thing, the manner of expressing them is quite another'.[42] Hence it would be wrong to take the formulations of the First Vatican Council as the only possible way of expressing what the Petrine ministry concretely means and what is permanently binding in it.

The fathers of the First Vatican Council experienced specific historical conditions that led them to formulate things the way they did.[43] The Council majority saw the Church besieged from all sides in an almost apocalyptic situation. They were traumatized by the Enlightenment, the French Revolution, the absolutism of modern states, by Gallicanism and Episcopalism, and wanted to make sure that the Church would remain capable of action in an extreme situation. This is why they reverted to the modern idea of sovereignty; they defined the primacy of the pope in terms of an absolute sovereignty, enabling him to act even if he should be prevented from communication with the Church. So their statements on primacy were conceived for extreme and exceptional situations.[44]

The understanding of the primacy in the sense of sovereignty does not mean – even according to the First Vatican Council – that the pope's power is unlimited. It is limited in several ways: by revelation itself and by binding tradition, by the sacramental structure and the episcopal constitution of the Church, as well as by human rights given by God. Therefore, the problem is not the actual dogma of the First Vatican Council but its maximizing interpretation both by its ultra-montanist advocates and by its critics.[45] This has turned what was considered an exceptional situation into a normal situation. The exceptional case has been, so to speak, stretched in time and made permanent. Therefore we should agree with J. Ratzinger when he says that the centralized image portrayed by the Church until the First Vatican Council did not stem directly from the Petrine ministry. The uniform canon law, the uniform liturgy and the designation of the episcopal thrones by the central power in Rome are all elements that do not necessarily belong to the primacy as such.[46]

If we separate the declarations on the primacy of jurisdiction from their historical forms, we can then find their binding, essential meaning, i.e. that the pope is free to act according to the specific and changing necessity of the Church. The primacy should therefore be interpreted in the light of the needs of the Church and applied accordingly.[47] It is in this sense that John Paul II in *Ut unum sint* speaks coherently of the need to find a way of exercising the primacy according to the new ecumenical situation of today.

Interpretation according to the Gospel

A fourth and last hermeneutical principle is the interpretation of the Petrine ministry according to the Gospel. The importance of this principle has been particularly highlighted in the dialogue with Lutherans, but Catholics also agree on its significance.[48] Real value in the Church has its roots in the Gospel, which was revealed once for all, and not in what is only an human invention.

In this sense the Catholic Church believes that the Petrine ministry has its foundation in the biblical witness and ultimately in Jesus Christ himself. For this we refer not only to the famous Petrine instances (Matt. 16.18f.; Luke 2.32; John 21.15-17), but also to the fact that Jesus gave Simon the name *kepha*, Petros (John 1.42), which means rock, and in doing so explained his function within the Church. We refer also to the role of Peter among the Twelve as their representative and spokesman, his role as leader of the primitive community in Jerusalem, and the whole Petrine tradition in the New Testament, expressed especially in the first and second letters of Peter, which already point beyond the earthly lifetime of Peter towards the post-apostolic and post-biblical time and tradition.

It is true that the exegesis of all these biblical instances is controversial. Historical interpretation of the Bible provides us with good reasons for our belief, but historical interpretation alone does not provide the ultimate foundation. The Gospel in its original meaning is not a book but the message witnessed in the Bible and, in the power of the Spirit, announced and believed in the Church. Thus the biblical witness cannot be severed from this witness of church tradition. Today a purely historical understanding of the Gospel, which looks only for the exact historical meaning of the words of the so-called historical Jesus, is obsolete. Historical exegesis is certainly legitimate, helpful and fundamental, but theological debate cannot be biblistic in a narrow sense and should not separate the scriptures from the living tradition. It should take into account both scripture and tradition, and make use of spiritual and theological hermeneutics.[49]

To tradition belongs the early Church's perception of the faithfulness of the community of Rome despite persecution and confrontation with Gnosticism, its steadfastness against Marcion and in the final establishment of the biblical canon, and the role of its bishops, who very early took over responsibility for the unity of the Church beyond the Roman community. These were all factors that convinced the Church that in the church of Rome and its bishop the promises given to Peter were realized and still at work. So from the third and fourth century on, the Church referred to the biblical witness which is given especially in Matt. 16.18.[50]

However, such a historical and at the same time theological and spiritual interpretation of the biblical witness is not only concerned with finding a formal foundation for the Petrine ministry, but also with emphasizing its theological meaning and its appropriate exercise according to the Gospel. Understood in the sense of the Gospel, the Petrine ministry cannot be interpreted as power but only as service. In fact, the Gospel says: 'whoever wishes to be first among you must be your slave' (Matt. 20.27). This aspect is reflected in the famous expression (and since Gregory the Great the title of the Bishop of Rome), 'servus servorum'.[51]

The Prooemium of the First Vatican Council, also mentioned by the Second Vatican Council, is along the same line.[52] Here the Petrine ministry is not expressed in juridical formulations but theologically understood as *episkopē*.[53] Pope John Paul II has referred to this interpretation in *Ut unum sint*. This could be an ecumenically helpful proposal for a new interpretation. Furthermore, Pope John Paul II has also referred to the martyr bishop Ignatius of Antioch, who described the primacy of Rome as the 'primacy of love'.[54] Thus the Pope himself has given an important indication of a new interpretation of primacy inspired by the Gospel. His interpretation is not one of jurisdiction based on the idea of sovereignty, but a spiritual one based on the idea of service – service to unity, service and sign of mercy and love.[55]

This closer reference to the Bible has helped to replace, in current usage, the expressions 'papal ministry' and 'papacy' with 'Petrine ministry' and 'Petrine service'. This linguistic change is quite telling. It wants to give the papacy – developed throughout history and in part also burdened by history – an interpretation and reception in the light of the Gospel, not renouncing its essential nature but setting it within a wider spiritual understanding, on the theoretical as well the practical level. The Petrine ministry is *episkopē*, meaning that it is a pastoral service after the example of Jesus the good shepherd, who gives his life for his flock (John 10.11). In this sense Peter admonishes his fellow elders: 'Be shepherds of God's flock under your care, serving as overseers – not because you must, but because you are willing, as God wants you to be; not greedy for money, but eager to serve; not lording it over those entrusted to you, but being examples to the flock' (1 Pet. 5.2-4).

Such a biblical and pastoral understanding does not exclude juridical authority and is not to be confused with a primacy of honour understood in a merely honorific sense. Pastoral responsibility without the means to execute it would be void and would not help the Church in the urgent situations where she most needs it, and a merely honorific primacy would be very far from the spirit of the Gospel. Thus a primacy of jurisdiction cannot be opposed by a pastoral primacy of service. Honour, in the legal language of the early Christian centuries, which was that of Roman law, meant the dignity and privileges attached to the power of a magistrate and thus denoted authority and power;[56] within the Church this has to be understood in the biblical sense of *exousia*, which is exercised as the service of *episcopē* and the *oikodomē* of unity within the Church.

In conclusion, we could summarize by saying that, with the help of an interpretation of the First Vatican Council in the light of the four hermeneutical principles outlined above, it is possible to uphold the binding and unchangeable essence of the Petrine ministry and, at the same time, to open up and explore the way and prepare a spiritual rereading and re-reception in our own church which – we hope – can facilitate a broader ecumenical reception as well. It has not been the intention of these reflections to give a concrete answer on how to shape the Petrine ministry in the future, but to pave the way for such an answer.

My hope is that, as in the first millennium, the Petrine ministry may take a form that, although differently exercised in the East and the West, could be recognized by both the East and the West within a unity in diversity and a diversity in unity. I do not delude myself. I am aware that the path ahead, according to human measurement, may yet be long. But I still hope that when we patiently and at the same time courageously do what we can, God's Spirit will help and accompany us so that we reach what he has in mind for the full visible unity of the Church.

Notes

1   H. U. von Balthasar, *Der antirömische Affekt*, second revised edition, Einsiedeln 1989.
2   See 'Antichrist', in: *LThK* I (1993), 745f.
3   See 'Papa angelicus', in: *LThK* VII (1998) 1323.
4   Cf. statements by Pope Paul VI and Pope John Paul II in J. A. Radano, '"Ut unum sint": The Ministry of Unity of the Bishop of Rome', in: *Angelicum* 73 (1996) 327–9.
5   A selection from the extensive literature: H. Asmussen and R. Grosche, *Brauchen wir einen Papst?*, Köln-Olten 1957; J. Meyendorff (and others), *The Primacy of Peter in the Orthodox Church*, London 1963; G. Denzler *et al.*, *Papsttum und Petrusdienst*, Stuttgart 1975; H. Stirnimann and L. Vischer (eds), *Papsttum und Petrusdienst*, Frankfurt a.M. 1975; A. Brandenburg and H. J. Urban (eds), *Petrus und Papst*, 2 vol., Münster 1977/78; *Dienst an der Einheit. Zum*

Wesen und Auftrag des Petrusamts, 1978; *Papsttum als ökumenische Frage*, 1979; J. M. Tillard, *L'Évêque de Rome*, Paris 1982; P. Granfield, *Das Papsttum. Kontinuität und Wandel*, Münster 1984; *The Limits of Papacy*, New York 1987; V. von Aristi, *Das Papstamt – Dienst oder Hindernis für die Ökumene?*, Regensburg 1985; J. Ratzinger (ed.), *Dienst an der Einheit*, Düsseldorf 1978; *Papsttum als ökumenische Frage*. ed. by the Arbeitsgemeinschafrt ökumenischer Universitätsinstitute, München-Mainz 1979. Cf. Notes 11–13.

6 'Lutheran–Catholic Dialogue: Malta Report' (1972) §§ 66f., in: *Growth in Agreement*, ed. H. Meyer and L. Vischer, New York 1984, 184; 'The Ministry in the Church' (1981) §§ 69–73, in: ibid., 269–71; *Papal Primacy and the Universal Church* (Lutherans and Catholics in Dialogue V), Minneapolis 1974; *Teaching Authority and Infallibility in the Church* (Lutherans and Catholics in Dialogue VI), Minneapolis 1978; *Lehrverurteilungen – kirchentrennend?*, Freiburg i.Br.-Göttingen 1986, 167–9; *Communio Sanctorum*, Paderborn-Frankfurt a.M. 2000, 77–99. 'Anglican–Catholic Dialogue: Venice Statement (1976)' §§ 19–23, *Growth in Agreement*, ibid. 96f.; 'Elucidation (1981)' § 8, ibid. 104f.; 'Windsor Statement (1981)', ibid. 106–18; 'The Gift of Authority (1999)' §§ 45–48.

7 A selection from the rich literature, especially R. Brown *et al.*, *Peter in the New Testament*, New York 1973; O. Cullmann, *Petrus. Jünger – Apostel – Märtyrer*, Zürich-Stuttgart 2nd ed 1960; F. Mussner, 'Petrusgestalt und Petrusdienst in der Sicht der späten Urkirche', in: *Dienst an der Einheit*, Düsseldorf 1978, 27–45; R. Pesch, 'Was an Petrus sichtbar war, ist in den Primat eigegangeni': in: *Il Primato del Successore di Pietro*, 22–111; J. Gnilka, *Petrus und Rom*, Freiburg i. Br. 2002.

8 UUS, 88.

9 Ibid. 95.

10 Ibid. 96.

11 P. Hünermann (ed.), *Petrusamt und Ökumene*, Regensburg 1997; O. Clément, *Rome autrement. Une réflexion orthodoxe sur la papauté*, Paris 1997; J. R. Quinn *et al.*, *The Exercise of the Primacy*, New York 1998; M. Buckley, *Papal Primacy and the Episcopate*, New York 1998; H. J. Pottmeyer, *Towards a*

Papacy in Communion, New York 1998 (German: Die Rolle des Papsttums im Dritten Jahrtausend, Freiburg i.Br. 1999).

12 Il primato del successore di Pietro. Atti del simposio teologico (1996), Città del Vaticano 1998; Il ministero Petrino e l'unità della Chiesa, Venezia 1999; Il primato del successore di Pietro nel ministero della Chiesa, Città del Vaticano 2002.

13 Information Service 2002/I–II, 29–42 (with an almost complete overview of all publications).

14 'Hinc sacrorum quoque dogmatum, is sensus perpetuo est retinendus, quem semel declaravit sancta mater Ecclesia, nec umquam ab eo sensu alterioris intelligentiae specie et nomine recedendum est' (DS 3020). Cf. DS 3043.

15 Denzinger–Hünermann (DH), Kompendium der Glaubensbekenntnisse und kirchlichen Lehrentscheidungen, Freiburg im Breisgau 1999, 3020; Dei verbum (DV) 8.

16 Cf. W. Kasper, Die Methoden der Dogmatik, München 1967.

17 J. Ratzinger, Das neue Volk Gottes, Düsseldorf 1969, 140.

18 Y. Congar, Diversité et communion, Paris 1982, 141.

19 The concept of reception is fundamental for ecumenical theology. Y. Congar, 'La réception comme réalité ecclésiologique', in: RSPhTh 56 (1972) 369–403; A. Grillmeier, 'Konzil und Rezeption', in: Mit ihm und in ihm, Freiburg i.Br. 1975, 309–34; W. Beinert, 'Die Rezeption und ihre Bedeutung in Leben und Lehre', in: W. Pannenberg and Th. Schneider, Verbindliches Zeugnis, vol. 2, Freiburg-Göttingen 1995, 193–218; G. Routhier, La réception d'un concile, Paris 1993.

20 DH 3016.

21 UR 11: 'When comparing doctrines, they [i.e. theologians] should remember that in Catholic doctrine there exists an order or "hierarchy" of truths, since they vary in their relation to the foundation of the Christian faith.'

22 DH 3050f.

23 P. Rodriguez, 'Natura e fini del primato del Papa: Il Vaticano I, alla luce del Vaticano II', in: Il primato del successore di Pietro nel ministero della Chiesa, op. cit. 81–111.

24 DH 3061.

25 DH 3112-3117.

26 Dogmatic Constitution on the Church, Lumen gentium 27.

27 Hans Urs von Balthasar, Der antirömische Affekt, chapter 2.

28   Such a view seems to correspond with the Orthodox view as
     outlined by O. Clément, *Rome autrement*. *Un orthodoxe face
     à la papauté*, Paris 1997, 59–64; 107.
29   DH 3052.
30   DH 3059.
31   DH 3065.
32   Decree on Ecumenism, *Unitatis redintegratio* 14.
33   Ibid., 16.
34   J. Ratzinger, 'Die ökumenische Situation – Orthodoxie,
     Katholizismus und Reformation', in: *Theologische Prinzipien-
     lehre, Bausteine einer Fundamentaltheologie*, München 1982,
     esp. 209: 'As for the doctrine of primacy, Rome should not
     claim from the East more than was formulated and lived in the
     first Millenium'. On this subject: M. Maccarrone (ed.), *Il
     primato del vescovo di Roma nel primo millennio*, Rome
     1991.
35   E. Lannes, 'Églises locales et Patriarcats à l'époque des grands
     conciles', in: *Irénikon* 34 (1961) 291–321; W. de Vries, *Rom
     und die Patriarchate des Ostens*, Freiburg-München 1963;
     'The Origin of the Eastern Patriarchates and their Relation-
     ship to the Power of the Pope', in: *One in Christ* 2/1 (1966)
     50–69; A. de Halleux, 'L'institution patriarchale et la
     pentarchie', in: *Rev. Théol. de Louvain* 3 (1972) 177–99; Y.
     Congar, 'Le pape, patriarch d'Occident', in: *Istina* 8 (1983)
     374–90.
36   J. Ratzinger, 'Primat und Episkopat', in: *Das neue Volk
     Gottes*, Düsseldorf 1969, 141–4; 'Primat', in: *LThK* VIII
     (1963) 761–3. In the meantime the Congregation for the
     Doctrine of Faith holds another position ('Note on the
     Expression "Sister Churches"', 2000), which is influenced by
     A. Garuti, 'Il papa patriarca d'occidente?', in: *Studio storico-
     dottrinale*, Bologna 1990; *Saggi di ecumenismo*, Roma 2003,
     121–40. The position of Garuti is criticized by F. R.
     Gahbauer, Art. 'Patriarchat', in: *TRE* 26 (1996), 85–91 and
     G. Nedungatt, 'The Patriarchal Ministry in the Church of the
     Third Millennium', in: *The Jurist* 61 (2001) 1–89, esp. p. 10,
     n. 17.
37   UR 14; 16.
38   J. Ratzinger, *Kirche, Ökumene, Politik*, Einsiedeln 1987, 76f.;
     81f.

39 Worth mentioning especially is the end of the Byzantine Empire and the disappearance of the emperor, who was to some degree the co-ordinator of unity; more recently, we should consider the emergence of the autocephalous national churches and patriarchates and the fact that the majority of Orthodox Christians live today in the diaspora in the western world.

40 From the Orthodox side cf. J. Meyendorff, *Orthodoxy and Catholicity*, New York 1966, 49–78; O. Clément, *Rome autrement. Un orthodoxe face à la papauté*, Paris 1997.

41 DH 3020.

42 Pastoral Constitution *Gaudium et spes* 62. This sentence takes up the speech Pope John XXIII delivered at the opening of the Council (*AAS* 54, 1962, 792). It was further developed by the Declaration of the Congregation for the Doctrine of Faith, 'Mysterium Ecclesiae' (1973), in: DH 4539f.

43 H. J. Pottmeyer, *Die Rolle des Papstums im dritten Jahrtausend* (Quaestiones disputatae, 179), Freiburg i.Br. 1999.

44 H. J. Pottmeyer, *op. cit.*, 44f.

45 Ibid. 66f.

46 J. Ratzinger, *Das neue Volk Gottes*, 142.

47 *Il Primato del successore di Pietro*, 501f.; cf. W. Brandmüller, 'Natur und Zielsetzung primatialer Interventionen im zweiten Jahrtausend', ibid., especially 377f. See also the remarks by D. Valentini, ibid., 381f.

48 Dogmatic Constitution, *Dei verbum*: 'It follows that all the preaching of the Church, as indeed the entire Christian religion, should be nourished and ruled by Sacred Scripture.' Significantly, the Council sees sacred scripture in the context of tradition and the doctrine of the Church (cf. ibid. 7–10).

49 All this is meant by the difficult and complex term '*ius divinum*'. It is widely recognized that the *ius divinum* does not exist in a pure and abstract sense but is concretely translated into history through the *ius ecclesiasticum* and the *ius humanum*. In this sense the *ius divinum* comprises what has acquired its definitive value on the basis of the holy scriptures in the history of the Church guided by the Holy Spirit. Cf. K. Rahner, 'Über den Begriff des "Jus divinum" im katholischen Veständnis', in: *Schriften*, vol. 5, Einsiedeln 1962, 249–77; G.

A. Lindbeck, in: *Primacy and the Universal Church*, 193–208; J. Freitag, Art. 'Ius divinum – ius humanum', in: *LThK* V (1996) 697f.

50 J. Ludwig, *Die Primatsworte Mt 16,18.19 in der altkirchk-licheh Exegese*, Münster 1952; W. Kasper, in: *Dienst an der Einheit*, 82–8.

51 Cf. DS 3061.

52 LG 18.

53 Cf. P. Rodriguez, *op. cit.*; P. Goyert, 'Primato ed episcopato', in ibid. 133f.

54 Ignatius of Antioch, *To the Romans*, Prol.

55 UUS 88-91.

56 G. Nedungatt, *The Patriarchal Ministry of the Church of the Third Millennium*, in: *The Jurist* 61 (2001), 43.

9

Spiritual Ecumenism

The Ecumenical Movement Today

The ecumenical dialogue has made great progress since the Catholic Church officially opened itself to the ecumenical movement during the Second Vatican Council. More important than individual results is what Pope John Paul II, in his encyclical *Ut unum sint* (1995), calls the rediscovery of brotherhood among Christians (42f.). Despite this positive progress, however, difficulties persist beyond those which could be considered normal and part of life. Although the conversations and meetings, visits and correspondence continue, the dialogue has somehow faltered. Situations and moods have changed, and in some ways one even has to speak of a crisis. There can be no doubt: the ecumenical movement is today at a turning point.

One reason among many others is that after clearing up many misunderstandings and establishing a basic consensus concerning the centre of faith, we have now reached the inner core of our differences: our institutional ecclesiological differences. In the encounter with the ancient Oriental and Orthodox churches this is represented by the Petrine ministry; in the encounter with the churches of the Reformation, it centres on the question of the apostolic succession in the episcopate. According to our Catholic understanding, both are constitutive for full church communion and, therefore, eucharistic fellowship depends on the solution of these questions. Institutions, and particularly institutions which are as ancient, venerable and traditional as those mentioned above, have their own momentum but also their own cumbersomeness. The way to an agreement, therefore, is not easy and is probably long.

What can we do? How should we proceed? In order to reach a consensus, neither public debate nor academic dialogue alone, however important and essential they may be, can be considered sufficient. In order to get matters moving again, an impetus is needed which is greater and stronger than human undertakings and academic debate can be by their very nature. In this critical situation we have to return to the very first impetus of the ecumenical movement. In the beginning the ecumenical movement was driven by a spiritual movement, by spiritual ecumenism, which is the power behind the 'Week of Prayer for Christian Unity' started mainly by the Abbé Paul Couturier, the grand apostle and pioneer of spiritual ecumenism.

With good reason the Second Vatican Council in its Decree on Ecumenism, *Unitatis redintegratio*, discerned in the ecumenical movement an impulse and work of the Holy Spirit (UR 1; 4). And with good reason the Council and the present pope call this spiritual ecumenism the heart of the ecumenical movement. For church unity cannot be achieved by human endeavour alone; the unity of the Church is the work and the gift of God's Holy Spirit. Only a renewed Pentecost, a renewed outpouring of the Holy Spirit, can bestow on us the unity of all disciples of Christ for which Jesus prayed on the eve of his death on the cross: 'That all may be one' (John 17.21). Ecumenical work, therefore, is a spiritual task and can be nothing other than participation in the High Priestly Prayer of Jesus. Spiritual ecumenism is thus the heart of ecumenism. This means prayer, especially common ecumenical prayer, for the unity of Christians, for personal conversion and individual renewal, for repentance and the striving for personal sanctification (UR 5-8).

To many Christians this seems to be an alibi. In some ways, however, such a 'programme' corresponds to the present state of the ecumenical dialogue. The schisms of the eleventh and sixteenth centuries did not occur only because of doctrinal questions. The question of truth interacted with many non-theological factors and different experiences, which led to mutual alienation and consequently to misunderstandings and different doctrinal positions as well.

Eastern and Western Christianity did not break apart at a certain point in history; there was a long process of mutual alienation. Even today, when we meet our Orthodox brothers and sisters, despite our extensive common heritage – our almost full communion in the same faith, as Pope Paul VI observed – we still sense a deep, historically conditioned difference in culture and mentality, which sometimes creates serious difficulties for dialogue. The Oriental churches are basically sceptical about the conceptual theology which has developed in the West since medieval scholasticism, particularly in modern times. For them, it is the doxological and apophatic theology and its underlying liturgical and mystical experience which are important.

In discussions with the churches of the Reformation we have touched upon the existential dimension of their theology in the doctrine of justification. The churches of the Reformation are not so much concerned with a doctrine of justification as with the existential significance of the message of justification. The message of justification is in some ways the subjective side of christology; it deals with what Jesus Christ means for me (*pro me*) and for us (*pro nobis*). The difficulty which many Christians have with the doctrine of justification and the fundamental consensus reached about it is that they can no longer experience and comprehend the profound shock of Luther's existential experience of the burden of sin, the threat of God's judgement and the liberation of the message of justification. Therefore the doctrine of justification will remain meaningless for them, and the disputes around it pure theological bickering, unless it can be rendered accessible again through an existential experience.

Finally, the special emphasis of spiritual ecumenism corresponds to our present intellectual milieu which, on the one hand, is influenced by post-modern relativism and scepticism and on the other also longs for spiritual experience and a spiritual alternative to our modern and post-modern lifestyle, which many feel to be empty and void. After the breakdown of, and disillusionment with, modern ideologies and utopias, there is a distrust of any doctrinal position, yet at the same time a search for spiritual experience, vague and residual as it often may be. In this context, we will only be able to make progress in our missionary endeavour if we return to the spiritual roots of Christianity in general and of ecumenism in particular and search for a renewed ecumenical spirituality.

Spirituality

The yearning for ecumenical spirituality also entails both a danger and a trap. Spirituality is currently a much-used and ambiguous concept. Often it has become a mere slogan. Sometimes spirituality is understood in a merely emotional sense as an escape from, and a substitute for, an objective confession of faith. This temptation has emerged in some enthusiastic movements, both in the past and in the present. Such a tendency, which seeks a spirituality apart from the objective faith of the churches, sooner or later becomes empty and void; it cannot help the churches to overcome their differences and it becomes ecumenically useless.

In order to avoid such misunderstandings we should first try to clarify the term spirituality and the 'matter' behind it. Spirituality is a word borrowed from French Catholicism. Literally translated, it means 'piety'. But this does not cover the whole meaning of the term. The *Dictionary of Christian Spirituality* defines spirituality as the attitudes, faith convictions and practices which determine the life of men and women and help them to reach extra-perceptory realities. More simply, it can be understood as the Spirit-effected way Christians conduct themselves before God. The term therefore includes faith, the exercise of piety and the conduct of life; it signifies a lifestyle guided by the Spirit. The *Ecumenical Dictionary* states that 'spirituality is the development of the Christian existence under the guidance of the Holy Spirit'.

This shows clearly that the term spirituality has two components: the one 'from above', which is beyond human reach, is the working of God's Spirit; the other, 'from below', is represented by the human conditions and circumstances of the Christian existence, the context which it tries to form and permeate spiritually. A tension necessarily emerges between the one Holy Spirit who is at work everywhere and in all, and the multiplicity of human cultural and social realities and forms of life. The tension between unity and diversity, therefore, is rooted in the very nature of the concept of spirituality. Moreover, the term spirituality implies the tension and conflict between the Holy Spirit and the spirit of the world, as it is understood in the Bible.

We could even say that, to a certain extent, the different understandings of spirituality are a reason for the divisions within Christendom. Christians did not diverge primarily because of debate and controversy about different doctrines, but through the way they lived. Different forms of living the Christian faith had become estranged, alienated to the point where they could no longer understand each other, and this led to divisions. Cultural, social and political conditions and constellations played a role in this process. This does not exclude the fact that the divisions also touched upon the question of truth; but historically the question of truth is always embedded in manifold human conditions, in different concrete experiences of reality, and is sometimes hopelessly entangled with them.

This is obvious both in the schism between the East and the West in the eleventh century and in the division within the West as a consequence of the Reformation of the sixteenth century. The Eastern and Western ways of life had already increasingly diverged linguistically, culturally and politically during the first millennium. They regarded each other with suspicion and a lack of understanding. The differences were often attached to questions which appear to us today either as trivial or as a legitimate diversity within a possible unity: leavened or unleavened bread, different rites, different canonical discipline (including the wearing of beards by the clergy), different liturgical calendars and, in particular, different dates for Easter, as well as different theological approaches which led to the controversy concerning the *filioque*, etc. All of these remain and reflect different existential and ecclesial forms of expression and life which in each individual case, particularly for the Eastern Church, raise the question of their whole spiritual identity. It is for this reason that some churches are finding it so difficult, or even impossible, to move on the question – central for all Christian communities – of a common date for Easter. Even the question of the date of Easter is often a doctrinal problem for them.

The situation was similar in the sixteenth century. Luther could no longer reconcile his spiritual experience, centred on the experience of justification *sola fide* and *sola gratia*, with a spirituality which expressed itself in a piety of indulgences and the whole 'system' of priestly, sacramental and institutional mediation of grace as it developed in the late Middle Ages. This form of practice of indulgences was doubtless misused in many cases; but even a purified and theologically redefined practice, which millions of pilgrims to Rome followed with great spiritual seriousness during the Holy Year of 2000, was met not only with a complete lack of understanding by many Christians of the Reformation, even those who are ecumenically open, but also sometimes with an existential and emotional unease and polemical rejection. And, despite all the rapprochement achieved so far, this is also true for the specifically Catholic forms of eucharistic worship such as the celebration of Corpus Christi, or the practice of Marian piety. There are clearly still not only doctrinal but also emotional barriers.

Different spiritualities therefore inherently carry the danger of division. It is by no means true to say, as some naively suppose, that doctrine divides but spirituality unites. There are such things as intolerance and obstinacy due to what is actually pseudo-spirituality. Unfortunately, many of our controversies were driven by such self-opinionated apologetic and dogma, and instead of leading to mutual understanding, only increased and cemented the gulf.

Ecumenical spirituality wants to counteract all this. In common with all other ecumenical approaches, it no longer starts with what divides us but with what we have in common. It starts with common Christian experiences and – today more than in the past – with common Christian challenges in our more or less secularized and multicultural world. These common experiences also enable us to understand our differences better. For a deeper ecumenical understanding and agreement, a spiritual empathy is needed, an understanding of a different and initially strange Christian and ecclesial form of life, a sympathetic and intimate understanding from the inside, not just with the mind but also with the heart. Ecumenical spirituality means listening and opening ourselves to the demands of the Spirit who also speaks through different forms of piety; it means a readiness to rethink and convert, but also to bear the otherness of the other, which requires tolerance, patience, respect and, not least, goodwill and love which does not boast but rejoices in the truth (1 Cor. 13.4-6).

On the basis of my own experience, I can say that ecumenical dialogue only succeeds where all this works to some extent. In order to succeed, trust must be built and friendships established. Where this is not possible, everybody is sufficiently intelligent to find objections to opposing arguments. Such dialogues will never come to a conclusion; one could say that they have an eschatological dimension. We have to leave it to the dear Lord whether they will ultimately lead to heaven or to hell. But when there is friendship and common spiritual ground, the situation changes. This may not, and normally does not, lead to an immediate consensus, but it helps us to understand better what the other really means and why a different position has been reached. It helps us to accept the other in his or her otherness.

Ecumenical spirituality, however, is not a magic formula which will easily solve ecumenical questions and the present ecumenical crisis. Different spiritualities do not just carry within themselves the danger of divisions. Spiritualities, which are faith incarnate in the world and in culture, also carry the danger of syncretism, i.e. the mixing of the Christian faith with religious and cultural elements which do not fit but falsify the faith. Spiritualities can also be appropriated for political reasons and aims, giving the Christian faith not only a national but also a nationalistic, chauvinist or ideologically pseudo-spiritual character. In some forms of religious fundamentalism this danger is all too obvious. But there are also forms of so-called spirituality, even so-called ecumenical spirituality, which one can only call superficial, mere emotional late-bourgeois trivialization of the Christian faith.

Every spirituality must be questioned about the spirit behind it, whether it is the Holy Spirit or the spirit of the world. Spirituality demands the discernment of spirits. Thus spirituality is not an exclusively emotional affair devoid of the question of truth; rather, it helps, enables and even compels us to seek the truth. An appeal to spirituality, therefore, does not mean a painless escape from theology. In order to remain healthy, spirituality demands theological reflection and theological discernment.

The Holy Spirit

The great masters of the spiritual life have left us a rich treasure of experience for the discernment of spirits. Best-known are the rules for the discernment of spirits in the retreat manual of Ignatius of Loyola. It is worth rereading them carefully from an ecumenical point of view; much ecumenical benefit could be derived from them. But I would like to choose a different, more systematic and theological way and, in three biblical and systematic steps, work out the nature and activity of the Spirit and then, on the basis of a reflective theology of the Holy Spirit, raise the question of what could be an appropriate ecumenical spirituality

Universal effectiveness

The basic meaning of both the Hebrew and the Greek word for spirit (*ruach*, *pneuma*) is wind, breath, respiration and – since breathing is the sign of life – life, soul and finally, in a derivative form, the spirit as the principle of human life, the place of a person's intellectual perceptions and attitudes of will. However, it is not a principle immanent in the human person; spirit is the life given and empowered by God. God gives it and can withdraw it again. Thus it is God's spirit which is the creative life-force in all things. God's spirit gives to humans their aesthetic sense and acumen, their insight and wisdom. It is the *spiritus creator* which is at work in the whole reality of the creation. 'The spirit of the Lord, indeed, fills the whole world, and that which holds all things together knows every word that is said' (Wisd. 1.7, cf. 7.22-8.1).

An appropriate doctrine of the Holy Spirit therefore has to start from a universal perspective. It must not hide behind church walls or withdraw into its own inner and innermost self. Pneumatology is only made possible by listening to the hints, the expectations, the joys and failures of life and in marking the signs of the times which are found wherever new life breaks forth and develops, ferments and boils, but also where hopes for life are violently destroyed, strangled, gagged or murdered. Wherever true life appears, God's spirit is at work.

According to Augustine, the Spirit is 'the gravity of love, the upward pull which resists the downward gravity and brings everything to fulfilment in God' (*Conf.* XIII,7,8). The Second Vatican Council saw this universal effectiveness of the Spirit not only in human religions but also in human culture and human progress (GS 26; 28; 38; 41; 44).

Pope John Paul II has continued this thought in his missionary encyclical *Redemptoris missio*. He says: 'The Spirit, therefore, is a the very source of man's existential and religious questioning, a questioning which is occasioned not only by contingent situations but by the very structure of his being.' Then he continues: 'The Spirit's presence and activity affect not only individuals but also society and history, peoples, cultures and religions. Indeed, the Spirit is at the origin of the noble ideals and undertakings which benefit humanity on its journey through history' (28). For, as Thomas Aquinas teaches, all truth, wherever it comes from, comes from the Holy Spirit (*Summa theol.* I/II, 109,1).

An ecumenical spirituality which is shaped by the Bible therefore cannot be one-sidedly introverted or purely ecclesiocentric. As ecumenism is not an end in itself, ecumenical spirituality too must look beyond itself. Jesus prayed that all may be one so that the world may believe (John 17.21). Ecumenism in general and ecumenical spirituality in particular must enable the Church to bear common witness to the world and more convincing Christian witness in the world. Thus spiritual ecumenism must seek out life and serve life. It must be as much concerned with everyday human life and everyday experiences as it is with the great questions of contemporary human life and survival, questions of justice, peace and the preservation of creation, as well as the world's religions and human cultural achievements. According to a principle deriving from the late Middle Ages and the thought of Ignatius of Loyola, God is to be found in all things. In this principle lies the legitimate concern of secular ecumenism, of ecumenical co-operation between Christians on social and environmental issues, etc. However, in order to preserve its own identity and not become purely secularist, such secular ecumenism must be inspired, nourished and directed by the two other criteria for the discernment of the spirits.

Christological basis
In the Bible the Spirit is not only God's creative power but also God's power over history. It speaks through the prophets and is promised as the messianic spirit (Is. 11.2; 42.1). It is the power of the new creation which turns the desert into a paradise and creates a place of justice and righteousness (Is. 42.15f.). 'Not by might and not by power, but by my spirit, says the Lord of hosts' (Zech. 4.6). Thus the waiting and groaning creation leads to the freedom of the children of God (Rom. 8.19f.).

The New Testament announces the coming of the kingdom of freedom in Jesus Christ. He is the creature of the Spirit (Luke 1.35; Matt. 1.18, 20); at his baptism the Spirit descends on him (Mark 1.9-11). The whole of his work on earth is under the sign of the Spirit (Luke 4.14; 18; 10.21; 11.20). The Spirit rests upon him, so that he can preach good news to the poor and proclaim release to the captives, recovery of sight to the blind and liberty for those who are oppressed (Luke 4.18). His resurrection happens in the power of the Spirit (Rom. 1.3), and in the power of the Spirit he is now present in the Church and in the world. 'The Lord is the spirit' (2 Cor. 3.17).

The soteriological activity of the Spirit finds its eschatological fulfilment in Jesus Christ, in his earthly life and his activity as the risen Lord. Therefore, Paul understands the Spirit to be the Spirit of Christ (Rom. 8.9; Phil. 1.19), the Spirit of the Lord (2 Cor. 3.17) and the Spirit of the Son (Gal. 4.6). The confession of Jesus Christ is therefore the essential criterion for the discernment of spirits. 'No one speaking by the Spirit of God ever says: "Jesus be cursed", and no one can say "Jesus is Lord" except by the Holy Spirit' (1 Cor. 12.3).

This is the essential christological criterion for an ecumenical spirituality. It counteracts the danger of spiritual relativism and syncretism, which tend to compare the spiritual experiences of the different religions in order to mix them up or choose eclectically from them. It safeguards the uniqueness and universality of the salvific significance of Jesus Christ. It is opposed to the unrealistic temptation to do without the christological mediation and claim direct access to God. It reminds us that 'No one has ever seen God. It is God the only Son, who is close to the Father's heart, who has made him known' (John 1.18).

An ecumenical spirituality, therefore, will primarily be a biblical spirituality, and will express itself in the common reading and study of the Bible, which for all Christians is the fundamental common witness of God's salvation in history fulfilled in Jesus Christ. It will always ponder the biblical accounts of the coming of Jesus, his liberating message and his freeing and healing acts, his service for others, his kenosis unto death, the whole of his person and his work, and use them as its criteria. In essence it is a biblical spirituality and, as the Pope said in his apostolic letter *Novo millennio ineunte* (2001), it always seeks the face of Christ. The ecumenical movement too means a *'ripartire da Cristo'*, a new start from Christ. The confession of Christ's uniqueness and universal salvific significance will keep the Christian faith from relativism and syncretism in its encounter with other religions, but also from arrogance. Discipleship of Jesus shows itself in modesty and humility, and in what Paul calls the fruits of the spirit: love, joy, peace, patience, kindness, goodness, faithfulness, gentleness, self-control (Gal. 5.22).

Jesus Christ is present through word and sacrament. Ecumenical spirituality therefore will also be a sacramental spirituality. It is based on our common baptism, by which we are already, through the one Spirit, members in the one body of Christ and live in a profound spiritual communion (1 Cor. 12.13; Gal. 3.28). By baptism we participate in the death and resurrection of Christ (Rom. 6.3-5), we are as new creatures (2 Cor. 5.17; Gal. 6.15), born anew into hope (1 Pet. 1.3), called to the permanent spiritual renewal of our lives, to a life not according to the spirit of the world but according to the Spirit of Jesus Christ. Renewal of our baptismal vows and liturgical commemoration of baptism is therefore a basic element of ecumenical spirituality.

Baptism is oriented towards eucharistic sharing. In the one eucharistic bread we become one ecclesial body (1 Cor. 10.17). This participation withstands all divisions (1 Cor. 11.17-22). It is therefore a deep pain for all who are engaged in the ecumenical movement that normally they cannot share at the Lord's table. This suffering of so many Christians must be a further impulse for all who are responsible for promoting Christian unity. This does not mean that in the meantime nothing can be done. It is one of the positive achievements of the ecumenical movement that a rapprochement in doctrinal issues on the eucharist and an intense exchange of eucharistic experiences and liturgical forms have taken place. This is not a small thing, for apart from the issue of the papacy, the historical controversies have been harshest concerning the mass, which the Reformers called an idolatry.

It would, however, be a wrong and cheap solution simply to forget these controversies, abolish them and fall instead into a pure ignorance and trivialization of the eucharistic mystery. The eucharist is a mystery of faith. Thus we can reach a consensus only by an exchange of faith lived out in a deep eucharistic spirituality. Much has been achieved in this respect, especially in ecumenical communities. Even now we can already share in spiritual communion when we attend a eucharistic celebration in a church or church community not in full communion with our own church. In particular situations of spiritual urgency and authentic deep desire, we are – as Pope John Paul II stated – able to welcome other Christians (UUS 46; *Ecclesia de Eucharistia* 46).

Finally, like Jesus, we can and may, in the Spirit, say 'Abba, Father' to God (Rom. 8.15; 26f.; Gal. 4.6). An ecumenical spirituality therefore is a spirituality of prayer, centring on the Week of Prayer for Christian Unity celebrated in January or in the week before Pentecost. Such prayer will always gather people, in the same way as Mary and the apostles gathered, to pray for the coming of the Spirit which will unite the peoples in one language, and to pray for a renewed Pentecost (Acts 1.13f.). We join Jesus in his prayer on the eve of his death, 'That all may be one' (John 17.21). Like Jesus himself, an ecumenical spirituality lives by prayer and, like Jesus on the cross, suffers and endures in prayer the experience of being forsaken by the Spirit and by God (Mark 15.34), the experience of our ecumenical difficulties and disappointments, our ecumenical desert experiences.

The life of the Church

Besides the Christological criterion there was also for Paul an ecclesiological criterion. Paul links the Spirit with the building-up of the congregation and service in the church. The Spirit is given for the general good; the different gifts of the Spirit therefore have to serve each other (1 Cor. 12.4-30). The Spirit is not a spirit of disorder but a spirit of peace (1 Cor. 14.33). The Spirit is given to all believers and to the Church as a whole. The Church as a whole is the temple of the Spirit (1 Cor. 3.16-17; 2 Cor. 2.16; Eph. 2.21), built up by all the faithful as living stones (1 Pet. 2.5). Thus the action of the Spirit can neither be confined to the institutions of the Church, nor be claimed as their monopoly; neither can the Spirit or the charisma be seen as separate from the sacramental structure and ministries of the Church, which are also gifts of the Spirit. The Spirit acts not through opposition but in togetherness and in working for each other. He is the enemy of all party business and all forming of factions. The highest gift of the Spirit is love, without which all other charisms are worth nothing. 'Love is not jealous and does not boast, is not arrogant or rude ... it bears all things and endures all things' (1 Cor. 13.4, 7).

This aspect in particular has been developed within the theological tradition. According to Irenaeus of Lyons, the Church is 'the vessel into which the Spirit has poured faith in its youthful freshness, and where it keeps it' ... 'where there is Church, there is also the Spirit of God; where there is the Spirit of God, there is the Church and all grace' (*Adv. haer.* III,24,1). And Hippolytus says: 'Festinet autem et ad ecclesiam ubi floret spiritus' (*Trad. Apost.* 31; 35). According to the whole of the Western tradition, mainly influenced by Augustine, the Spirit is the love between the Father and the Son, at the same time the innermost and the outermost part of God, because in him and through him God's love has been poured into our hearts. Thus the Spirit is the principle of the life of the Church; the Spirit's function in the Church can be compared with the function of the soul in the human body (LG 7).

Ecumenical spirituality therefore is ecclesial, i.e. community spirituality. The ecumenical movement did not start from an ecclesiological and dogmatic relativism and liberalism; on the contrary, it started and was supported and accompanied by a 'ressourcement', a return to the very sources of church life, the witness of the Bible, the liturgy, the fathers. So ecumenical spirituality will strive for the 'sentire ecclesiam', will seek a deeper understanding and awareness of the nature, tradition and especially the liturgy of the Church, and try to make the objective reality of the Church its own subjective reality. It lives by the witness and celebration of the liturgy.

Normally, ecumenical spirituality is cultivated in ecumenical groups and gatherings. However, these groups should not separate themselves from the larger community of the Church. They have their particular role within the Church and for the Church. Ecumenical spirituality suffers from the wounds caused by the divisions of Church, from which it bleeds. Thus it is the critical conscience of the Church, reminding her not to withdraw into a confessional self-sufficiency, but rather to undertake courageously all possible and responsible steps to promote Christian unity through an 'exchange of gifts', taking and using the riches of other traditions and thus seeking greater ecumenical unity in order to achieve the whole concrete fullness of catholicity. An ecumenical spirituality will therefore be an examination of conscience in the existing reality of the Church, always thinking ahead prophetically. However, it will not run away from reality, but labour patiently and persistently to find consensus. It will attempt to keep the unity of the Spirit (Eph. 4.3).

The prophetic role also has a positive and constructive aspect. Those groups which live an ecumenical spirituality of communion anticipate a church lifestyle which should become the paradigm for the whole Church. Pope John Paul described such a spirituality of communion as the recognition of the other in his or her otherness.

A spirituality of communion means an ability to think of our brothers and sisters in faith within the profound unity of the Mystical Body, and therefore as 'those who are a part of me'. This makes us able to share their joys and sufferings, to sense their desires and attend to their needs, to offer them deep and genuine friendship. A spirituality of communion implies also the ability to see what is positive in others, to welcome it and prize it as a gift from God: not only as a gift for the brother or sister who has received it directly, but also as a 'gift for me'. A spirituality of communion means, finally, to know how to 'make room' for our brothers and sisters, bearing 'each other's burdens' (Gal. 6.2) and resisting the selfish temptations which constantly beset us and provoke competition, careerism, distrust and jealousy. Let us have no illusions: unless we follow this spiritual path, external structures of communion will serve very little purpose. They would become mechanisms without a soul, 'masks' of communion rather than its means of expression and growth. (*Novo millennio ineunte* 43)

Without such a spirituality of communion, institutional communion becomes a mere machine without a soul. But with such a spirituality of communion the very goal of the ecumenical movement is anticipated. It will not be a uniform church, but a unity within legitimate diversity, a unity according to the model of the Trinity: one God in three persons, existing in an intimate exchange of love.

Ecumenical Dialogue

The three criteria for the discernment of the spirits are very wide. They are not limiting, they open up. They are upheld by the Spirit of love which drives out fear (1 John 4.18) and overcomes the concern for one's own identity which tends to block, confine and smother the ecumenical movement. These three criteria make for an ecumenical dynamism and a dynamic ecumenical spirituality.

It is true that, like every Christian spirituality, ecumenical spirituality is anchored in the revelation which has come through Jesus Christ once and for all (Heb. 9.28), which is its ground and measure. But what kind of criterion is this? It is by no means an inflexible measuring-stick. It is the life and death of a person in whom, according to the witness of Holy Scripture, the fullness of the Godhead dwells (Col. 2.9), so that the letter to the Ephesians can speak about the unfathomable richness of Christ (Eph. 3.8). No human concept, no dogma can fathom these riches. All our knowledge is partial (1 Cor. 13.9); the dogmas of the Church are true because they point with absolute certainty beyond themselves to the unfathomable mystery of God.

The aim of dogmatic statements is not the stated formula itself but God's truth to which it points (*Summa theol.* II/II, 1,2 ad 2). According to an apt scholastic wording, articles of faith are a 'perceptio divinae veritatis tendens in ipsam' (*Summa theol.* II/II, 1,6). Thus, the Church is the people of God, on the way, in the faithful assurance and absolute certainty that they are being held in the truth, yet nevertheless recognizing that they are also on the way, being led ever more deeply into the truth which has been revealed once for all. The Second Vatican Council says that 'through the centuries the Church has constantly been striving for the fullness of divine truth' (DV 8).

This induction into an ever greater and deeper truth is the work of the Holy Spirit; he is to lead us into the whole truth (John 16.13). The Spirit does this in various ways; according to the Council, one of the ways is spiritual experience, including the ecumenical spiritual experience. The ecumenical dialogue is not only an exchange of ideas but an exchange of spiritual gifts and spiritual experiences (UUS 28). Every Christian can do this, in his or her place and manner, for everyone is an expert in his or her own way, i.e. somebody who has had an experience and wants to pass it on. Similar to what Paul said about every gathering of the congregation, it is true to say about the ecumenical dialogue that 'when you meet, each of you contributes' (1 Cor. 14.26).

Ecumenical dialogue absolutely does not mean abandoning one's own identity in favour of an ecumenical 'hotch-potch'. It is a profound misunderstanding to see it as fostering doctrinal relativism. The aim is not to find the lowest common denominator. Ecumenical dialogue does not aim at spiritual impoverishment but at mutual spiritual enrichment. In ecumenical dialogue we discover the truth of the other as our own truth. So through the ecumenical dialogue the Spirit leads us into the whole truth; he heals the wounds of our divisions and endows us with full catholicity.

During recent decades we Catholics have learnt a lot from the experiences of our Protestant brothers and sisters about the significance of the word of God, about Holy Scripture and its exegesis; in turn, they are learning from our sacramental reality of signs and from our way of celebrating the liturgy. In our relations with the Oriental churches we can learn from their spiritual wealth and their respect for the mysterious; in return, we can share our pastoral experience and our experience in dealing with the modern world. In the words of Pope John II, which have practically become a slogan nowadays, the Church can learn again to breathe with both lungs.

Ecumenical dialogue does not aim to convert others to our side. Naturally, individual conversions cannot and must not be excluded; one has to treat them with great respect for the underlying decisions of conscience. However – and this is true for individual conversions as well – it is not a question of conversion to another church but of conversion of all to the full truth of Jesus Christ. In this sense, there is no ecumenism without conversion and church renewal (UR 7), and such conversion is not an isolated act once for all but a continuing, never-ending process.

The ecumenical movement calls us to this conversion. It leads to the examination of conscience and cannot be separated from personal conversion and the desire for church reform (UUS 16; 24f., 83f.). When we move closer to Jesus Christ through the exchange of our different confessional experiences and our different approaches, and grow into the full stature of Jesus Christ (Eph. 4.13), we become one in Jesus Christ. He is our unity. In him we can also realize historically the whole fullness of catholicity after overcoming our divisions.

If we ask what this unity in fullness will look like, the answer does not lie in a comprehensive, fully differentiated and cleverly devised system; nor does it involve a more comprehensively speculative or more comprehensively institutional system in which differences are abolished in ways similar to Hegel's dialectics. In this regard, dialogue differs fundamentally from dialectics.

Dialogue strives for reconciliation. Reconciliation does not abolish the different position of the partner; nor does it take over the partner or absorb him. On the contrary, reconciliation recognizes the partner in his or her otherness. Becoming one in love means that the identity of the other is not abolished or absorbed but rather confirmed and fulfilled.

The experience of unity in love is the model for Christian and church unity. Ultimately, it is grounded in the trinitarian love between Father, Son and Holy Spirit. This is the archetype of church unity; the unity of the Church is like an icon of the Trinity (LG 4, UR 3).

In line with the thought of Johann Adam Möhler, we therefore have to distinguish between tensions based on legitimate differences, which belong to the richness of catholicity, and contradictions which isolate one element of truth from the whole and absolutize it so that it becomes a *hairesis*, i.e. an isolated selection, a narrow position which breaks away from the richness of the Gospel and thus stands in contradiction to the fullness of catholicity. It is therefore the aim of ecumenical dialogue to remove such misunderstandings and divisive differences and reconcile them again, i.e. reintegrate them into the whole of the Gospel.

There can be no unity as long as any given church maintains that the accepted and binding truth of another church is contrary to the Gospel. Yet recognizing the other in his/her otherness does not entail a boundless pluralism or a dogmatic indifferentism. Not at all. On the contrary, it implies that we recognize the other in his or her otherness, and that we recognize – in different forms and formulas – the same truth, the truth that is so rich that it cannot be fully expressed in one formula, but only with complementary formulae. Thus abolishing divisive differences will not eventually leave us with a system of unified concepts and formulae. Even 'normal' human communication does not work in such a rational way, although ultimately it always presupposes an act of trust, that both mean what they say and that, even if occasionally they use different words, they mean the same thing. Even strictly scientific thought has ultimately to be content with complementary models like waves and corpuscles.

The unity of the Church cannot be some abstract system that, in a lucky hour, will be discovered and agreed upon in a theological dialogue. There is no doubt that theological agreement is necessary. But in the end unity can only be understood and accepted as a spiritual experience, an experience that, naturally, cannot be only individual but must have ecclesial character. It will be an act of trust in the fact that the other, with different forms and formulae, different images, symbols and concepts, means and believes the same mystery of faith that we retain in our tradition.

According to theological teaching, such a consensus is the work and sign of the Holy Spirit (LG 12). Consensus therefore is declared by a spiritual judgement of the Church. It does not just drop from the sky. It has to be prepared by many preliminary consensual processes at different levels of the life of the Church. Through them, and through the disputes they may instigate, the Spirit of God prepares the unity of Christians. It is not up to us to set deadlines; the Spirit alone determines the time.

Ecumenism was from its very beginning a spiritual phenomenon. Where ecumenical consensus has been possible, it has always been experienced as a spiritual gift. A future consensus of the universal Church, for which we hope, can only be bestowed as a renewed Pentecost experience. Opening the Second Vatican Council, with its clear ecumenical perspective, Pope John XXIII spoke about such a new Pentecost. To think that the Spirit would not bring to an end and to fulfilment the work he initiated, would be pusillanimity. Ecumenism needs magnanimity and hope. I am convinced that, as long as we do all we can, God's Spirit will one day give us this renewed Pentecost.

10

The Church and Contemporary Pluralism

A New Situation for the Church

It is often said that our society is a free and pluralistic one, and we are all happy to be living in such a free and pluralistic society in which we can determine and order our life without constraint. In such a society, religion, ideology and public opinion are not imposed by an authoritarian state or an almighty state party; on the contrary, different religious, denominational and political viewpoints, diverse lifestyles and attitudes coexist and various associations, parties, interest groups and freely chosen initiatives compete with each other. The churches represent but one feature of this pluralistic society.

Initially this was a new situation for the churches. Christianity had been a state religion from the time of the emperors Constantine and Theodosius in the fourth century. Although society in the Middle Ages was much more multifarious than is usually thought, it was homogeneous in its main religious and moral principles. Any deviation from the Church and her faith was considered tantamount to questioning the unity of the empire. The sixteenth-century Reformation represented no fundamental change to this situation; the principle '*Cuius regio eius religio*' remained valid. The monarch decided on the confessional affiliation of his people; those who either did not want to obey or – compelled by conscience – could not obey were forced to emigrate. From this perspective, there was no difference between Catholic and Protestant states: in Catholic states, life was difficult for Protestants, just as it was for Catholics in Protestant states.

The radical change in this situation traces its origins to the devastations of the wars of religion in Europe in the sixteenth century, where religion was no longer a uniting bond but the very reason for conflict. The only foundation left for a new order of peace was for the Christian religion to renounce its universal claim in the sphere of public life. It became a partial system, increasingly cast aside from the public sphere and confined to the private arena. This is the essence of modern secularization, which does not repudiate religion as such, but for the sake of peace seeks to restrict it to private life and extricate it from the public domain.

The Church – and I will talk mainly about the Catholic Church – had problems for a long time with the modern principle of freedom and even more so with pluralism. In the nineteenth century the liberal understanding of freedom of conscience and religious freedom was officially condemned. It was only with the Second Vatican Council (1962–65) that a new effort was made to come to terms with the new situation.

An Opening through the Second Vatican Council

The Second Vatican Council tried to overcome the previous defensive attitude towards modernity, and set itself the task of defining the Church *in* the modern world. Indeed, the Pastoral Constitution is entitled 'The Church in the Modern World'. In many respects, it brought about a revision – not of dogmas, but of practical and pastoral attitudes towards the modern world.

The open-mindedness of that document is already expressed in its often quoted first sentence: 'The joy and hope, the grief and anguish of the men of our time, especially of those who are poor or afflicted in any way, are the joy and hope, the grief and anguish of the followers of Christ as well' (GS 1). This sentence delineates an open disposition in solidarity with the modern world. The heading of the Pastoral Constitution expresses this change; it does not say: The Church *and* the Modern World, but: The Church *in* the Modern World.

Nevertheless, the concept and aim of pluralism still play a subordinate role within the Constitution. The emphasis is not on the problem of pluralism but on the deep and rapid changes in the modern world, the related growth crisis and uncertainties of many people, and the transition from a rather static order to a more dynamic and evolutionary understanding of reality (GS 4f.).

When addressing the problem of pluralism, the very first consideration taken up in debate on this issue concerned a pluralism which is not only possible but even desirable within the Church: plurality in liturgy, forms of piety, theology and local churches. Moreover, the Council took into consideration the pluralism of separate churches and ecclesial communities. This awareness of the pluralism within the Church and among the churches has since then radically changed the shape of Catholicism; today, it is no longer the monolithic reality that it was perceived to be in the past. Those who visit churches in Latin America, Africa or Asia have some idea of how varied life in the one Catholic Church is today. Ecumenical dialogue finds its place within the wide range of experience in the Church.

Two passages in the conciliar document also speak about pluralism within society. Firstly, in relation to education, it argues for an independent and free school system as opposed to the one envisaged by an ideologically inspired state (GS 6f.). This argument needs to be understood against the historical background of the sixties and in the context of the Cold War, when the Church was confronted with a totalitarian, atheistic system of education. The second mention is of cultural pluralism in general. The Council speaks of a pluriformity of cultures, because there is not only one culture, but various cultures.

> For different styles of living and different scales of values originate in different ways of using things, of working and self-expression, of practising religion and of behaviour, of establishing laws and juridical institutions, of developing science and the arts of cultivating beauty. Thus the heritage of its institutions forms the patrimony proper to each human community. (GS 53)

The Second Vatican Council declared in detail its position on religious pluralism in the 'Declaration on the Relation of the Church to Non-Christian Religions' (*Nostra aetate*, NA). The Council stated that the Church rejects nothing of what is true and holy in these religions. Rather, she speaks about them with respect and seeks dialogue and co-operation with them (NA 2). This is particularly the case for relations with Judaism, which throughout history had often been marked by misunderstandings, prejudices and polemics, even persecution. Against this background of atrocities and the tragedy of the Holocaust, the Declaration

denounced all forms and manifestations of anti-Semitism, out-
bursts of hatred, and persecution, and at the same time it recalled
the Jewish heritage of Christianity (NA 4). Since then, interreligious dialogue, especially the dialogue with Judaism, has
become a defining characteristic of the life of the Church.

In fact, since the Second Vatican Council dialogue has become a
fundamental expression and feature of Catholicism. There are
different dimensions of dialogue. On the one hand, there is an
internal dialogue within the Church herself, while on the other
there is an external dialogue with the other churches and church
communities, with other religions, and also with modern culture,
arts and science, politics and the media. This dialogue is not just an
external method, or even a strategy, of ecclesial politics; dialogue
consists not only of sophisticated reflection and an exchange of
ideas, but is, rather, an expression of the dialogical structure of
human existence and the perception of truth. Pope John Paul II
describes dialogue as 'an indispensable step along the path towards
human self-realization, the self-realization both of each individual
and of every human community' (UUS 28). As human beings, we
not only undertake dialogue, we are dialogue, we are by nature
dialogical beings. This is even more true for our Christian
existence, for biblical revelation is God's dialogue with human
beings (DV 2).

The Intensification of the Pluralist Situation

The Second Vatican Council undoubtedly set a new tone and
ushered in new emphases and perspectives that have changed the
historic shape of the Church in the modern world. Yet, when we
read the conciliar texts today, almost 40 years after the conclusion
of the Council, we become aware that the situation has again
changed and become considerably more complex.

In the Council's declarations, cultural pluralism is still understood as pluralism in terms of geographically separate cultures and
societies, existing alongside each other. However, cultural pluralism as it confronts us today more or less everywhere in the Western
world is often described by the catchwords 'multicultural society',
and is quite different. It now consists not of separated societies but
of different cultures, lifestyles, ethical value systems, religions and
confessions co-existing within any given society.

In Europe the new situation emerged after the forced displacement of populations in the wake of the Second World War. Christian denominations no longer lived in a state of regional separation, but found themselves living in the same communities; indeed, individually distinct Catholic or Protestant milieus are found only in pockets. The migration movements that have since taken place have marked a more intensive presence of non-Christian religions in Europe; Islam in particular, with its quite different culture, but also Asian religions are dispersed throughout the Western world. In the United States the situation has been shaped in the last decades by Hispanic immigration. The danger in these developments is the disintegration of previous cultural identities. The debate about immigration is therefore centred on the question of how much pluralism a society can bear.

However, it is not only immigration from outside which is the problem, but the inner processes in our Western civilization. The common values and shared concepts of Western societies have become weaker. Their reserves have shrunk. The Christian values and ethical norms which were generally accepted have to a large extent lost their function as leading ideas, as well as their influence and importance in society. The clearest sign of the upheaval is the breakdown of what had been up to now the generally accepted roles of the sexes, the emergence of different understandings of the family and diversified opinions on abortion, euthanasia, divorce, etc. The processes of individualization have increased. The range and diversity of possibilities for people to determine and shape their own life and lifestyle are quite unparalleled in history; there is a considerable increase of individual freedom, although the outcome of this new situation for individuals is more often interrupted and broken biographies than creative innovation.

Such highly complex societies are very demanding in terms of cohesion, community life and social stability; in fact, modern pluralist societies are extremely fragile and imperilled entities. They involve, in particular for young people, considerable orientation problems and extended phases of maturation. But the problem affects us all. Each of us lives in different worlds: family, professional, economic and political worlds, all with different regulatory systems. This leads to conflicts of roles and norms between the standards of family, professional and economic life and those of the Church. So the conflict between the Church and societal standards involves not only abstract institutions but concrete people, committed and practising Christians who, as lawyers, judges, doctors and so on, are also subject to different secular norms. Pluralism cuts across our own personal existence.

Pluralism as a Philosophical Programme

From a contemporary philosophical point of view, the idea of pluralism has been taken up by so-called post-modern philosophy. The starting point is the perception that the present enormous body of scientific knowledge can no longer be totally comprehended by any one person. A universal genius able to embrace everything is no longer possible. For post-modern philosophy, the bewildering extent of human knowledge is no longer held together by a narrative framework, a leading idea or a general faith conviction. On the contrary, universal systems, which reached their high point with Hegel's idealism in the nineteenth century, are now burdened with the judgement of having provided the ideological background for the totalitarian systems of the twentieth century.

These theories raise the empirical and existent pluralism to the rank of a fundamental pluralistic programme. Truth is now only understood in terms of the pluralism of truths; truth exists only in the plurality of truths. 'The' truth, even if it is testified in non-violent ways and through open dialogue, is considered to be a totalitarian claim. Often it is considered as a product of the European Enlightenment, and consequently as disguised eurocentrism and an expression of the claim of Western hegemony. Even universal human rights founded on the dignity of all human beings, which for a long time had rightly been considered as progress in the history of freedom, are challenged as a Western invention. Post-modern thinkers criticize one-sided rational thinking based on clarity and precision, which seeks to understand everything within an all-embracing unity. Opposed to it is an aesthetically imaginative and colourful symbolic thinking. Mythological thinking has once again become fashionable.

The prophet of post-modernism is Friedrich Nietzsche and his nihilism. Nihilist belief, he writes, holds that 'there is no truth' (Schlechta edition, vol. 3, 675); it is 'unbelief in the metaphysic world' (ibid. 678). Truth is an appraisal, a surmise, a prejudice, a fiction, an illusion, the will for power. 'Truths are illusions, of which one has forgotten that they are illusions' (ibid. 315).

The Pluralist Religion Theory

This all-relativizing, sceptical and nihilistic position calls into question all religious communities and especially the Church. Ideological pluralism seems to me to be currently the real and fundamental challenge for the Church, and – I am convinced – the fundamental challenge in a wider sense as well. In the meantime, ideological pluralism has also manifested itself within theology (J. Hick; P. Knitter; L. Swidler and others). According to a number of theologians upholding the pluralist religion theory, our cognition can only recognize the 'phainomenon' of things, not the 'nooumenon'; that is, we perceive only what things are to us, not what they are truly and inherently.

Thus we perceive only what God means to us. We cannot grasp God's nature in itself. The mystery of the divine appears in multiple forms of revelation and in different religions. In the final analysis, the divine mystery remains forever the great unknowable 'behind' all religions. From this perspective, it is impossible to examine the many and multifarious images and representations of God in terms of their objective truth. Every religion is relative; no religion can claim to possess the final and full word when it comes to God. All – including Christianity – have a provisional character. There can be only representations, concepts, images, ideal forms of the divine that direct us towards the transcendent reality, but there cannot be a Christian claim to absoluteness, where the transcendent reality manifests itself. Jesus Christ is relativized as a religious genius through whom human beings become aware of their divine sonship.

The pluralist religion theory that emerged from the basic equality among the religions does not, however, imply that all religions would actually have the same value and be recognized in their diversity without distinction. That sort of superficial relativism is quite remote, for religions are notorious for offering not only important and deep-seated insights, but also destructive elements such as superstition and inhuman practices which force us to make distinctions.

For the proponents of the pluralist religion theory, the criterion for this distinction and evaluation is not theoretical but ethical and practical. The decisive criterion is the respective capacity of a particular religion to integrate people and various areas of human life into a process that leads from 'self-centredness' to 'reality centredness', with preference being given to that religion which corresponds most closely to, and furthers most adequately, the dignity of the human being.

This can certainly be *one* criterion; but it cannot be the only or the decisive one. Moreover, any practical judgement about what is truly human will differ according to what I consider to be human, and this is not only a practical but also a theoretical question, a question of truth. The question about the truthfulness of reality cannot therefore be avoided. Furthermore, religious statements can have a sense and a meaning for me only if God really 'is'. Only if he 'is' is the talk about God more than an empty consolation or a vain promise; only if he 'is' can he effectively mean something to me.

If the truth question is not raised, we then have a purely aesthetic understanding of the world, in which things are judged according to subjective experience or subjective decision for what seems to correspond best to one's own idea of happiness. Personal taste becomes the decisive criterion. You help yourself at the à la carte market of possibilities and put together your own religion with set pieces from various religions. Thus many combine Eastern reincarnation concepts with the Christian faith, although they are really not compatible.

A Critique of Pluralism

The difficulties, problems, conflicts and dangers inherent in a pluralistic situation make the emergence of a critique of pluralism understandable. This critique comes not only from theology but also from sociology and philosophy. There is a right-wing and conservative critique of pluralism as well as its left-wing and so-called progressive counterpart.

The left-wing critic calls attention to the fact that, under the guise of pluralism, pressure is exerted, mainly by the media, towards adaptation and standardization of certain so-called modern forms of behaviour and opinions; through market globalization this leads to the monopoly of new all-dominating standards of capitalism, exclusively animated by profit motives. But the globalization of the market economy is not the only problem. There also exists the soft tyranny of political correctness and, in the churches, a theological correctness which in turn establishes new taboos. Infringements against these new taboos are punished by public opinion, or at least by its published voice. Pluralistic tolerance can be very intolerant and when it becomes an ideology it turns into its opposite.

The right-wing critic fears the abyss of anarchy and the decay of traditional common values and sometimes tends towards the no less dangerous recommendation of an authoritarian state or a new kind of chauvinistic nationalism, xenophobia, religious fanaticism. Unfortunately this critic also sometimes tends towards a new confessionalism, marked by a withdrawal into a given form of confession and opposition to the ecumenical approaches of the last decades.

Against an indifferent pluralism in the last decade the question of identity has been reawakened in all religions, cultures and denominations: Who are we? Who am I? This question is legitimate, and indeed constitutive for one's personal as well as communal identity. Nobody wants to perish in an anonymous, faceless, globally uniform civilization. So the question of identity is important and constitutive. But badly understood it can lead to new delimitations and can result in fundamentalism. Thus the pluralistic coexistence of religions, each commanding an absolute claim on truth, has considerable explosive potential, leading ultimately to the 'clash of civilizations' sometimes prognosticated (S. P. Huntington).

Our pluralistic situation is therefore not as harmless as it may seem. Situations can arise, and they do, where dialogue comes to an end. For no dialogue is possible when the other does not want it, or is incapable of it, or, in the extreme, deliberately seeks violent conflict. One must realistically take such antagonistic situations into account.

For Christians these circumstances are not such a new lesson. There have been and continue to be situations of persecution against Christians. There are aggressive sects with whom dialogue is just impossible. If we turn to the Bible we learn that until the end of time in this world Christians will continue to face the challenge of contradiction and conflict. For the reality is that we do not live in a harmonious pluralistic context but in a conflictual pluralistic world where courage and bravery are necessary, and where in extreme but always possible cases one's personal identity can be maintained only by martyrdom. So we come now to the theological points of view.

The Theological Challenge

Even for those who are only mildly familiar with the New Testament, the pluralist religion theory must obviously raise basic questions. It could not be said more clearly and distinctly: this theory may correspond to a currently widespread mentality, but it fundamentally calls into question the testimony of the Bible, and not only – as many might think – a church or even a specific Catholic dogma. The challenge is real not only for Catholic, but also for Orthodox and Protestant theology. Thus there is no way of ignoring this observation: within the mentality of ideological pluralism, religious pluralism is *the* challenge today for Christianity and for the Church.

From its very first page, the Bible affirms that God created human beings in his own image and likeness (Gen. 1.27). That means that every human being, irrespective of ethnic and cultural affiliation, irrespective also of his/her religion, possesses an unconditional, even unique, dignity. Therefore, fundamental human rights apply universally and to every individual person. In adhering to this universalism and the absolute that is present in every human person, Christians lay and defend the foundations of a universal order of peace in the world.

This universalism also applies to the salvific mission of the Church. Jesus has sent his disciples into the whole world, to all nations, to all people (Matt. 28.19; Mark 16.15; Luke 24.27; Rev. 1.8). The mission of the Church is therefore universal. It is not linked to a particular people, or to a particular culture or language, or to a particular political or economic system. The Church is, so to speak, the oldest 'global player'. She transcends all ethnic, national and cultural differences and seeks to unite all peoples, languages and cultures, and indeed understands herself as a sign and instrument of peace among peoples, languages and cultures.

Next to universality is unity, even uniqueness, understood as oneness. The Bible bears witness to the *one and only* God (Deut.

6.4; Mark 12.29), who is the Father of all human beings, good and bad alike (Matt. 5.45). It confesses the *one* Lord Jesus Christ (1 Cor. 8.6; Eph. 4.5). In no other name is there salvation (Acts 4.12). He is the *one and only* mediator between God and humankind (1 Tim. 2.5). He is the *one* high priest who has redeemed us *once and for all* (Heb. 7.27). This message is entrusted to us *once and for all* (Jude 3). For that reason, there can be only *one* true Church; confessing the *una sancta ecclesia* is common to all churches. This common confession is the basis of the present ecumenical movement, the purpose of which is the restoration of full visible church unity.

Unity and universality are fundamental categories of the Bible which cannot be extracted from the biblical witness without destroying its roots and affecting its core. Those who profess that unity, if they are consistent with themselves, must sail against the wind of the spirit of the times – whether they want to or not. Experienced sailors know that this seems impossible only to beginners; they themselves confront it as a challenge and an art that offers joy and satisfaction. In fact, history has shown that it has not always been constructive for the Church to be just the spoiled child of the world in which she lived; she has always been strengthened through various challenges.

Fundamental Theological Reflection

We are certainly not advocating a return to a time before the Second Vatican Council, throwing the dialogical model overboard and falling back into the old apologetic and controversial theological track. There is no return to the nineteenth century with its opposition between the Church and modernism. After the 'razing of the bastions' (Hans Urs von Balthasar) a retreat into the ghetto is no longer possible. In the history of the Church too, if we want to move safely, we can only go forward and not backwards. The Church's presence in the world, as envisioned by the Second Vatican Council, remains a permanent task. The decisive guidelines on how to perform that task are outlined by the Council itself in its 'Declaration on Religious Freedom'. Indeed, the most passionate debate on the most forward-looking breakthrough took place on this issue.

Church doctrine until the Second Vatican Council was based on the principle that only truth, and not error, had the right to exist. From that perspective, the Church in the nineteenth century rejected religious freedom understood in the liberal sense. The Catholic state represented an ideal for many. Change was essentially brought about through a contribution from North American theology, especially by John Courtney Murray (d. 1967). North America was not and is still not burdened with the European ideological debate of the past; it has a liberal tradition of its own, which differs from the French Enlightenment. This new North American experience offered a major contribution to the Council and ultimately to the universal Church.

The main question concerned how to reconcile the claim for truth, which is essential for Christian faith, and the modern principle of freedom. The clearest answer and the best expression of the innovative insight are found in an intervention in the council hall by the then Archbishop of Krakow, Karol Wojtila. As a philosopher, he was familiar with modern thought and he tried to link it to Thomist philosophy. He explained that we possess the truth only in freedom. Though truth is not a mere subjective reality but something that is given to us, nevertheless it does not exist in itself, it exists – as Thomas Aquinas taught us – in human subjects. But, conversely, freedom does not exist in any and every attitude and is even the opposite of arbitrariness; freedom is oriented towards the truth. For truth liberates us from momentary emotions and interests, from rapidly changing fashions, from the pressure of public opinion; truth widens the horizon for freedom. Truth – as the fourth Gospel says – will set us free (John 8.32). Thus truth and freedom are correlated and presuppose each other.

The same can be explained and deepened by a reflection on the dialogical structure of human existence. As mentioned before, dialogue is constitutive for personal identity. Our personal identity emerges not as a lonely Robinson Crusoe on a remote island but only in relation and dialogue with others. But such a dialogue is possible only between partners who have their respective identities. Two indistinct fog-banks cannot experience an encounter, they become blurred into each other. Thus dialogical openness is quite different from lack of distinction; identity and dialogue are correlative. Through dialogue the human person is in search of the truth. Therefore, truth in love and love in truth are the intimate fulfilment of the human person.

Revelation corresponds to this search for truth and love. God speaks to us and addresses us like his friends; he reveals himself as love, and love as the ultimate truth about himself and about human existence. Love is the summary of all revelation and this implies that each and every human being is respected, accepted and loved by God. Christian faith therefore is not imposed; God wants the free 'Yes' of his creatures. Faith is a free gift of God as well as a free human response made possible by that gift; it is therefore a free act. God's truth sets us free.

The consequence of this is that the right of truth, rightly defended by the pre–conciliar position, presupposes at the same time the right of the subject, and actually constitutes it. The freedom to seek the truth, and to confess it once it has been recognized, is therefore inalienable from a Christian point of view; it is a fundamental human right. The Christian faith can thus affirm its unconditional and universal claim to truth only in so far as it acknowledges and defends the freedom of all. This conciliar view has become the basis of the human rights policy of the current pontificate; it has – as expressed by one who should know, Mikhail Gorbachev – decisively contributed to the fall of the Berlin wall and the end of the Communist system.

The Christian claim to truth, rightly understood, is not totalitarian; on the contrary, it is radically anti-totalitarian. But Christianity's claim of absoluteness is also opposed to what can be called pluralistic totalitarianism. So it does not have to surrender itself in a pluralist society; it can assert itself and at the same time affirm and defend the rights of all others who are seeking the truth.

Given these reflections, it is almost superfluous to comment that the constellation – as the Pope stated in his encyclical *Fides et ratio* (1998) – has fundamentally changed since the nineteenth century, and has even been reversed. Today, the Church and modernity, the Church and modern science are no longer adversaries; they are now allies in the fight for truth, for the truth capacity of the human person and for his/her right to truth. The Church does not question empirical pluralism; indeed, she acknowledges its right, although at the same time she questions and wants to help in preventing and overcoming the dangers immanent in ideological pluralism.

The Diaconal Church

The place of the Church within the pluralistic world can best be described in terms of the 'diaconal Church'. With these words I do not mean what many would want them to signify, namely that the Church today should no longer insist on the truth, but should adopt a merely pastoral and therapeutic approach. For it is clear that if what has been said so far is true, the Church cannot be understood simply as a social service agency and a social emergency organization, as if people could be helped independently of the truth, and as if it were not precisely the truth and nothing but the truth, as the Gospel affirms, that sets free (John 8.32). Witnessing and proclaiming the truth is the priority pastoral task. Therefore, with the words 'diaconal Church' I imply an understanding of truth in its liberating, and in that sense therapeutic and pastoral, character.

This understanding results from the way Jesus himself bore witness to the truth. His was a unique and altogether unheard-of claim to truth, which was perceived as scandalous by his opponents. His teachings in the Sermon on the Mount are repeatedly prefaced: 'But I tell you' (Matt. 5.22, 28, 32, 34, 39, 44). He claims to be the truth in person: 'I am the way, the truth and the life' (John 14.6).

On the other hand, among his disciples he is 'like a servant' (Luke 22.27). As the Gospels testify, he is the man for others; he did not come to rule but to serve and to give his life 'for many' (Mark 10.45 par.). In the words of the ancient Christological hymn, though he was in the form of God, he did not count equality with God a thing to be grasped, but emptied himself as a servant, humbling himself even unto death on a cross. As the one who emptied himself fully, God has exalted him and bestowed on him the name which is above every name, so that every tongue should confess him as Lord (Phil. 2.6-11). It is precisely through his self-consuming service to the end that he is the Lord of the universe and embodies the new 'universal law' of love.

These biblical excerpts could easily be multiplied. They could also be theologically deepened from a trinitarian perspective. In our context, it suffices to bear in mind that in Jesus we encounter the claim to truth in an absolute sense, not in terms of imperial sovereignty, but in the form of a service that is emptied of self. The absoluteness of the Gospel has to do with the absoluteness and the unconditional nature of love, which neither casts aside nor absorbs the other, but rather withdraws, makes room for the other and thus acknowledges his/her identity and enriches him/her. At stake is the truth in love (Eph. 4.15). Truth without love can be hard and repulsive; love without truth, just as tolerance without truth, is insincere, empty and meaningless.

Understood in these terms, the affirmation of the uniqueness and absoluteness of the Christian order of salvation is not an imperialistic thesis, which represses or absorbs other religions. It neither validates nor consents to any imperialistic understanding and programme of mission, though in history it has been sometimes misunderstood and misused in that sense. Rather, it sees itself as service to others.

If the thesis of the universality, uniqueness and absoluteness of the Christian order of salvation is understood as such, by its very nature it also at the same time safeguards and defends the inalienable right of every individual. It is precisely its determined opposition to all relativism and syncretism that validates a tolerant and respectful, as well as dialogic and diaconal, relation with other religions. This position is far removed not only from all relativism but also from all narrow fundamentalism.

This dialogic and diaconal relationship has three aspects: Christianity acknowledges, respects and defends all that is true, good, noble and holy in other religions and cultures (Phil. 4.8) (*via positiva seu affirmativa*); it criticizes prophetically what in them is prejudicial to God's honour and to human dignity, when the divine and the human are mixed together so that neither God nor humanity are respected in their own particular dignity (*via negativa seu critica et prophetica*); finally, it extends an invitation to other religions and cultures to meet Jesus Christ and through participation in its own fullness to attain their own fullness and perfection (*via eminentiae*).

In that threefold way, the Church is called to a specific service to humanity, a service that she alone can carry out: for the truth of love, forgiveness, reconciliation, mercy, is the most intrinsic message of the Gospel that no other institution can offer. Especially in our troubled times, this message of absolute love and mercy is needed. Only when we relate to each other not only in a righteous but also in a merciful and charitable way, are we able to withstand the 'pluralist stress' and endure it humanly.

This message considers seriously the single individual in his/her uniqueness and at the same time in his/her social dimension. On the one hand, it takes seriously his/her individuality and personality; it does not simply integrate him/her in a totality or a global system of a general nature. In that sense, justice is done fully to the plurality of human existence and to each cultural reality. The individual is neither a case nor a number. The Christian message embraces plurality and even defends it.

On the other hand, it seeks to avoid the danger of individualism, isolation and loneliness. Mere pluralism can become cold and disconnected, cold unto death, disconnected unto personal and social disintegration. Love unites; love is solidarity. Therefore, it looks after the *bonum commune*, the common good, in which alone the well-being of the individual is guaranteed. It seeks the globalization of solidarity, and is itself boundlessly and universally enmeshed in that solidarity. It does not build a Great Wall of China around its own rich territory, but on the contrary feels responsible for the poor and the poorest lands of the earth.

Plurality within the Church

When pluralism is embraced it also becomes a challenge for the life and shape of the Church. Of course, there can be no ideological and religious pluralism in the Church as such, for the Church is the community of believers. There can only be one faith. But throughout history there has always been a plurality of styles, forms of piety, rites, theology, etc., and this will increase considerably in the future. It is not a necessary evil and should not be perceived as a sign of weakness; rather, it could be a sign of life and inner richness. The Church should knowingly permit such a plurality and seek to shape it in a constructive way, not try to suppress it through disciplinary measures which are in any case futile. The principle should be: 'In necessariis unitas, in aliis libertas, super omnia caritas' ('In what is necessary unity, in all else liberty, and in everything charity').

For this reason the principle of personality and the principle of solidarity also involve the Church. Only by applying these principles within her own sphere can the Church be credible as a diaconal Church. Reform and renewal are still needed in this area; there is still 'housework' to be done.

To do justice to the principle of personality, the Church is required to do justice not only to the cultural diversity of humanity, but also to the increasing differentiation of individual lives, lifestyles and life histories, including their disruptions. She has to intensify the use of *epikeia* and *oikonomia* (economy) in the practical interpretation of her laws. She should not pursue the truth heartlessly; while the truth is binding for all, it should be interpreted in a pastoral and benevolent way according to concrete reality and with respect for the dignity of each individual situation.

Such pastoral flexibility is possible only if there is a better balance between universal church norms – undoubtedly necessary on fundamental issues – and the legitimate autonomy of local churches, and when there is an analogous application of the principle of subsidiarity. Such a plurality of local churches within the one universal Church does not at all negate the ultimate value and vital importance of the unity of the Church, nor does it need to deteriorate into the narrow-minded provincialism of some local churches. Nothing could be worse in our globalized world than such provincialism, nationalism or narrow ethnocentrism. While there is no question of renouncing unity and universality, we have to exclude the interpretation and implementation of unity understood as uniformity. The ultimate model of the Church is the Trinity; so we have to understand the unity of the Church in terms of trinitarian unity, which is a unity in three persons, and we have to shape the Church along the lines described by the Second Vatican Council, as the people of God 'brought into unity from the unity of the Father, the Son and the Holy Spirit' (LG 4).

The same is true with regard to the principle of solidarity. Applied to the Church, it means that she should develop a means of communicating and undertaking dialogue which corresponds better to her *communio*-structure; the Church should be – as Pope John Paul II put it in his apostolic letter *Novo millennio ineunte* (2001) – a house and school of *communio*. Thus church leadership must look for a means of communication, consensus building and reception, and for as much participation as possible by all believers. There should be public expression of opinion, open discussion and debate in the Church.

This presumes a strengthening of synodical structures, for every church authority has three dimensions. Firstly, a personal dimension and responsibility: neither the pope, nor the bishop nor the

pastor is simply the representative, 'general secretary' or spokesman of any church body; he has his personal responsibility, which
is not delegated to him from below but derives from the sacrament
of ordination. Secondly, this incontestable personal responsibility
before God and the community is integrated in the collegial
dimension and is shared with all others who bear such authority
and responsibility. Except in situations of urgency, the personal
right and duty of decision-making normally presupposes a process
of common collegial decision-making. Thirdly and finally, in
decision-making one has to take into account the communal
dimension, that is, one has to listen to the witness of the faithful
and their *sensus fidei*.

We need unity among the disciples of Christ, so that the world
may believe (John 17.21); we also need loyalty in our church when
a decision is made. But normally it is only through dialogue and
communication that we can reach and preserve unity and find
common ground and unanimity amidst legitimate plurality. In
dialogue of this sort, tensions and even conflicts may and will arise
and become public. But such tensions and conflicts will be worse
and create even more tension and distrust when public dialogue is
suppressed. The open discussions we had during the Second
Vatican Council did no harm at all to the Church; on the contrary,
they enhanced its credibility. Indeed, they made the Church more
interesting and engaging.

In the present context, by proclaiming her message of truth in
love, the Church can be a credible sign and instrument of peace and
reconciliation. She can show that unity and plurality do not
necessarily exclude each other, but that they are correlative and
complementary, and that their tendency is to keep each other in a
healthy balance. Thus the new situation does not only signify
danger for the Church; it also – and even more so – represents a
radical opportunity to realize her fundamental nature as a
community of believers in a more original, genuine and authentic
way, and, in the best sense of these words, to become thereby a sign
for the world.

This should not be understood as a naive, harmonious position,
which is untenable in any case, given the problems and tension
within the Church and, even more so, the tensions and conflicts in
society. With regard to conflict within the Church, we know that
from the very beginning there have been schisms, and they can also

happen today. With regard to conflict in society, we must be conscious that by her faith the Church is immune to the utopian vision that everybody would eventually want to join her. A fundamental pluralism, and even antagonism, has never been eradicated in the course of history. Christianity must expect to be contradicted until the end of time. Thus its approach to pluralism should be wise and calm and should never take the form of sect-like fanaticism. Only at the end of the time will the weeds be separated from the wheat (Matt. 13.30).

We do not need a church which conforms to rapidly changing fashions, but neither do we want a church which only focuses on a pessimistic approach to modernity. Pope John XXIII, at the beginning of the Second Vatican Council, contradicted all the prophets of doom who were always forecasting the worse. There is no reason for such fear and lack of confidence. As Christians we should be realistic and see the dangers and temptations of our modern world, but we should also be sufficiently self-confident and courageous to accept them as a challenge and call to mission and action. What our complicated and imperilled pluralistic world needs in order to survive is neither naive optimism nor prophecies of doom. What is needed – and what we as Christians can contribute to the survival of authentic freedom and offer as an inspiration for hope – is the calm but firm and courageous witness of truth in love.

Index

Abramowski, L. 28
absolution 106
Acts
  1.13: Pentecost 166
  1.15: Christian brotherhood 76
  2.1–13: mission and the Holy
    Spirit 97
  2.42 community 55
  2.44: community 55
  4.12: no other name 183
  4.23: community 55
  10.23: hospitality 76
  10.44–47: action of the Spirit
    103
  11.1: Christians as brothers 76
  11.15: work of the apostles 103
  15.8: Holy Spirit 103
Ad gentes 61, 103
Adventists 25
Afanassiev, N. 59
al-Azhar, Cairo 40
Althaus, Paul 58
Ambrose 109
Anglican Communion 21, 23, 90,
  122, 127, 139
Anno ineunte 76, 81
Antichrist 136
Apostles 55
Apostolic canons 60, 80
apostolic succession 73, 132
Apostolicam actuositatem 103
Apostles' Creed 56, 98, 115
Aquinas, Thomas 36, 57, 98–9,
  109, 110, 117, 118, 162, 184
Arabic culture and the West 36
Arianism 110
Aristi, V. von 150

Armenians 18
Asmussen, H. 149
Athanasian creed 110
Augsburg 124, 126, 133
Augsburg Confession 3, 23
Augustine 57, 71, 99, 109, 162,
  166
Averroes 36
Avicenna 36

Balthasar, H.U. von 118, 120, 123,
  142, 149, 151, 183
baptism
  into the Body of Christ 41, 43,
    51, 55, 59, 165
  and the Holy Spirit 101, 106
Baptism, Eucharist and Ministry
  (Lima documents 1982) 22,
  23, 35, 64
Baptists 25
Barth, K. 120, 123
Bartholomew I, Patriarch 112, 113
Basil 109
Beinert, W. 151
Benedict VIII, Pope 111
Berdajev, N. 120
Berengarius of Tours 57
Bible 131–2, 147, 148
Bishop of Rome *see* Petrine
  ministry
bishops *see* episcopacy
Bishops' Conferences (2000) 80
Body of Christ 58
  and baptism 41, 43, 51, 55, 59,
  165
Bolotov, V. 119
Bonhoeffer, Dietrich 58

Bowen, F. 95
Brandenburg, A. 149
Brandmüller, W. 153
Brown, R. 150
Buber, Martin 35
Buckley, N. 150
Bulgakov, S. 119, 120
Bulgaria 20

Calvin, John 30, 108
Camisaca, M. 118
Catechism of the Catholic Church
113
Catechismus Romanus 62
Catholic Church *see* Roman
Catholic Church
Catholic Eastern churches 86, 87,
88–9, 91, 94
charismatic movement 25, 26,
104
Charlemagne 111
Chomjakow, A.S. 58
Christianity and other religions 40,
179, 187
christology *see* Jesus Christ
christology of the Spirit 102
Christus dominus 61, 68, 79,
103
Church
image of the triune God 129–30
'true nature of' 58, 64–71, 100–
4, 132
see also communio/communion;
local churches; Orthodox
churches; Reformation
churches; Roman Catholic
Church
church councils 45
Church and Justification (1994)
124
church laws 102–3
'Church in the Modern World,
The' 174
Church of Sweden 139
Clément, O. 152, 153

Colossians, 2.9: fullness of
Godhead 168
Commission on Faith and Order
73, 107
communio/communion 26, 27, 42,
43–4, 50–74
and Catholic ecclesiology 64–71,
115
communio sanctorum 56–7, 62,
115
and the Eastern/Orthodox
churches 18, 21, 77–80, 90
in the Holy Spirit 26, 96–8, 116,
167–8
misunderstandings of 52–4
theological foundations of 54–9
'vertical' and 'horizontal' 58–9
Communism 19, 87
confirmation 106
Congar, Yves 28, 31, 48, 57, 58,
71, 92, 93, 101, 117, 118,
120, 140, 150, 152
Congregation for the Doctrine of
the Faith 2, 15, 34, 80–1, 82,
126, 139, 141
and the Petrine ministry 139,
141
and the Reformation churches 2,
15, 34, 126
and 'sister churches' 80–1, 82
congregations 62
consecration 84–5, 107, 108
Constantine, Emperor 173
Constantinople 111
conversion 17
Copts 18, 46
Cordes, P.J. 118
1 Corinthians
1.9: communion with Christ 55
1.10: unity 69
2.10–15: Spirit 117
2.16: mind of Christ 166
3.16: temple of the Spirit 98,
115, 166
6.11: baptism 106

7.7: gifts of God 104
8.6: one Lord 183
10.16: eucharist 55, 60
10.17: one body 165
11.17–22: one body 165
12: gifts of the Spirit 26
12.1–11: Spirit of Christ 103
12.3: Spirit of Christ 100, 164
12.4–31: gifts of the Spirit 98,
     104, 166
12.13: body of Christ 51, 55, 59,
     106, 165
13.4, 7: love, a gift of the Spirit
     166
13.4–6 rejoicing in the truth 160
13.9: all knowledge is partial
     168
14.26: each of you contributes
     169
14.33: Spirit of peace 166
16.20: Christians as brothers 76
2 Corinthians
  1.5, 7: suffering and comfort 55
  3.17: 'The Lord is the Spirit'
     101, 102, 164
  5.17: new creatures 165
  6.16: temple of the Spirit 98, 115
  8–9: community 55, 96
  13.13: Holy Spirit 55, 115
Corpus Christi 160
Council of Chalcedon 12, 18, 46,
     48, 109, 114
Council of Constantinople 48, 98,
     109
Council of Ephesus 48, 111
Council of Florence 9, 87, 92
  East–West schism 76, 81
  filioque 109, 111
Council of Nicea 12, 48, 79, 92
Council of Trent 6, 48, 63, 123, 128
Couturier, Abbé Paul 156
creeds 46, 56, 110
  see also filioque
cultural identity 36, 177, 181
cultural pluralism 158–9, 176–7

Cyprian of Carthage 59
Cyril of Alexandria 18, 109
Cyril of Jerusalem 107

'Declaration on Religious Freedom'
     183
Dei Verbum 31, 67, 153,
     169
  the Holy Spirit and truth 48,
     102, 103
  and revelation 37, 40
  scripture 105
del Colle, R. 31
democracy 52, 54
Denziger-Hünermann 54, 61, 69,
     70, 109, 110, 111, 151, 152,
     153
Denzler, G. 149
Deuteronomy, 6.4: one and only
     God 183
diaconal church 186
diaconia 42, 43
dialogue 184
  between cultures and religions
     36, 40, 175–6
Dictionary of Christian Spirituality
     158
Didache 107
Dignitatis humanae 38–9
Disciples of Christ 25
diversity 68–9
Divinum illud 99
divisions 158–9, 160
dogma 48, 168–9
Dominus Iesus (2000) 13, 15, 34,
     41, 65
Drey, Johann Sebastian 4
Drumm, J. 121

Easter, date of 159
Eastern bloc 2–3
Eastern churches see Orthodox
     churches
Ebeling, G. 31
Ebner, Ferdinand 35

'*ecclesia semper reformanda/
purificanda*' 47–8, 71
Ecclesiam suam 34
ecumenical dialogue 33–49, 155
    consequences of 43–7
    ecclesiological foundation 41–3
    and the Holy Spirit 14, 24, 155–
    76
    methods of 45–7
    personal presuppositions 47
    philosophical presuppositions
    35–7
    at the present time 1–5, 14–27,
    59, 134–5, 155–6
    questions and problems 47–9
    structures of 45
    theological foundations 37–40
Ecumenical Dictionary 158
Ecumenical Directory 45, 73
Elert, Johann 58
Enlightenment 19, 52, 145, 178
Ephesians
    1.10: Jesus the aim of all creation
    38
    2.21: temple of the Spirit 98,
    115, 166
    3.8: richess of Christ 168
    4.3: unity of the Spirit 55, 98,
    167
    4.5: one Lord 69, 183
    4.7–12 church 54
    4.13: full stature of Christ 170
    4.15: truth in love 187
    epiclesis 106–7, 107–8
Epiphanius of Salamis 109
episcopacy 16, 22, 60, 65, 67, 73–4
    and local churches 63–4, 69
    and pastorate 62
    and primacy 83–5
Episcopalism 145
Erasmus 38
ethical issues in ecumenism 23
Ethiopians 18
eucharist 72
    and the Holy Spirit 106–8

and local churches 60, 79
    one body 55, 57, 165
    in the Reformed churches 61
Evdokimov, P. 107, 118, 119,
    120

faith 122, 123, 127, 159, 185
Faith and Order Commission 23,
    31, 132
Fides et ratio 185
filioque 19, 24–5, 46, 96–7, 107–
    17, 158
First Vatican Council 7, 9, 21, 48,
    63
    and the Petrine ministry 137,
    140–6, 148, 149
Flogaus, R. 120
Florovsky, G. 58, 59
forgiveness 47, 132
Forte, B 119, 120
Fourth Lateran Council 9, 111
Franconian synods 110
Free churches 25, 53
freedom 184, 185
    of the Holy Spirit 24, 27, 97,
    102, 103
Freitag, J. 154
French Revolution 54, 145

Gahbauer, F.R. 93, 152
Galatians
    2.9: communion 55
    2.10: community 55
    3.26–28: body of Christ 51, 55,
    165
    4.4: Jesus the fullness of time 38
    4.6: Spirit of Christ 100, 102,
    164, 165
    5.13: 'serve one another in love'
    27
    5.22: fruits of the spirit 164
    6.2: each other's burdens 116
    6.15: new creatures 165
Gallicanism 145
Garuti, A. 82, 93, 94, 152

Gaudium et spes 8, 9, 37, 38, 46,
    162, 174, 175
Genesis, 1.27: Man in the image of
    God 37, 182
Glaeser, Z. 91
globalization 14, 15, 36, 180–1
Gnilka, J. 150
Gnosticism 63, 147
God
    creative spirit of 162
    the Father and the Son 109–10
    judgment and mercy of 133
    is love 26, 115
    and man 37, 182
    monarchy of the Father 112–13
    in pluralist religion theory 179–80
Gorbachev, Mikhail 185
Goyert, P. 154
grace 122, 123, 127, 159
Granfield, P. 150
Great Catechism 62
Greece 20
Gregory the Great 147
Greshake, G. 93, 117, 120, 121
Grillmeier, A. 28, 151
Grosche, R. 149
*Growth in Agreement. Reports and
    Agreed Statements of
    Ecumenical Conversations on
    a World Level* 50
guilt 132

Halifax, Lord 90, 95
Halleux, A. de 28, 94, 152
Hebrews
    7.27: one high priest 183
    9.28: salvation through Christ
        168
Hegel 178
Henry III, Emperor 111
Hertling, I. 58, 120
Hick, J. 179
hierarchy 53–4, 63, 83–6, 104
hierarchy of truth 45–6, 141
Hilberath, J. 121

Hippolytus 107
Hollenweger, W. J. 31
Holocaust 175
Holy Spirit
    and charisma 103–6
    christology of 102
    in the Church 24–7, 96–108,
        115–17, 166–8
    in creation 101, 162
    and *filioque* 24–5, 96–7, 108–17,
        159
    freedom of 24, 27, 97, 102, 103
    and Jesus Christ 4, 24–5, 41,
        100–3, 163–6
    and *koinonia* 55
    Pentecost 97, 100, 102
    and the sacraments 101, 106–8
    spiritual ecumenism 155–76
    and spirituality 160, 161–8
    trustworthiness of 5
    and the word of God 105–6
Hooft, Visser't 34
human beings
    in the image of God 37, 182
Hünermann, P. 150
Huntington, S.P. 181
Hyppolytus 166

identity 15, 188
Ignatius of Antioch 60, 148, 154
individualism 36, 177, 188
indulgences 131
infallibility 47, 48, 137, 139
institutions 53
intercommunion 3
Irenaeus of Lyon 98, 101, 166
Isaiah
    11.2: the Spirit 163
    42.1: the Spirit 163
Islam 36, 177

Jerome 62
Jerusalem church 55–6, 69
Jesus Christ
    anointing of 101, 102

and Chalcedon 18, 46
fulfilment of human desires 37–8
'fully subsists only in the
  Catholic Church' 16, 40
as the head of the Church 71
and the 'historical Jesus' 147
and the Holy Spirit 4, 24–5, 41,
  100, 101–2, 163–6
and justification 122, 127, 132,
  157
and *koinonia* 55
and Mariology 46
meaning for us today 133
the person for others 39
as revelation 38, 168, 179
true man and God 37, 38, 46
John XXIII, Pope 7, 34, 77, 100,
  172
1 John
  1.3: Father and Son among us
    26, 55
  4.8, 16: 'God is love' 26, 115
  4.18: love drives out fear 168
2 John, v.13: 'sister churches' 75
John's Gospel
  1.13: incarnation 169
  1.18: the Son made known 164
  1.33: baptism 106
  4.11: 'well of living water' 105
  6.32–59: eucharist 108
  6.63: Spirit 108
  8.32: truth sets us free 184, 186
  10.11: the good shepherd 148
  10.15: Jesus and the Father 37
  10.16: one shepherd 49
  10.30: Jesus as son of God 37
  14.6: the way, the truth.... 38,
    186
  16.13: fullness of the truth 12,
    40, 125
  17.21: that all may be one 4, 14,
    156, 163, 190
  17.21–23: unity of Father and
    Son 55
  17.22: that all may be one 27

  21.15–17: Peter 146
John of Damascus 56, 109
John Paul II, Pope
  and ecumenical dialogue 14, 42,
    43, 155, 170
  and the Joint Declaration on
    Justification 126, 130
  and the Orthodox churches 77,
    112
  and the Petrine ministry 19, 69,
    90, 137, 138–9, 146, 148
  and the Spirit 162, 167–8
Joint Catholic-Orthodox
  Commission for Theological
  Dialogue 19
Joint Declaration on Justification
  21–2, 29, 46, 48, 71, 122–35
Joint Declarations of Pope John
  Paul II with Patriarchs
  Dimitrios I and Barthomew
  77, 92
Joint International Commission
  Balamand 1993 88, 94
  Baltimore 20
  Freising 1990 88
  Munich 1982 60
Jubilee Year 2000 2, 159
Judaism 175–6
Jude 3: once and for all 183
Jüngel, Eberhard 123
justification 21, 46, 71, 122–34,
  157, 158
Justification by Faith (1985) 124

Kasper, W. 117, 118, 119, 120,
  150, 154
kenosis 38
Knitter, P. 179
koinonia 54–6
Küng, Hans 123

Laetentur caeli 76, 88, 92
laity 54
Lannes, E. 91, 94, 152
Latin America 25

Lehmann, K. 30
Lehrverurteilungen –
    Kirchentrennand? (1986) 124
Leo the Great, Pope 109
Leo III, Pope 110
Leo XIII, Pope 33, 77, 99
Leuenberg Church Fellowship 64
Leuenberg Community 22–3
Levinas, Emmanuel 35
Lindbeck, George 123, 154
local churches
    in *communio* 79, 90, 189
    and episcopacy 63–4
    and eucharist 60, 79
    as in the New Testament 68
    and the Reformation churches
        62
Lombard, Peter 62
Lossky, V. 31, 113, 117, 119
love 115, 166, 185, 188
    and truth 44–5, 185, 187
Lubac, Henri de 57, 92, 118
Ludwig, J. 154
Luke
    1.35: Holy Spirit 101, 163
    2.32: glory to Israel 146
    4.14: Christ and the Spirit 163
    4.18: Christ and the Spirit 101,
        163
    5.4: 'Put out into the deep' 74
    5.11 James and John 55
    6.31: Do to others... 37
    10.21: Christ and the Spirit 163
    11.20: Christ and the Spirit 163
    22.27: like a servant 186
    24.27: mission to all people 182
Lumen gentium 7–8, 9, 10, 28, 31,
    32, 65, 142, 151, 154
    consecration and jurisdiction 83,
        84, 85
    diversity 68, 69
    Holy Spirit 100, 101, 102, 171,
        189
    laity 54
    local churches 61, 68, 79, 103

Mariology 46
sanctification 104
semper purificanda 46, 66
'sister churches' 77, 79
trinitarian *communio* 50, 58,
    170
the true Church 41, 64–5
unity 63
Luther, Martin 30, 38, 61, 99, 122,
    158
    On Christian Freedom 23–4,
        27
Lutheran World Federation 21–2,
    21–3, 29, 48, 122–35
'Lutheran-Catholic Dialogue:
    Malta Report' 1971 124, 150

Maccarrone, M. 152
Malachias 137
Malankara 18
Marcion 147
Mariology 46, 160
Mark
    1.9–11: baptism and the Spirit
        163
    10.30: Love your neighbour 37
    10.45: Jesus gives his life for
        others 37, 186
    12.29: one and only God 183
    16.15: mission to all people 182
Matthew
    1.18, 20: the action of the Spirit
        163
    5.22, 28, 32, 34, 39, 44: 'but I
        tell you' 186
    5.45: Father of all 183
    7.12: Do to others... 37
    12.25–27: Jesus and the Father
        37
    12.48: Christians as brothers 76
    13.29, 30: wheat and weeds 13,
        191
    16.18: Peter 146, 147
    18.15: Christians as brothers 76
    20.25–27: ministry 54

20.27: 'whoever wishes to be first...' 147
23.8: Christians as brothers 76
28.19: mission to all people 182
Maximus the Confessor 110
Meerson, M. A. 120
Mennonites 25
Mercier, Cardinal 90
Methodists 25, 127
Meyendorff, J. 91, 92, 149, 153
Meyer, H. 28, 30, 91, 123
Middle Ages 136, 173
mystics and theologians 98, 99
ministry 27, 54, 73, 115, 132
  in Protestant churches 61–3, 64, 71
  in the Roman Catholic Church 63–4
  and Second Vatican Council 63
  see also episcopacy; Petrine ministry
mission 39–40, 123, 182
Mohler, A. 11
Möhler, Johann Adam 4, 27, 48, 57, 71, 102, 117, 121, 129, 171
Moltmann, J. 118, 120
monastic communities 53
Mortalium animos 11, 33
Moscow 20
Mühlen, H. 120
Murray, John Courtney 184
Mussner, F. 150
Mustici corporis 99

Nedungatt, G. 93, 152, 154
neo-Romanticism 53
New Testament church 68, 69, 75–6
Newman, John Henry 11, 48, 102
Nietzsche, Friedrich 178
Niketas of Remesiana 56
Nostra aetate 38, 175, 176
Novo millennio ineunte 32, 73, 164, 168

Old Testament 105
ordination of women 23
Orientalium ecclesiarum 77, 78, 82, 85, 89
Origen 109
Orthodox churches 2–3, 18–21, 59–61, 67, 75–91, 156–7
  Diaspora 79
  and filioque 24, 96–7, 107, 108–17, 158
  and the Petrine ministry 24, 82–6, 155
Oxford Movement 33

Palamas, Gregory 113, 120
Pannenberg, W. 30, 118, 120, 123, 151
papacy see Petrine ministry
Parys, M. van 95
Pastor aeternus 143
Patriarch Athenagoras 76
patriarchates 82, 83
  five early patriarchates 78
Paul, Apostle 138
Paul VI, Pope 7, 19, 34, 76, 137, 156
Péguy 49
Pelagianism 123
penance 106, 131
Pentecost 97, 100, 156, 166
Pentecostal movement 25, 26, 104
Peri, V. 92, 94
Pesch, Otto Hermann 123
Pesch, R. 150
Peter, Apostle 137, 138, 141, 146–7, 148
Peter, Carl 123
1 Peter
  1.3: born anew into hope 165
  2.17: Christians as brothers 76
  2.4: living stones 98
  2.5: living stones 166
  3.15: hope of unity 5
  5.1: glory to come 55
  5.2–4: shepherd's of God's flock 148

5.9: Christians as brothers 76
2 Peter
  1.4: divine nature 55
Petrine ministry 3, 21, 24, 42–3,
    57, 63, 65, 67, 69–70, 73–4,
    82–6, 132, 136–49
  and the Orthodox churches 19–
    20, 60–1, 82–6, 89, 90, 93,
    143–5
  and the Reformed churches 71
Philemon 6: faith 55
Philippians
  1.5: Gospel 55
  1.19: Christ and the Spirit 164
  2.6–11: every tongue confess him
    Lord 186
  3.10: suffering and resurrection
    55
  4.8 : all that is true 187
Philips, G. 65, 93
Photius 110
Pius IX, Pope 141
Pius XI, Pope 11
Pius XII, Pope 33, 34, 99
  Instruction of the Holy Office of
    1949 34
pluralism 173–91
  as a philosophical programme
    178–9
  pluralist religion theory 179–80
  within the Church 188–91
Podalsy, G. 120
Pontifical Council for Interreligious
    Dialogue 40
Pontifical Council for Promoting
    Christian Unity 17, 19–20,
    108, 112, 125–35, 139, 140
popes see Petrine ministry
Pottmeyer, H.J. 150, 153
prayer 47
Presbyterorum Ordinis 101, 103
priesthood
  of all the baptized 26, 115, 132
  hierarchical 26, 115, 132
Priscillianism 110

'Pro Oriente' Foundation, Vienna
    18, 108
proselytism 39–40
Protestant churches see
    Reformation churches

Quinn, J.R. 150

Radano, J.A. 149
Rahner, K. 119, 120, 123, 153
Ratzinger, J. 4, 28, 43, 82, 83, 93,
    121, 140, 143–4, 146, 150,
    152, 153
Redemtoris missio 162
Reformation 131, 136, 173
Reformation churches 2, 3, 25, 41,
    47–8, 61–4, 71, 157, 158
  and ecumenism 21–4, 34, 127
  and ministry 61–3, 64, 155
  and sacraments 107, 108
  as 'sister churches' 80–1
religious freedom 38–9
revelation 37, 168, 185
  in pluralist religion theory 179–
    80
Revelation (N.T. Book)
  1.8: Alpha and Omega 182
  13.1–10: the Beast 136
  22.20: Maranatha 107
Ritschl, D. 119
Rodriguez, P. 151, 154
Roman Catholic Church
  ecclesia semper purificanda 47–8
  and ecumenism 16, 33–4, 38–9,
    40, 41–2, 43, 50, 59, 122
  'subsistit in' 16, 34, 40, 41, 65–
    7, 68
  'wounded by division' 16–17
  see also Second Vatican Council
Roman primacy see Petrine
    ministry
Romania 3, 20, 87
Romans
  1.3: resurrection 163
  1.4: resurrection 101

3.9: all under the power of sin 100, 102
6.3–5: death and resurrection of Christ 165
8.9: Spirit of Christ 100, 102, 164
8.15: Spirit of God 165
8.19: God's sons to be revealed 163
8.22: completion of the work of the Spirit 5
8.26: Spirit of God 165
12.4: body of Christ 55
12.4–8: gifts of the Spirit 98
13.10: fulfilment of the law 37
16.14: Christians as brothers 76
Rosenzweig, Franz 35
Ruthenians 87

sacraments 55, 67, 106
and word 61, 62
Sacri canones (1990) 89
Sacrosanctum concilium 58, 61, 68, 79, 101, 103
Saier, O. 120, 121
St Irenaeus of Lyons 12
salvation 113
Satis cognitum 33
Schäfer, R. 121
Schelkle, K.H. 92
Schlette, H.R. 118
Schmemann, A. 60, 120
scriptures 105–6, 131–2
and tradition 147
Second Council of Lyon 9
Second Vatican Council
and ecumenism 6–13, 34, 38–47, 50, 122
and the hierarchy of truths 45–6
and the Holy Spirit 4, 25–6, 100–6
interpretation of documents 11–13
and the laity 25–6
and local churches 68
and ministry 63
and modern pluralism 174–6
and the nature of the Church 58, 64–71, 100–4
and the Orthodox churches 76–82, 83–6, 89, 94
and the Petrine ministry 137, 141, 142, 143, 144, 148
and the scriptures 105–6
and tradition 11–12
Second World War 177
Secretariat for Promoting Christian Unity 34
self-realization 35, 37
Serbia 20
Sermon on the Mount 186
'sister churches' 75–81, 76, 86, 91, 92
Slavorum apostoli 76, 95
Slenzka, R. 108, 119
social contract 52
Soloewjev, V. 120
spiritual ecumenism 4, 17, 44, 156–76
spirituality 157–61
Stirnimann, H. 149
Suttner, E. Ch. 91, 94
Swidler, L. 179
Synod of Bishops 1985 58
Synod of Pistoia 54
Syrians 18

Taft, R.F. 94
Tertio millennio eunte 116
Tertullian 109
Theodosius 173
theological faculties 45
Thessalonians1
5.26: Christians as brothers 76
Thessalonians2
2.1–12: the Enemy 136
Tillard, J.M.R. 60, 121, 150
1 Timothy
2.5: only mediator 183
4: ministry 104

Titus
  1.5: ministry 62
  3.5: baptism 106
Tomos agapis 76, 92, 93
tradition
  and interpretaion of Councils
    11–12
  and scriptures 147
Trinity 26, 46, 56, 112, 113, 114,
  115, 116, 129, 189
truth 169, 184, 185
  hierarchy of 45–6
  as Jesus Christ 47
  and love 44–5, 185, 187
Tübingen 4, 27, 57, 129

Ukraine 3, 20, 87
uniatism 2–3, 20, 86–90, 94
Unitatis Redintegratio 6–13, 28,
  50, 67, 152, 156
  diversity 68
  and the eucharist 61
  Holy Spirit 34, 41–3, 44–5, 58,
    66, 74, 103
  need of conversion 41–3, 44–5,
    74, 170
  and the Orthodox churches 76,
    77–9, 83, 85, 86
  unity 41–3, 63, 68–9, 165, 183,
    188, 190
  and diversity 68–9, 103, 130,
    158, 171
Urban, H.J. 28, 149
Ut unum sint (1995) 12, 19, 28, 34,
  35, 69, 77, 94, 156, 176

brotherhood 43, 51, 155
Holy Spirit 16, 66, 67, 169
need of conversion 42, 74
the Petrine ministry 70, 138,
  146, 148, 150

Valamo Document 1988 61
Valentini, D. 153
Vischer, L. 28, 107, 118, 119, 149
Vitali, M. 118
Vries, W. de 93, 152

Wagner, H. 30
wars of religion 173–4
'Week of Prayer for Christian
  Unity' 156, 165
Wendenburg, D. 28, 120
Wisdom
  1.7: the spirit of the Lord 162
  7.22–8.1: the spirit of the Lord
    162
Wojtyla, Karol see John Paul II,
  Pope
word of God 25, 105–6
  and sacraments 61, 62, 67
World Council of Churches 33, 34,
  60, 132
  Toronto Declaration 1950 2
World Day of Prayer in Assisi
  (1986, 2000) 40
World Missionary Conference at
  Edinburgh (1910) 33

Zechariah, 4.6: the Spirit 163
Zizioulas, J. 60